LIONEL TRILLING

MODERN LITERATURE SERIES

GENERAL EDITOR: Philip Winsor

In the same series:

(continued on last page of book)

LIONEL TRILLING

Edward Joseph Shoben, Jr.

FREDERICK UNGAR PUBLISHING CO.
NEW YORK

Library of Congress Cataloging in Publication Data

Shoben, Edward Joseph.
  Lionel Trilling.

  (Modern literature series)
  Bibliography: p.
  Includes index.
  1. Trilling, Lionel, 1905–1975—Criticism and
interpretation.   I. Title.   II. Series:

PS3539.R56Z9   818′.5209   81–40472
ISBN 0-8044-2815-8   AACR2

For Ann
who made it possible
and
To Abigail
in loving hope for her future

Acknowledgments

The obligations which I have incurred in the writing of this little volume exceed the space available for their acknowledgment. A few, however, simply cannot go un-mentioned. I owe the first expression of gratitude to Diana Trilling, Lionel's wife for forty-six years and a critic, in her own right, of considerable dimension. One of the joys of this rewarding task has been the renewal of my acquaintance with her, and both her warmth and her helpfulness have exceeded all reasonable expecta-tions. She also is the main source of biographical in-formation about her husband, whose social grace and interpersonal accessibility clothed an intense sense of privacy. Second, my heartfelt appreciation goes to num-bers of students with whom I have shared these chapters in various drafts and who have both identified in a kindly and helpful fashion my tendencies toward opac-ity and at least some of my lapses from either logic or accuracy. What defects remain are certainly not their fault but mine. Third, a number of friends have read one or more sections of this book and provided me with aid and comfort for which I simply lack the wit to thank them adequately. I count on their forgiveness as I have been able to count on their help. They include Ilena Dunlap, Johanna Gallers, Richard S. Goldberg, Harvey Goldstein, Sharon Milan, and Lois Parker. They all have a proper claim to credit for much of what may be of merit here, but they have no responsibility for

errors or stupidities. Both, despite grim efforts to avoid
or to eliminate them, may appear.

One final word: I have dedicated this essay to my
wife and to my granddaughter. The inscription to the
former has a bald literalness that masks private and rich
complexities and intensities that I pray she fully understands. The inscription to the latter, who was born
while this little work was in progress, grows out of the
unexpected hopes and loving yearnings that new grand-
fatherhood quickens. I shall be particularly proud if
this book of mine provides a bridge by which Abigail
may one day cross the years to become acquainted with
Lionel Trilling's mind and character.

Contents

Preface

When a clinical psychologist writes a book about a literary critic, some explanation obviously is in order. In the present case, the necessary explanation entails three statements that I am delighted to put on the public record.

In the first place, I have been bewildered and troubled for years by the great gulf that yawns between psychology and serious reflections on literature, between the social sciences and the humanities. Both concern themselves with human functioning and with the qualities of human experience; both aim at increasing our understanding of ourselves and our relationships to others and to the realities of culture, and both reflect the uses of the mind and the imagination in our efforts to achieve that always deficient comprehension of our status and our conduct as human beings. Lionel Trilling stands out as a literary figure who, if he did not bridge that chasm in the enterprise of thought, certainly narrowed it. Committed to Freud, skeptical but sympathetically informed about Marx, and intimately familiar with the contemporary efforts of such social scientists as David Riesman and Daniel Bell, he insisted that the self defines the central subject matter of literature, and that the conflict between the self, ever seeking a greater degree of autonomy and free expression, and the culture, at once nurturant and nay-saying, lies at the heart of the human drama. As one whose professional des-

tiny it is to hold frequently the damp hand of other
people's misfortune, I agree. In the unshared reflections
in which I occasionally indulge in my consulting room,
I often am terrified by the perception of how fragile is
the skin of civilization that covers the idiosyncratic and
self-serving drives, impulses, and passions of my pa-
tients. Just as frequently, I find both my compassion
and my rage aroused by the ways in which the influences of society have cruelly cabined the spontaneity,
the emotional capabilities, and the imaginations of the
people with whom I work.

What may seem odd is that a great deal of the
understanding I may possess of these poignant matters
derives as much from the literary record of human destiny as from my own discipline of psychology. This
state of affairs may issue from nothing more than the
fact that my personal intellectual awakening, if it ever
occurred, took place during my undergraduate years
under the auspices of some stimulating teachers of literature. I am more inclined to believe, however, that
writers like Shakespeare and Melville understood more
of the vicissitudes of the human heart, more of the
subterranean forces that color our experience for good
or ill, than most (which is *not* a synonym for "all")
psychologists. The superiority of outstanding literary
insight stems, I think, from the capacity of the disciplined and informed imagination to perceive experience
in its essence and as a totality, a whole, whereas psychologists typically content themselves with more precise but fractional forms of comprehension, eschewing
great leaps of the imaginative reason in favor of an inch-
worm's units of progress, in the faith that these small
increments will profitably cumulate. Both procedures
strike me as essential. What I regret is that they so
seldom enter into an enriching dialogue with one another.

In the mind of Lionel Trilling, something, at least,
of that dialogue went on for half a century. In his es-

says and books, the extensions of a remarkable mind, that dialogue becomes available to any who can read. As a participant in that interchange, I have learned much that puts me in Trilling's debt. In a very real sense, this effort of mine represents an acknowledgment of that debt and a desire to share with others my considerable benefits as Trilling's debtor.

Second, a clinician cannot escape the great puzzles: about the meaning of that dream of happiness human beings are heir to; about how life's contradictions can be managed with a measure of contentment and its buffets sustained without breaking the spirit; about the sources of enjoyment and pride we can find even in the face of our own mortality and our own curious and damaging self-destructive and socially disruptive tendencies. Neither could Trilling. His concern for the complexities of personal experience and for the quality of life as people encounter it on a day-to-day basis underlay all his reflections on the authors, works, and issues to which he turned his attention. That concern, always immediate and warm, coupled with the creativity with which he mined the literary veins available to him, make him, for me, a model and an exemplar in the twentieth century of the tradition that deserves to be called humanistic. In addition to the fertility and provocative power of his mind, Trilling exhibits in his published work a *character*—a set of reflected-upon values in action—that, I confess, I envy to a degree and that I admire enormously. The world, I believe, would be a more engaging place if it were populated by a few more Lionel Trillings.

Finally, I spent the years from 1950 to 1965 as a faculty member at Columbia University. Trilling, thirteen years my senior, had already achieved the acclaim due him for the work culminating in *The Liberal Imagination* when I arrived on Morningside Heights, still a bit callow, a trifle brash, and marked by levels of ignorance that time has done too little, I'm afraid, to reduce. Although I never knew him well, Trilling was extraordinarily generous and sweetly responsive to me, and his friendliness and occasional gentle guidance meant a good deal to me personally and to my intellectual development. I've rarely enjoyed such comfortably stimulating talk as at our infrequent lunches together at the Faculty Club or during occasional gentle discussions in his office or mine. Neither a full-fledged friend nor a disciple (Trilling wanted no disciples), I found my affections almost as much invoked as my respect for his personal qualities and my esteem for his intellectual powers. If (as I hope is the case) my admiration shows in the pages that follow, I make no apologies and simply quote Trilling himself: "objectivity . . . begins with what might be called a programmatic prejudice in favor of the work or author being studied." The point is that, once again, Trilling's character figures as largely in his work as does his mind, and both his mind and his character have something of worth to say to our much-chivied civilization.

1

Lionel Trilling:
The Opposing Self

White-haired, his deep-set eyes characteristically haunted, Lionel Trilling roamed the front of his Columbia College classroom. The magisterial reputation as literary and social critic that he brought with him evoked an atmosphere of formality. Yet, without attempting to deny it and with an all but articulate and quietly insistent pleasure in decorum, he colored the climate of formality with a relaxed ease. Appearing (but only appearing) to turn randomly through the pages of James Joyce's *Dubliners*, he read aloud in a softly modulated baritone: "He lived at a little distance from his body." The always evanescent smile warmed the haunted eyes, and there was a sudden joyous glow that every undergraduate in the class felt, whether or not he understood it in some more intellectual sense. "Marvelous phrase," Trilling exclaimed. "Isn't that the essence of alienation?" He then commented, still moving in his leisurely fashion about the room, on an association between the habit of one of the characters in *Dubliners* of keeping a rotting apple in his desk and Friedrich Schiller's statement that he could only write poetry if a rotting apple were emitting its fragrance from his tabletop. And that led to a typical, good-humored but thoroughly serious warning against preciousness and too academic an approach to literature. "If anyone connects any of these rotting apples to the

Fall," Trilling grinned, "he immediately loses twenty points on the next exam."

Representative as it is, this commonplace vignette catches many of the central qualities of Trilling as a human being—his courtly combining of formality and relaxation, the mystery of the hag-ridden eyes, and the ready smile that always failed to realize itself fully. The story reflects his love of fun that clearly exceeded an intellectual's taste for sheer wit, and it at least suggests the delight he found in seriousness without solemnity. It hints at his sense of the richness and crucial value of linkages between the experience of literature and the experience of life. It vibrates with his refusal to burden works of art with imposed symbols, to force them onto procrustean beds of aesthetic or literary theory, as against investing the effort to see each of them as, in the phrase of Matthew Arnold's that he so prized, "an object as in itself it really is."

If *mind* was and remains the dominant motif in Trilling as teacher and as writer, what accounts for his influence and his importance is the intimacy with which mind married passion. When he wrote of E. M. Forster's "two ideals" of truth and passion, the first symbolized by "some vaguely ancient pagan time" in Greece, and the second by the "ruffianism of the Renaissance" in Italy,[1] he spoke in significant part from self-knowledge and a felt commonality. In quoting Forster's "those ghosts who are still clothed with passion or thought are profitable companions," he reveals something vital and distinctive in himself.

Such self-revelation didn't happen often. Trilling was a deeply private person. His use of "I" in his essays is far more an acknowledgment of responsibility for the ideas and judgments he advances than it is a means of self-disclosure, and, in his relationships, he was at once highly available but essentially inaccessible. Most people who knew him only casually or only in his roles as professor, colleague, or co-participant in a professional conference, were quite aware that to talk with him was to command his full attention, that to ask his help was to receive it. Few, however—probably no more than his wife Diana and perhaps such rare and old friends as Jacques Barzun and James Grossman—caught more than glimpses of an intense inner life. Nevertheless, one cannot read him, just as one could not know him at any distance, without realizing that Trilling's feelings surged powerfully within him and that he was a man who cared profoundly about people, values, and ideas.

Indeed, his capacity for enjoyment was basically a function of his large capacity for feeling and for caring. While he was too much a born-and-bred New Yorker to qualify as an outdoorsman or to respond to nature after the manner of the Wordsworth he so deeply admired, he liked to wade a trout stream, and he appreciated the skills that a fly rod requires. Although without the cultivation of a true gourmet, he enjoyed a variety of foods and wines. Cordially and genuinely interested in a remarkably wide range of people, his fascination with personalities quite different from his own and with their distinctive ways of fraternizing was only partly professional. A reflection of his preoccupation with manners, with what he called the "hum and buzz of implication" that informally but fundamentally "draw the members of a culture together," it also emerged from his committed concern for human "variousness and possibility."[2]

For closely related reasons, he sometimes found an uncomplicated and joyful pleasure in mindless movies, and his fondness for what he regarded as second-rate literature seemed based in a contented suspension of his critical faculties and a resultant freedom, almost a license, to toy with ideas and forms that levied little on his seriousness. Laughter, including his own, so long as it was without derision, was important to him. It occurred often and sometimes memorably. During the course that Trilling taught jointly with Barzun in cultural history, a student once mentioned, while the class was discussing Malthus, the famous motto of the Order of the Garter: *Honi soit qui mal y pense.* Barzun immediately quipped, *"Honi soit qui Malthus pense,"* which evoked from Trilling a wry, *"Honi soit qui mal thus puns."* On another occasion, bewildered by students' boredom with Stendhal's *The Red and the Black*, he asked if Julien Sorel did not evoke their empathy through mirroring their own drives and aspirations. Overwhelmingly, they replied that they had little use for Julien's self-serving ambitions; what they wanted was decent, socially useful work to do. "I felt," he said, "like an aging Machiavelli among the massed secretariat of the U.N."[3] In the middle of the fifth of the Charles Eliot Norton lectures, which were to become *Sincerity and Authenticity*, the book into which Trilling most fully and most openly poured his most passionate convictions, he observed that "Irony is one of those words, like love, which are best not talked about if they are to retain any force of meaning." Looking up from his text, he grinningly commented, "Other such words are sincerity and authenticity."[4] More than most of us, Trilling understood the sense of personal ease and even gaiety that results from not taking oneself *too* seriously.

But his passionate nature also had its raspy side. Although controlled, it defined in his eyes a virtue for which, therefore, there was no need for apology. He appears never to have quoted Cardinal John Henry Newman's concept of the gentleman as one who refrains from hurting others, but that notion was deeply and functionally rooted in his own code, his own courtliness. It lent fire to those occasions when he deliberately went on the attack. His virtual demolition of V. L. Parrington and Theodore Dreiser illustrates this seldom-exercised capability.[5] When he makes his pox-o'-both-your-houses case against C. P. Snow and F. R. Leavis for their roles in the "two cultures" controversy, he directs the white heat of his outrage with a laser beam's

precision and controlled destructiveness.[6] The intensity
of his assault is even greater when he charges the likes
of Norman O. Brown, R. D. Laing, and David Cooper
with cant and hypocrisy, with being neither sincere nor
authentic.[7] At other times, his assaults had the quality
of irritability, a touch of gentled and justified snide.
While praising James Pope-Hennessy's life of Moncton
Milnes, for example, Trilling cannot inhibit a few "objections . . . of a . . . carping kind":

I do not know who . . . instructed the English writers of
nineteenth-century biographies that Wordsworth is the
very type of sentimentality and taught them that whenever
they refer to sentimentality they should call it "Words-
worthian sentimentality." Mr. Pope-Hennessy has not freed
himself of this bad practice. . . . He [tells] us that a certain
Mrs. Twistleton had been born Ellen Dwight, "the daughter of a member for the Province of Massachusetts in the
House of Representatives." The best opinion holds that by
the nineteenth century Massachusetts was already what in
this country we call a State. . . . Mr. Pope-Hennessy refers
to (Hawthorne) as the author of . . . *The House With
the Seven Gables,* which is not unlike referring to *The Mill
Upon the Floss,* or a *Tale About Two Cities,* or *Much Ado
Concerning Nothing.* . . . he speaks of [Hawthorne's *English Notebooks*] as having been "very sanely edited" by
Professor Randall Stewart, as if the *Notebooks* were a natural temptation to editorial frenzy, an impression which he
confirms by speaking of them as having been "sponsored"
in England by the Oxford University Press; in my experience, the O.U.P. publishes rather than sponsors books, and
I cannot understand why it should have changed its practice on this one occasion.[8]

Good fun, but fun with a decided bite in it.

The biting fun has its rationale. Favoring and finding value in David Riesman's concept of the inner-
directed character, those persons who have internalized the ideals of adult authority, especially the
aspirations and demands of "good" parents, Trilling
cites the conventional Latin tag that so often has

served as the motto of the inner-directed personality: *Ad astra per aspera* ("to the stars through difficulty"). He also suggests the translation, "To the heights by means of asperity," for, he says, "a kind of asperity marks the dealings of the inner-directed man with the world, his fellow men, and himself."

The man of business as well as the scientific or artistic genius, or the religious leader, or the philosopher, were all at one in their submission to inner-direction. The belief that energy, self-control, and self-reverence would achieve miracles was held not only by the dullest spirits of [the nineteenth century] but also by the noblest. We must think of the Alger books as being the expression not merely of a strenuous philistinism but of a general culture in which strenuousness was valued in all walks of life. There was a connection between the passions of a Bounderby and a Beethoven.[9]

For all his charm and gentlemanliness, for all his genuine sweetness, Trilling thrived on controversy and strenuously involved himself in it. As he remarked of William James, he "hated war but he loved the idea of fighting," and he often quoted James's statement that, "If this life be not a real fight in which something is eternally gained for the universe by success, it is no better than a game of private theatricals from which one may withdraw at will. But it *feels* like a fight."[10]

And yet there is a tension, a profound and disturbing ambivalence, that constitutes the engine powering Trilling's work, both as writer of fiction and as critic. In evaluating George Saintsbury, "a critic in whom I find it hard to discover merit," he said of his response to literature that, "almost by its very lack of ideas and of interest in ideas, by the very indiscriminateness of its voracity, it expresses an emotion that might seem to pass for an idea—for it affirms the swarming, multitudinous democracy of letters, and testifies to the rightness of loving civilization and culture in and for themselves and of taking pleasure in human communication almost for its own sake and of the order and peace in which men may listen to each other and have time and generosity enough to listen even to those who do not succeed in saying the absolutely best things." And Trilling's celebration of Edmund Wilson rests on Wilson's "awareness that what constitutes the matter of literature is the discordant and destructive reality that threatens the peace which makes literature possible."[11]

If life feels like a fight, the legitimate purpose of the battle is to achieve and to maintain those forms and that degree of peace essential to creative effort, and the context always strains, always challenges, always threatens: ". . . no cultural situation is ever really good, culture being not a free creation but a continuous bargaining with life."[12] For one who prizes individuality, who struggles unremittingly for the increased autonomy of the self, who delights in the human "variousness and possibility" that only *persons* can embody, it is not easy "to love civilization and culture in and for themselves," when one knows only too well how civilization and culture cabin and shape and restrict the growth of selfhood. This, however, was the tension with which Trilling lived and with which he concerned himself, both as a literary figure and as a man.

Accounting for this abiding ambivalence on the basis of publicly available knowledge is hard to do. Much has been made, undoubtedly correctly, of his being a New Yorker and a Jew, but no other New York Jew became Lionel Trilling. He was born on the Fourth of July, 1905, in New York City, the only son of David W. and Fannie Cohen Trilling. His father was a native of Bialystok, then in Lithuania, now a city in northeastern Poland, always a place dominated by first Czarist and later Soviet Russia. Although the English-sounding name suggests one conferred by immigration authorities when David arrived, a boy in his early teens, at Ellis Island, it is entirely authentic. Relatively late in his life, Trilling discovered namesakes in many places, all tracing their lineage from a distinguished rabbi of Bialystok.

That passage through Ellis Island, according to Diana Trilling, is associated with a cloud of disgrace and failure under which Lionel's father lived all his life, and about which his son learned only in his mid-twenties. Displaying a degree of precocity as a child, David Trilling seems to have been destined for a scholarly career, probably as a member of the rabbinate. At his Bar Mitzvah, however, the ceremony of his entry into manhood, he somehow broke down. It seems likely that he stumbled and forgot, despite the prompters all around him, the prayer and the chant from the Haf-Torah required of him. Apparently embarrassed to the point of humiliation, his family appears to have shipped him off to the United States, an unwanted exile.

In response to his rejection and his shame, he somehow acquired at least the veneer of a gentleman, even a touch of the dandy. Diana Trilling recalls that his wife spoke of his having been an excellent and enthusiastic dancer, and that his son remembered him as a strong swimmer. His English was fluent and unaccented; and outside his family, he maintained an attitude of warmth, courtesy, and charm. Inside it, he was intensely hypochondriacal, and his emotions occasioned anxiety by virtue of both the ease with which they could be touched off and their intensity once unleashed. Occupationally, he established himself as a moderately successful custom tailor, but because, he said, he wanted his son to think of himself as the offspring of a manufacturer rather than a workman, he at some point went into business as a wholesale furrier.

A long series of mistakes culminated in the late 1920s in his disastrous decision to make handsome and expensive raccoon coats—for chauffeurs. Closed automobiles had by then almost universally replaced the older open models, but Mr. Trilling was sure that they were a short-lived fad. While the passengers in open "touring" cars could protect themselves against the cold with rugs, drivers enjoyed no such option; the costly coats were virtual essentials for their health as well as their comfort, and they were sure to sell. When Lionel expressed doubts and asked his father why he didn't cultivate college students as potential customers, David condescendingly explained that students could hardly afford expensive garments like his. No one could shake his curious and characteristically wishful faith in the economic resources of chauffeurs. Meanwhile, as members of his family arrived in America, he took care of them for various periods of time, performing a duty that never freed him, through adequate expiation, from the severe embarrassment that he had caused or the shaming sense of failure that he lived with.

Fannie Trilling, on the other hand, was a sturdy and protective presence in her son's life. Although her parents were also East Europeans, she had been born and spent her early girlhood in London's East End. Her Anglophilia ran deep. She read omnivorously until her eyes failed in her late eighties, and she deeply impressed her daughter-in-law by the growth and adaptiveness she displayed during the last thirty years of her life, when she steadily and thoughtfully modified her views and values. When Lionel was apparently no more than four or five, his mother shared with him her dream of his taking a PhD at Oxford; and when, because of a deficiency in mathematics, he was not admitted in good standing as a freshman at Columbia in 1921, she unhesitatingly and successfully called on the appropriate university officer to have the decision altered. To her confidence, to her loving support, and to her stimulating aspirations for him, her son quite directly attributed much of the drive, the tenacity, and the fundamental self-respect that carried him through dark years and crises to the degree of eminence that he eventually achieved.

Lionel Trilling's parents, then, were middle-class,

respectable, and affectionately respectful of the potentials for progress they perceived in their adopted America. His father bore the considerable burden of managing a guilty secret, but was a distinctive and colorful if highly trying figure. On one occasion, while living at home as a student, Lionel returned to the house to find his father rifling his desk and reading his mail. In response to his son's not-often-expressed fury, the elder Trilling explained in hurt tones, "I'm not reading your mail. I'm just interested in your life." His mother, ambitious for her boy, protected him against his father's communicable anxieties and peculiar fantasies. When Lionel, for example, won a part in a school play, she kept her husband out of the room while she heard his lines. If the family lived a somewhat restricted life socially and culturally, rarely eating in restaurants or going to the theatre, they never felt excluded because of their Jewishness, and his mother especially could deal comfortably with gentiles. Fannie Trilling maintained a kosher household, but she was entirely acceptant of her husband's taste—away from home—for ham and shellfish; and Friday-night suppers, featuring Sabbath candles, apparently represented more a compound of tradition and habit than a matter of piety or conviction.

The extent, then, to which Lionel absorbed a Jewish element into his self-concept remains unclear. In his essay on "Wordsworth and the Rabbis,"[13] he disclaims any talent as a Hebraist, either as a boy attending Hebrew school in essentially a pro forma fashion or as an adult. He speaks of his knowledge of the Jewish tradition as "all too slight," and he characterizes as "primitive" his account of the world view, the values, and the distinctive propensity for mysticism of the rabbis in the *Pirke Aboth* or *Sayings of the Fathers*. Yet his familiarity with the *Aboth* is obviously intimate, and he records his admiration for Max Kadushin's *The Rabbinical Mind* with greater warmth than sheer scholarly brilliance could provoke, or than even his acknowledgment of fondness for an old teacher makes appropriate. Four observations suggest that once again ambivalence defines a major motif in Trilling's life.

To consider effectively these four instances, we must understand something of Elliot Cohen and *The Menorah Journal*, and the role that the man and the magazine played in Trilling's youth. Cohen, after demonstrating outstanding talent as a literary scholar and critic at Yale, gave up on graduate work when he realized that a Jew in the 1920s was simply not going to be appointed to an American university post in English. Charismatic, witty, and endlessly energetic, he became managing editor of *The Menorah Journal* and gathered around him a clever and strikingly capable group of young people as staff and contributors. The *Journal* had been founded by Henry Hurwitz as a kind of extension of the Menorah Society that he had started at Harvard. His purpose was to deal with the sense of exclusion felt by Jewish students and by Jews of an intellectual disposition generally from a wide range of educational and cultural opportunities. Although the magazine was his creation, and although he maintained it through his stubborn and successful insistence that it be financed by the Jewish community, Hurwitz was too solemn, too stiff, and too sedate in both manner and outlook to determine the *Journal*'s character. The mercurial Cohen, at once glittering and substantial, dominated it and, from 1923 to 1931, gave it a quality of irreverent liveliness that embarrassed Hurwitz but made it deeply attractive to youthful and aspiring artists, writers, and social critics. Little older than his animated young staff, Cohen established unchallenged seniority and leadership by his drive, his wit, his wide range of knowledge, and his almost smothering attentiveness to the development of each of his junior colleagues. Some years later, on the strength of the same qualities, Cohen founded *Commentary*, a magazine of somewhat broader appeal but still conceived as a Jewish publication serving the Jewish community and reflecting primarily its needs, interests, and concerns.

Trilling was one of the little group that came under Cohen's strong influence, and it was in *The Menorah Journal* that, still an undergraduate and not quite twenty, he published in 1925 a story entitled "Impediments."[14] It deals with the relationship between the first-person narrator, himself an undergraduate, and a fellow student named Hettner. Hettner is "a scrubby little Jew with shrewd eyes and full, perfect lips that he twisted out of their crisply cut shape." Hettner wants talk, acceptance, friendship. The narrator hides behind "the convenient barrier" that he is erecting "against men who were too much of my own race and against men who were not of my own race and hated it." He fears that Hettner will "attempt to win into the not-too-strong tower that I had built myself, a tower of contemptible ivory perhaps, but very useful." One night, Hettner visits the narrator in the latter's dormitory room. Drinking gin and tea, the two "engage in battle" until morning, Hettner driving for relationship, for the acknowledgment of Jewish commonality, the narrator repelling him with flippancies. At last, Hettner goes to the door; "not very loud, as though he were prefacing a long tirade that must begin low to reach its height of fury, [he] said, 'What a miserable dog you are.' " The accusation and the hatred are deserved and are understood so, but it is quite clear that the tower of contemptible ivory will remain intact. A protective fortress is equally necessary against the fully committed Jew and against the anti-Semite. Complexity marks the ambivalence, but the ambivalence is undeniable.

Second, we have Trilling's own oblique comments on his Jewish childhood and associations. They are made in the context of a tribute to Robert Warshow, a brilliant movie critic and student of popular culture, who died suddenly at thirty-seven. Trilling reflects on the nature of Warshow's involvement with the Jewish community during the years that the younger man worked under Cohen in an editorial capacity at *Commentary*. "I should say," Trilling writes, "that it was essentially not very different from my own." Warshow, presumably following a pattern very much like Trilling's, "acknowledged, and with pleasure, the effect that a Jewish rearing had had upon his temperament and mind, and he was aware of, and perhaps surprised by, his sense of connection with Jews everywhere—and found that the impulses of his intellectual life came from sources that were anything but Jewish, that the chief objects of his thought and feeling were anything but Jewish. At the same time, he had, and thought he should have, a very considerable awareness of the life of 'the Jewish community' and a genuine if detached interest in it."[15] If this statement has the ring of genuineness, it also carries strong overtones of limitation. The protective personal fortress has lost some of its obvious armament and proclaimed impregnability, but its functions still are exercised, although more generously and more suavely.

Third, this impression is reinforced by Trilling's account of his refusal of an invitation from Elliot Cohen to serve on an advisory board for *Commentary* at the time the magazine was just beginning. Trilling wrote to Cohen, explaining that he "had had his experience of the intellectual life lived in reference to . . . the Jewish community" and that he had no desire to repeat it. Others might affiliate with the new publication for all sorts of legitimate reasons; "for me it could now only be a posture and a falsehood."[16] Despite the anger and expressed contempt that his letter evoked from many of the members of *Commentary*'s staff, he resolutely held to it. Indeed, the episode marked one of the barriers that Trilling's friendship with Warshow had to surmount.

Finally, there are Trilling's recollections of the period from about 1923 to 1931, when he was one of those clever young people clustered with such verve around Elliot Cohen at *The Menorah Journal*. What gave that group its coherence, what stimulated and supported its high morale, was "the idea of Jewishness." That idea had no religious significance; "we were not religious." It had no connections with Zionism; "we were inclined to be skeptical about Zionism and even opposed to it . . . during the violence that flared up in 1929 some of us were on principle pro-Arab." What was sought was "authenticity . . . a sense of identity." What authenticity and a sense of identity meant was "that the individual Jewish person recognizes naturally and easily that he *is* a Jew and 'accepts himself' as such, finding pleasure and taking pride in the identification, discovering in it one or another degree of significance. From which there might follow an impulse to kinship with others who make the same recognition, and perhaps the forming of associations on the basis of this kinship." The sincerity of this formulation can remain entirely beyond challenge, but it appears quite inconsistent with the view expressed in "Impediments," with the notion that the impulses of one's intellectual life and the objects of one's thought and feeling are "anything but Jewish," or with Trilling's refusal to serve on *Commentary*'s advisory board because to do so would amount to "a posture and a falsehood." That inconsistency and its implication of ambivalence seem intensified by the mild and somewhat covert hostility, or at least the negative self-criticism, in the activities of *The Menorah Journal*'s young, clever, liberal, and secular staff—satirizing "the sodden piety" in so much of Jewish literature, teasing Jewish life generally, writing "vivacious stories of modern sensibility in which the protagonists were Jewish," etc. Nor is either the inconsistency or the implied ambivalence lessened as a function of the purpose of these vigorous efforts—"to help create a consciousness that could respond to the com-

plexities of the Jewish situation with an energetic un-
abashed intelligence."

But the reference to "the Jewish situation" provides a useful clue. For the first four decades of the
twentieth century, whatever pride in their culture,
whatever strengthening perception of belonging to an
ancient and honorable tradition of dignity and accom-
plishment, that American Jews could bring to their own
self-definition, they could hardly avoid that toxic frag-
ment in their identity that was thrust upon them by a
profoundly prejudiced and anti-Semitic society.[17] That
external identification not only entailed an exclusion,
both deeply felt and entirely actual, from many aspects
of American life; because of its massiveness and pervasiveness, it carried the force of an accusation that
seemed somehow justified. The emotional and spiritual
effects of this experience were typically debilitating and
frequently ruinous. The interest of Cohen and the
young people gathered around him at *The Menorah
Journal* was less in the phenomena of anti-Semitism
than in these "emotional or characterological effects,
which they undertook at least to neutralize."[18]

In many important ways, Trilling's Jewishness
seems far less a central component of his self-concept
than a crucial exigency imposed by the bigotry of the
culture: *Ad astra per aspera* once again. Helped in one
fashion by the example of his parents, especially his
mother, when he was small, in quite a different fashion
by his peers and by Elliot Cohen in the decade of his
twenties, Trilling learned to respond to that exigency
with tenacity, courage, and intelligence. Jewishness was
for him a part of his "hard inheritance," the mastery of
which shaped his character and gave direction to some
of his key concerns. It was the basis for his response to
the line from Goethe with which Freud closed his post-
humous *Outline of Psychoanalysis*: "What you have
inherited from your fathers, truly possess it so as to
make it your very own." In making his Jewishness his

very own in the context of American society in the
twenties and thirties, Trilling sensitized himself to
Freud's conception of the eternal warfare between the
self, straining after its own realization, and the nay-
saying culture, and he laid the groundwork for his interest in tragedy, with its entailment of "some meaning-
ful relation between free will and necessity."[19] We are
almost certainly touching here the roots of his sense of
the intransigeance of social reality, and of the value of
imagination in coping with it. Similarly, his distrust of
panaceas, of Utopias and fanaticisms—his insistence
on confronting issues in all their complexity—found its
base in his coming to grips, at the historical moment in
which he did it, with his Jewish identity. As it did for
others, it created large and threatening problems for
him, and he maintained a constant awareness that those
problems could not be successfully, appropriately, or
decently solved by denying or otherwise attempting to
escape that identity. The tension could not be resolved;
it could only be managed.

The processes for its management were enlarged
and honed by his education at Columbia College.
When Trilling enrolled at Morningside Heights, he
entertained literary ambitions. He dreamed of being a
novelist and even had plans in that direction. Looking
back on his career shortly before his death, he wrote,
"I am always surprised when I hear myself referred to
as a critic . . . It always startles me, takes me a little
aback . . . and raises an internal grin . . . Criticism . . .
was always secondary, an afterthought; in short, not a
vocation but an avocation." Even as an undergraduate,
he was manifesting his lifelong concern "not with
aesthetic questions, except secondarily, but rather with
moral questions, with the questions raised by the
experience of quotidian life and by the experience of
culture and history." Out of this concern emerged his
tendency, for which many of his literary colleagues have
found it hard to forgive him, "to be a little skeptical of

literature, impatient with it, or at least with the claims of literature to be an autonomous, self-justifying activity." What mattered when he first went to college (and what continued to matter) was the possibility of changing and correcting the structure of society and the dynamics of culture through conscious intention and the application of intelligence.

"Intelligence" in 1921 at Columbia College was a great and special word. It had been given a banner and something of a creed by the title essay of John Erskine's *The Moral Obligation to Be Intelligent*; and it was Erskine who had instituted and directed, over the intense opposition of many of his faculty colleagues, the General Honors program that had a profound impact on Trilling and many others. A virtually forgotten man in America's cultural life, Erskine enjoyed a zestful and distinguished career marked by the publication of over forty books. Many of his novels, such as *The Private Life of Helen of Troy, Galahad,* and *Adam and Eve* retain both their readability and their merit. His autobiographical volumes, especially *My Life as a Teacher* and *My Life in Music,* continue to illuminate entertainingly some of the central tendencies in the intellectual and artistic life in America from shortly after the turn of the century through the Second World War. He wrote verse, social commentary, literary scholarship and criticism, opera libretti and music criticism, and a history of the New York Philharmonic Society and its distinguished orchestra. After he was forty, he won a minor but favorable reputation as a concert pianist; and between 1928 and 1937 he took leave from his professorship in the English department at Columbia to serve as the president of the Juilliard School of Music. More than anyone else, it was he who built that institution into the great cultural resource that it is today.

Above all else, Erskine was a teacher, fully committed to the notion that education is or should be a special form of companionship over generations, serving two purposes. One is the personal development of "courage, without which no one ever speaks out," "determination to go through to the end," and a "firmness of purpose" that emerges from and is disciplined by a sense of how one's life is inevitably and necessarily shared with others. The other purpose is citizenship, both the informed capability and the readiness to participate in the affairs of society, in the shaping of the polity. Here are the moral bases of the obligation to be intelligent about oneself and about one's social world, and the method of acquiring intelligence, conceived in this way, lies through a "delighted" and intimate familiarity with the great intellectual and artistic works of the past, primarily books but not excluding music and the visual arts. Erskine's General Honors program, which embodied his faith, consisted simply in having relatively small groups of undergraduates meet for two hours (which often stretched spontaneously into much longer periods) each week to discuss one of the great works of Western culture with two faculty members "selected for their disposition to disagree with each other." There were no lectures and no surround of literary scholarship. The *Odyssey*, the *Aeneid*, Dante's poem, or a play by Shakespeare was read as if it had just appeared on a best-seller list and was dealt with on the basis of its direct meaning for contemporaries. What Erskine was reaching for was partly an analogue to the spirit with which the "audience thronged the ancient theatre to enjoy a new work by Aeschylus or Sophocles." They "were not classical scholars [but] merely the human beings for whom the play was written." Partly, Erskine was attempting to provide students with the bases for a common intellectual life. Overwhelmingly, he was seeking an experience of "delight" that would promote the growth of intelligence in his special sense. Obviously, this enterprise at Columbia was the father of such Great Books ventures as have taken form at St. John's College in Annapolis and in Santa Fe, at the University of Chicago under the presidency of Robert Hutchins, and under the auspices of the Encyclopaedia Britannica.[20]

When Trilling entered General Honors, he was a participant in a heady and controversial project to which he brought his novelistic ambitions. "I did not count myself among those who were intelligent," he says:

I would have been the first to say that I was observant, even perceptive, of certain things, that I was intuitive; and I rather prided myself on a quality that went by the name of subtlety. But intelligence I scarcely aspired to: it did not seem to me that this was a quality that a novelist needed to have, only a quick eye for behavior and motive and a feeling heart. But . . . I was seduced into bucking to be intelligent by the assumption which was prepotent in Columbia College that intelligence was connected with literature and that it was advanced by literature.[21]

The intelligence that he was "seduced into aspiring toward" had three central informing ideas. The first lay at the heart of the humanistic tradition: that "men who were in any degree responsible for the welfare of the polity and for the quality of life that characterized it must be large-minded men, committed to great ends, devoted to virtue, assured of the dignity of the human estate and dedicated to enhancing and preserving it; and that great works of the imagination could foster and even institute this large-mindedness, this magnanimity." The second bore on the question of background and social-class membership: "The Columbia mystique was directed to showing young men how they might escape from the limitations of their middle-class or their lower-middle-class upbringings by putting before them great models of thought, feeling, and imagination, and great issues which suggested the close interrelation of the private and personal life with the public life, with life in society."[22] The third expressed itself in the faith that great works of thought and imagination

were *accessible*, that their value lay in the stimulus that
they provided not merely to specialized scholars but to
the human beings for whom they had been written. Shot
through the fabric of Columbia College and the General
Honors program was the great question that dominated
intellectual life at the close of the First World War and
that had a special liveliness and visibility in the publishing and academic center that was New York City:
After the great international upheaval, what were the
polity and the culture to be like, and who was to make
their terms?

Trilling not only found himself "bucking to be intelligent." Partly because the career of a novelist was as
economically uncertain in the 1920s as it is now, but
more because of the excitement and gratification in his
undergraduate experience, he found himself wanting to
teach literature. His was emphatically *not* the calling of
the professional scholar, although he respected and
admired scholarship. What he wanted was to perpetuate the spark-inducing discussions of General Honors
and to extend, now as a professor rather than as a
student, the consideration of those intellectual and
moral values inherent in direct involvements with literature. He had found a congenial milieu that was taking
seriously the humanistic tradition of personal magnanimity and social involvement, and he determined to
remain a part of it.

He also had found, at first in an almost inarticu-
late form, his conception of criticism. In the ambience
of Columbia College and in the talk in General Honors,
he had discovered how the interpretation of the great
works of the past could be both *interesting and cogent*[23] relative to the great and ongoing questions of
contemporary society: What forms and consequences
will characterize modern politics and modern culture?
What will be the quality of modern life? How can those
concerned with the imagination and with the life of the
mind contribute to a more tolerable, a more generous

world? These are not the questions with which formal scholarship typically deals, although formal scholarship is not irrelevant to them. They are, however, very much the questions which education must attend to, and Trilling's interest in education, begun then, continued as a strong one[24] and formed the basis of his seriousness and of the responsible enthusiasm that he invested in his role as a teacher.

In addition, his developing conception of criticism and his interest in education, probably interacting with his ambition to write fiction, led him to think of the most general audience possible for his own work. Unlike many who elect professorial careers, perhaps especially in the profession of English-teaching, Trilling from the beginning was less concerned with communicating with his academic peers and more with reaching the widest range available of people who respond to ideas and who participate in the life of the imaginative reason. To his last day in a classroom, teaching, particularly the teaching of undergraduates, significantly fulfilled that desire.

During this same period, Trilling had his first encounters with two powerful influences on his thought and outlook, Sigmund Freud and Karl Marx. To Freud, as a systematic thinker, he remained essentially committed, although he was never doctrinaire as a Freudian, and he certainly was not blind to some of Freud's deficiencies as an interpreter of literature.[25] Only for a short time did he consider himself a Marxist. Neither of these great figures provided him with a doctrinal authority so much as they forced upon him "the sense of the actuality and intimacy of history, of society, of culture" and made him feel "the necessity . . . of discovering the causative principles of these entities." What appealed to Trilling in both Freud and Marx was their convincing "programmatic rejection of the settled, institutionalized conception of reality and how it works . . . their discovery of principles of causation which lead to the conclusion that the settled, institutionalized reality is a falsehood, or . . . a mask. . . . They taught the intellectual classes that nothing was as it seemed, that the great work of intellect was to strike through the mask." They also, of course, "worked a revolution in the world-picture that was available to anyone who undertook to think at all," and for Trilling, Freud especially, but Marx too, "enforced a relationship to the past which was more comprehensive, more intimate, and more *active* than any that had existed before . . . they . . . intensified the relation of the individual to society, and to culture, and to the whole of mankind."[26]

In a number of ways, his familiarity with Freud increasingly shaped and gave a language to some of Trilling's most intimate experience and lent a distinctive color to some of his central values. With Marx, two quite different circumstances proved important. The first centers in the profound implication of Marx's thought in the Russian Revolution, only four years old when Trilling first enrolled at Columbia, and in the structure of the Soviet Union as the issue of the revolution. This state of affairs gave Marxian ideas an inevitable ideological cast; Marxian theory became thoroughly confounded with Soviet practice, and one could hardly read Marx without thinking of the revolution and its aftermath. The aftermath included intense and dramatic struggles inside the Soviet Communist Party. One of these battles pitted Leon Trotsky, intellectually a direct heir of Marx, and a revolutionary leader favored by V. I. Lenin as his successor as head of the new Union of Soviet Socialist Republics, against Josef Stalin, a highly capable administrator and astute politician, who commanded little of Trotsky's respect among the intellectuals as a Marxian theorist. When Lenin died in 1924, Stalin successfully ousted Trotsky and soon established himself as a powerful dictator. He violated a fundamental Marxian tenet—the ultimate "withering of the state"—in his policy of "consolidating socialism within one country" and in his strong and deliberate encouragement of nationalism. He reorganized the military along czarist disciplinary lines; he instituted highly conservative divorce and abortion laws, and he insisted on criteria of political "correctness" in the enterprises of education and the arts. Between 1934 and 1939, Stalin dealt with dissidence in the Soviet Union by means of a series of ruthless purges. Large numbers of once high-placed officials were executed; the total number of victims figured clearly in the millions, and the Soviet secret police, the instrument of the purges, became a symbol of terror. Before the world and in his own nation, Stalin always cited Marx as the almost scriptural authority for his actions. As a result, the confusion of Marxian theory with Soviet practice deepened into a confusion between Marx's ideas and Stalin's policies and techniques.

In the United States, a small and open Communist Party, which derived its political positions from Marx's theory, became difficult to distinguish from Stalin's sympathizers, who were primarily concerned with furthering the interests of the Soviet Union through secret organizations under direction by Russian agents. Although drawn to Marx's ideas, Trilling was revolted by totalitarian developments in the U.S.S.R. and even more outraged by manifestations of Stalinism, a thoroughly corrupt form of Marxism, in America. One of his most deeply felt and troubling preoccupations, until Stalin died in 1953, centered on the so-called fellow travelers—those Americans who were ordinarily better educated than most and liberal in their views and, though not Communist Party members, "went along" with Stalin, both in his domestic policies in Russia and in the functions of his underground apparatus in the United States, because of what they perceived as the importance, perhaps Utopian in its significance, of "the Soviet experiment."[27] The phenomena of the fellow traveler, Stalinism, and the authoritarian turn so quickly taken in the Soviet government complicated Marx's ideas almost as soon as Trilling became acquainted with them. They also deeply divided the liberal community, and Trilling's passionate antipathy to the complicating factors set him at odds with many members of that community with whom he otherwise could have made friendly common cause.

On the other hand, Marx gave Trilling a concept that enriched and broadened his experience, at *The Menorah Journal*, of grappling with "the idea of Jewishness." The concept was that of social class. His still rudimentary exposure to Marx made possible his perception that "One couldn't . . . think for very long about Jews without . . . using the category of social class. It was necessary not merely in order to think about Jews in their relation to the general society but in order to think about Jews as Jews, the class differences among them being so considerable and having so complex a relationship to the general concept of Jewishness that had at first claimed one's recognition and interest." The notion of social class as applied both to the idea of Jewishness and to the structure of the Jewish community acquired an energizing power. Trilling reports that it made society—that it made America—available to his imagination as it could not have been had he "tried to understand it with the categories offered by Mencken or Herbert Croly, or . . . Henry Adams." It connected his experience of Jewishness to an involvement in the Marxist intellectual radicalism of the thirties after the stock market crash of 1929. In the context of the radical movements of that time, he became familiar with the "moral urgency, the sense of crisis, and the concern with personal salvation that mark the existence of American intellectuals," and he discovered the realities that John Dos Passos forcefully documented in *The Big Money*. "Intellectuals who chose the life of liberty and enlightenment . . . [could be] destroyed by the cold actualities of this ideal existence . . . radicalism is not of its nature exempt from moral dangers."[28] As usual, complexity and difficulty, and the ambivalence that complexity and difficulty occasion, arose for Trilling out of his contemplation of human variousness and possibility. Ambivalence was the price of his growth and the basis for his freedom from the doctrinaire.

In 1925, Trilling was graduated from Columbia College. He remained at Columbia for another year to take his master's degree, and in 1926 went to the University of Wisconsin as a teaching assistant in Alexander Meiklejohn's Experimental College. That experience of the heartland widened his New Yorker's perspective on America; he was captivated by Madison as a university small town and by the countryside around Lake Mendota as a symbol of midwestern beauty, and he fully confirmed his decision to teach by his success and enjoyment in the classroom. But although genuinely drawn to Wisconsin and the academic life that he tasted there—they "would have given him a very sweet and gracious contentment"—he also feared something about the place and its culture. In "Notes on a Departure,"[29] a handsomely crafted and moving short story that he published in 1929, and that is clearly derived from this year in the Middle West, he speaks of the profound feeling "that the town was going to make him do things he must not do. It sought to include him in a life into which he must not go."

It seems reasonably clear that he was strongly tempted to forswear his Jewish identity, to assume the outward show of a gentile, as his name, appearance, accent, and manner made possible. To do so would have been the condition of full acceptance and a possible career at the University of Wisconsin and in the world that Madison represented. "To prevent this he . . . made use of a hitherto useless fact. He . . . said, 'I am a Jew,' and immediately he was free." Freedom, however, came only at a price: "if he embodied the sep-

arateness of his race . . . he found . . . too, that he had
assumed its antiquity. . . . 'If you will be as apart as a
Jew, be also as old as a Jew.' " Trilling's protagonist—
did not Trilling himself?—felt "old, wise, and empty . . .
a heavy senility seemed to touch him lightly all over."
The level of anguished conflict that he had reached reflects itself in his language. He was only twenty-four
when "Notes on a Departure" appeared, and it was
written out of an experience that occurred before he
was quite twenty-two. At one point, he

passionately denied all the logic he had used to strangle
what had been left of the green, irrelevant, unreal youth in
himself. For a little while, for another year, it might still
linger with him. Might it not? Ah, indeed, might it not?

He did not yet want the heavy weight, never to be
shaken off, of the real; he did not want the burden of the
good and peaceful things, of the necessary terrible things.
He wanted yet to spin out a world. He did not want the
burden and weight of good peace; he wanted to woo, in the
way of youth (at once sick and healthy), defeat and bitterness and high suffering, without the knowledge, fast creep-
ing in upon him, of what they truly were.

Trilling had passed through an ordeal of great intensity, and its stresses had at least two vital consequences for his character. First, he had made a choice
and established a basic point of honor: even if he
could, he would not forsake his Jewish origins. Second,
having made the choice, he laid down the bases for his
independence from the Jewish community. The echoes
of this Wisconsin experience reverberate some seventeen years later in Trilling's contribution in 1944 to a
symposium on the relationship of the Jew to American
society in the *Contemporary Jewish Record*.[30] His remarks hold special interest because they were made
toward the end of World War II, after he had published
his books on Matthew Arnold and on E. M. Forster,
and after his extended involvement with *The Menorah
Journal* and with Elliot Cohen.

After declaring that "I do not think of myself as a 'Jewish writer,'" Trilling says, "In what I might call my life as a citizen my being Jewish exists as a point of honor . . . the point of honor consists in feeling that I would not, even if I could, deny or escape being Jewish." And he quickly continues, "Surely it is at once clear how minimal such a position is—how much it hangs only upon a resistance (and even only a passive one) to the stupidity and brutality which make the Jewish situation so bad as it is." But having put himself on the record in this straightforward fashion, he charges the American Jewish community with "an impasse of sterility" and comes to a sharply critical, even a harsh conclusion:

As the Jewish community now exists, it can give no sustenance to the American artist or intellectual who is born a Jew. And so far as I am aware, it has not done so in the past. I know of writers who have used their Jewish experience as the subject of excellent work; I know of no writer in English who has added a micromillimetre to his stature by "realizing his Jewishness," although I know of some who have curtailed their promise by trying to heighten their Jewish consciousness.

On the road to this judgment, Trilling strikes a personal note, referring to his association with *The Menorah Journal*:

The effort of this journal . . . was . . . a generous one; but its results were sterile at best. I was deep in—and even contributed to—the literature of Jewish self-realization of which Ludwig Lewisohn was the best-known exponent. This was a literature which attacked the sin of "escaping" the Jewish heritage; its effect, it seems to me, was to make easier the sin of "adjustment" on a wholly neurotic basis. It fostered a willingness to accept exclusion and even to intensify it, a willingness to be provincial and parochial. It is in part accountable for the fact that the Jewish social group on its middle and wealthy levels—that is, where there is enough leisure to allow a conscious consideration of social

and spiritual problems—is now one of the most self-indulgent and self-admiring groups it is possible to imagine.

Trilling's writing in this brief statement has a tense
quality that appears almost nowhere else; and, although
his characteristic self-effacing and tone-softening devices—such as his acknowledging the "gracelessness"
of his position—reduce in some measure the tension, he
evinces a rare truculence. His point of honor aligns him
with a community that "does not *want* enough and is
nothing more than a resistance to an external force."
This state of affairs locks him in combat with those
who share his origins and the ethnic elements of his
identity. Trilling accepts this painful conflict with the
grim aggressiveness of a man who has been deeply
tested and who has emerged with his integrity intact.
Given the opportunity to escape his Jewish heritage,
he refused it as incompatible with honor. The election
to stand on the bedrock of his origins not only freed
him from temptation; it freed him from the self-
imposed exclusiveness of the "self-indulgent and self-
admiring" components of the Jewish community.

To understand this Wisconsin episode, its formative influence on Trilling, and its relationship to later
developments in his career as a "New York Jewish intellectual" is to understand some of his firmness of
character and something of the interplay between mind
and character in his personality. It also marks as mistaken, envious, or both, the portrayals of Trilling by
contemporaries like Alfred Kazin.[31] Respectful of
Trilling's subtlety and "the intense devotion behind the
wonderful book on Matthew Arnold," Kazin disparages
him for his "more than the usual literary connection to
things English," for "a self-protectiveness as elegant as
a fencer's," for his perceived consciousness "of social
position," for the "adopted finery in his conversation."
"No one," he charges, "could have been more discerning or less involved." Kazin's summary is that Trilling
"would always defend himself from the things that he

had left behind." What he supposedly had left behind, of course, was his status as an immigrant tailor's son, the background that should have disposed him toward a committed if intellectual radicalism, and—most of all —his Jewishness.

It seems quite clear that Trilling was leaving nothing behind. He was synthesizing his origins and his experience into a distinctive and independent selfhood. That process went on throughout his life, and the individuality that gave him value entailed his managing within himself the tensions and the contradictions of his culture. No matter how sympathetically or generously he might respond to a group, an idea, or an ideology, he reserved the room, which he felt he had earned, to search for its shortcomings and its perils. All human enterprises are subject to imperfections, often of a dangerous sort, and one of the tasks of criticism lies in the identification and the naming of the limitations and the hazards that attend creative effort in art, thought, and politics. Loyalty, Trilling had learned, frequently consists in simultaneously maintaining commitment and opposition, and selfhood always begins in defining oneself as "other," as different from even the groups in which one holds affectionate membership. Kazin and others, exuberantly finding their own identity in affiliation with an ideology or a subculture, have simply failed to recognize these elements in the human condition.

In 1927, however, Trilling had still a long developmental way to walk. When he returned to New York from Madison, he encountered an especially difficult time, alleviated only by his meeting with Diana Rubin, whom he married in 1929. She was beautiful. Her mind was quick and well-furnished, and her temperament both complemented and responded to his own. She developed her own career as critic and essayist, and their forty-six years together were deeply and warmly shared. Their first decade, however, as Mrs. Trilling has documented, was heavily shadowed and shot through with anxieties.

On a term-to-term arrangement, Trilling taught at Hunter College under the unfavorable and insecure conditions of the relationship the New York City colleges at that time had to the Tammany Hall system of patronage. Facing the necessity of a doctorate as the credential for full-fledged college teaching, he enrolled in the Graduate School at Columbia, and he increased his involvement at *The Menorah Journal*. For a long year, he worked as Elliot Cohen's assistant, apparently pleasing neither Cohen nor himself, although the personal relationship with Cohen remained intact. From 1930 through 1932, he taught evening classes at Hunter, earning slightly over $3 per hour for undergraduate and slightly over $5 per hour for graduate courses. Enrollment had to meet predetermined levels if the classes were to be given, so when insufficient graduate registration threatened, friends would sign up, recovering the fees of $15 from the Trillings out of the revenues from the course. When Trilling won a $1,800 fellowship at Columbia in 1931, he had to have special permission to continue his work at Hunter.

This was the period, of course, immediately following the stock-market crash of October, 1929, and the onset of the Great Depression. Diana's father lost everything in the market's failure; Lionel's father lost his fur business shortly thereafter. Shouldering the responsibility for his parents as well as themselves, the Trillings sustained a further blow when Diana developed a hyperthyroid condition that first made her dangerously ill and then required nearly ten years for her to regain her full strength and energy. In 1932, Ashley Thorndike, the chairman of the English department at Columbia, appointed Trilling to an instructorship. The action was as inexplicable as it was welcome; Thorndike had taken little notice of the obscure and harried graduate student who had not yet made significant progress toward his Ph.D. The post, however, paid $2,400 for teaching four courses concurrently with doctoral work. In addition, Trilling took any job he could wangle to meet the unremitting flow of debts: he reviewed books; for ten-dollar fees, he gave talks to women's clubs; he tutored needful students who could afford it; and he offered courses for private organizations like the Junior League.

His teaching seems to have suffered little under these strains, but his doctoral dissertation became a source of damaging frustration. It had been amorphously conceived as an intellectual biography of Matthew Arnold. Looking back, Trilling was "appalled" to "remember the state of ignorance and naivete I was in when I ventured upon this enterprise."[32] Ill-prepared himself, he found little support in the department of English for a project so big and so lacking in scholarly specificity. Accounting for Arnold's ideas seemed to entail a consideration of the entire intellectual history of the nineteenth century, and, even if one could somehow manage so formidable a task, there was little evidence that anyone else would care. Emery Neff, who directed Trilling's doctoral effort, was neither unfriendly nor unhelpful, but his own concerns with Arnold were essentially peripheral, and his student was, in fact, giving him little to encourage. Pressed for money, worried about his wife, and involved in an undertaking that proved always more difficult and more demanding than he had anticipated, Trilling was depressed, and his self-confidence was badly undermined. There were days when he set out for the library and wound up unseeingly at the movies, sitting through double features like a waif with nowhere else to go. Struggling against a disturbing although not total case of writer's block, he dully ground out uninspired chapters for presentation to Neff. Neff dealt with him gently, but repeatedly sent him back for another try.

Disaster fell after four years of this kind of grim

and fruitless round. The department notified him that his instructorship would not be renewed. The reason given was that the faculty understood that, "as a Freudian, a Marxist, and a Jew," he could not be happy at Columbia. When Trilling indicated that he *was* happy on Morningside Heights, the reply was that he clearly would be "more comfortable" elsewhere. There was undoubtedly an anti-Semitic element in the department's action, just as there was an anti-Marxist and an anti-Freudian cast to it. But Trilling at that time was also a frightened and heavily burdened graduate student who had not impressed his seniors, either with his intellectual competence or with the attractive facets of his temperament. His fortunes were at a depressingly low ebb; his self-esteem was tottering, and his relationships within the department were too distant for him to be known except by his unusual ethnic identity and his unorthodox interest in Marx and Freud.

A few days passed before Trilling responded directly to his notice of termination. During that period, he apparently brooded on his mother's high expectations for him and on his father's long intimacy with failure. When he finally took action, his behavior was out of character for both the thoroughly undistinguished graduate student he had been and the graciously urbane and deservedly honored professional he was to become. One by one, he called on the senior members of the department—Raymond Weaver, Mark Van Doren, Ashley Thorndike, Emery Neff, men of large authority as well as achieved eminence. He neither begged nor reasoned nor argued. Speaking with atypical forcefulness, he told each of them that they were making a serious error. They were dismissing the person who would bring distinction to the department and who would maintain and extend its prominence in the academic world; they would have to search long and hard to find any one else nearly so promising or so sure of success. It was not an act, played for the occasion;

Trilling meant what he said, and in an important sense he was making a promise—as much to himself as to the persons he addressed. Somehow, miraculously, he proved convincing. His instructorship was renewed for a year.

A dam had burst. The dispirited confusions about the Arnold project disappeared immediately. The depression lifted, and the case of writer's block cleared. In acting so decisively and at such great risk, Trilling had rediscovered his self-confidence, his self-discipline, and his wit. His instructorship was renewed thereafter by virtue of his performance and his new mode of self-presentation; and in two years he successfully submitted his dissertation for the Ph.D. degree.

Trilling himself was never sure of what had happened or of what were the sources of his acting in a fashion so foreign to his personality, and so unpredictable from his habits. He suspected that his previously mousy behavior had evoked the aggressive impulses of his senior professors: when one appears to beg so insistently for abuse, it is difficult not to oblige him. When, out of desperation, Trilling presented so different a self, they treated him as a man meriting respect and courtesy. It is also possible that his unexpected and forceful declaration of a profound self-confidence put a legitimate if tentative claim on their belief, and the faculty simply gave him the opportunity either to prove or to hang himself. Such dynamics may indeed have been the governing ones. Diana Trilling suggests a different explanation, not antithetical to these others, that finds its base in her husband's curious sense of self-worth, derived from the value that his parents had invested in him. Almost magical in its workings, possessed of strong affinities with the "sentiment of being" in Wordsworth, which later held so much fascination for him, this intuitive sense of his own worth is illustrated by an episode from his childhood. Returning home one day from school, he was set upon by a gang of boys who hurled snowballs, many of them containing stones, at him. Although frightened, he did not run. Continuing his course, he told himself that, like Balder, the Norse god of light, who could be harmed only by mistletoe, he was invulnerable. None of the snowballs reached its mark, and the street assault was not pressed. When driven to desperation's edge, when sufficiently *in extremis*, Trilling could somehow lay hold of that perception of his own being and find it in both the courage and the stimulus to his imagination to behave effectively. But his effectiveness was clearly *not*, as many have thought, the result of his being Fortune's darling, a stranger to hardship, insecurity, and self-doubt. It came through the stern cultivation of self-knowledge and integrity, and its cost may have had a great deal to do with the ghosts that always inhabited his eyes, even when they smiled.

Uncertainties still remained about his possible appointment to an assistant professorship. In 1938 and 1939, there were Jews at Columbia, but their numbers were remarkably small. They included Isadore Rabi, the Nobelist in physics, Meyer Schapiro, an art historian whose scholarly eminence was unsurpassed, and Irwin Edman and Felix Adler, philosophers whose intellectual achievements were reinforced by advantageous friendships in society and in the academic community. There were few, if any, others, and there certainly were none in the English department. Trilling had already ample evidence of the reluctance of his senior colleagues to break that barrier. Such, however, was his objective, and his drive toward the doctorate was, in his mind, simply preliminary to accomplishing it.

At that time, for the degree to be awarded, a dissertation had to be published. W. W. Norton agreed to take *Matthew Arnold* but only with a subsidy. The Trillings borrowed the necessary money, and the requirement was met. With the book just out, Trilling one day by chance encountered Irwin Edman. Edman, inquiring about his thesis, asked if he had sent a copy to Nicholas Murray Butler, the president of Columbia from 1902 to 1945. No, Trilling hadn't thought of doing so. But the president, Edman explained, *expected* his faculty to send him copies of their publications, and the procedure was well understood. First, using the campus mail, one wrote to the president, requesting permission to send him a copy of one's new work; two days later, without waiting for a reply that would not be forthcoming, one sent him the book, inscribed "To President Butler, Respectfully . . ." Protesting a bit vehemently, Trilling followed the protocol that Edman outlined.

Butler was an almost lengendary figure. When he first became Columbia's president, he acquired the leadership of a relatively small institution of modest reputation. In two decades, he had made it into a comprehensive university of genuine eminence in the academic world and set in motion the momentum that accounted in large part for its continued growth in both size and prominence. A close friend of financiers, politicians, and statesmen, he had aspirations to the presidency of the United States. In 1912, he was vice-presidential candidate on the unsuccessful Republican ticket. An internationalist and a strong advocate of world peace, he was instrumental in the founding of the Carnegie Endowment for International Peace, and in 1931 he shared with Jane Addams the Nobel Peace Prize. Butler despised Communism, and his dealings with suspected Communists and Communist sympathizers among Columbia's faculty and student body earned him the reputation of a repressive tyrant. That reputation may have been somewhat harsh, but it was quite consistent with his dominating administrative style. In a manner no longer possible in American universities, Butler in a very real sense *ruled* Columbia. However he may occasionally have abused it, Butler understood the uses of power and was an adept in power's exercise.

In the early spring of 1939, Butler, in response to *Matthew Arnold*, sent the Trillings one of his engraved invitations to dinner at the president's home. It obviously was something of a command performance. Trilling rented tails and a white tie; his wife bought long white gloves and a ball gown. On the appointed evening, they arrived at the presidential residence to find themselves simultaneously out of place in such illustrious company and the reason for its assemblage. Frank Fackenthaler, provost of the University, may have been present; Herbert Hawkes, dean of Columbia College, and Ernest Hunter Wright, newly appointed chairman of the English department, certainly were. After dinner, the ladies went with Mrs. Butler to her sitting room; the men joined the president for brandy and cigars in the library. Butler got quickly to his point. He had recently been in correspondence with the chancellor of the University of Berlin about an exchange of professors of philosophy. Columbia had proposed sending Felix Adler; the chancellor had written to indicate the unacceptability of a Jewish appointee. Looking with baleful firmness from Hawkes to Wright, Butler said, his tone making his purpose entirely clear, "I wrote back: 'At Columbia, sir, we recognize merit, not race.'" A few weeks later, in the summer, Butler, invoking his "summer powers," appointed Lionel Trilling an assistant professor of English, the first Jew to become a member of that department's faculty.

Trilling had found his intellectual home. He was promoted to an associate professorship in 1945 and became a full professor in 1948. In 1965, he was awarded the George Edward Woodberry Chair in Literature and Criticism, and he was named University Professor in 1970. When he retired in 1974, he continued to teach at Columbia on a part-time basis until shortly before his death on November 5, 1975. Through those years, from 1939 to 1975, he kept the promise that he had made in 1936, when he staved off, by his highly uncharacteristic act, his dismissal from an instructorship.

In fulfilling that promise, Trilling persistently followed an unorthodox course. When he received his appointment from President Butler, Columbia ranked—as it has continued to rank—among the most productive universities in the United States on the score of research and scholarship. Its ethos was clearly that of "publish or perish," and, if the literal rule of publication as a basis for professorial advancement was applied relatively loosely, the dominant spirit put a high premium on the faculty's original contributions to the disciplines that they represented. At the center of that emphasis lay the assumption that each professor's work would be addressed to his professional peers, that it would appear in recognized scholarly journals, and that the judgment of disciplinary peers, based on this kind of technical and formal scholarly effort, defined the essential grounds on which decisions about such matters as salary increases and promotions would be reached. The central responsibility of a faculty member, in other words, was to advance his discipline and to represent his special field of interest within it in a distinctive fashion. This conception of the professorial role led to a tendency to look with some suspicion on creative endeavors that could be regarded as "popular" or that were intended for a general audience rather than for a specialized and academic one, and it relegated teaching to an important but secondary consideration. Within the teaching function, the conducting of graduate seminars and the direction of research by graduate students enjoyed greater prestige than the instruction of undergraduates. Even at the undergraduate level, giving classes in one's own field was (and is) perceived as more significant than participating in interdisciplinary courses serving the ends of liberal or general education.

John Erskine's legacy had created a special situation at Columbia by virtue of his success with the General Honors program. The university had its share of great teachers who were also scholars of from adequate to outstanding reputation. But Erskine combined scholarly adequacy not only with brilliant teaching but with a career as a popular novelist and a popular commentator on American life. Although he was not the only American professor to transcend in his personal accomplishments the academic *Zeitgeist,* he was something of a rarity, and his influence on Trilling seems clearly facilitative and important. Trilling was undoubtedly correct in his judgment that "Erskine was not a person of the finest intellectual temper; he stood on the edge of flamboyance and at a distance from significant achievement in his undertakings as poet, novelist, musician, and critic."[33] But that evaluation overlooks the favorable conditions that Erskine had developed for Trilling's pursuing his own self-determined career path, and it must be understood in the context of Trilling's highly positive experience in General Honors during his own days as an undergraduate. General Honors, probably more than any other single influence, had formed his commitment, despite the chanciness entailed by his being a Jew, to a professorial life.

This background bears directly on his special way of keeping the promise to enhance the distinction of the English department that he had made to Thorndike and Neff, Van Doren and Weaver—and above all, to himself. He set himself at once to becoming not only an outstanding teacher, but an outstanding teacher of undergraduates. Few instructors could match him as a relaxed, clear, and witty lecturer. More importantly, he maintained throughout his career an eagerness to engage in the kinds of discussions with students that brought literature into intimate relation with their lives and that created for them windows on a larger world than they had previously known. His remarkable ability to *listen*, to understand empathically the concerns of undergraduates and the difficulties that they encountered in their reading, gave him special value and accounted for some of his popularity as a teacher. He quietly but relentlessly insisted on effort; he concentrated on the works that defined the content of his courses rather than on "student needs," and he was unsparing in his confronting the difficulty and the complexity of the ideas that the works both embodied and evoked. But he communicated, unmistakably, his own discriminating love of literature; he never failed to demonstrate effectively the ways in which literature is indeed, in Arnold's phrase, a criticism of life, and he made the consideration of literary materials a deeply and significantly human and personal experience. Nor did he forget Erskine's special stress on the element of "delight" as a condition for finding in literature the stimulus to intelligence and to a greater comprehension of culture and of one's own place and functions in society. Intellectual range, social cogency, and seriousness colored by gaiety were the hallmarks of Trilling's undergraduate classes for thirty-five years.

For him, they contrasted with his graduate seminars, which he ran with characteristic competence but with far less joy. The difference lay in the response and purposes of the students. His undergraduates shared with him in some degree his concern for the polity, for the character of the moral life, for the interplay between the individual and his culture. His graduate students, on the other hand, looked toward professional careers and were typically preoccupied with technical issues, with formal and biographical details, and with such immediate problems as identifying suitable topics for doctoral dissertations. Although sympathetic, helpful, and responsible in his relations with graduate students, Trilling found graduate instruction a not uninteresting but burdensome obligation. For him, it contained little of that warm opportunity for significant thought about manners and morals, about the quality of life in different cultural circumstances, about the nature of human experience and human destiny that characterized his work with undergraduates.

If, as a university faculty member, he invested himself as a teacher in an unusual way, he similarly followed a deviant road as a writer. Even in the dark and uncertain years in quest of his own doctorate, Trilling had "no wish to be a scholar," and his involvement with his dissertation on Matthew Arnold was animated by a "determination that the work should find its audience not among scholars but among the general public, that it was to be a work of criticism, not of scholarship." He enjoyed telling the story of how, at his final oral examination for his Ph.D., one of his examining professors leaned across the table toward him and remarked "severely that what I had presented was no doubt a good *book* but was by no means a good *dissertation*."[34] Committed, despite the character of the academic climate, to that distinction between "books" and "dissertations," Trilling, after his inner-directed fashion, hewed exclusively to his own line. *Matthew Arnold*, which appeared in 1939, was followed in 1942 by *E. M. Forster*, a critical appraisal of Forster's novels and short stories. In 1947, he published *The Middle of the Journey*, his only novel. Meanwhile, during the decade of the forties, he wrote the essays that he collected in 1950 under the title of *The Liberal Imagination*. That book brought him immediate and widespread recognition. Established as a literary critic of the first rank and of distinctive range in the kinds of topics to which he addressed himself, and in the nature of his insights into the human condition, he found his career assured. For the next twenty-five years, with grace and an unassuming confidence, he walked the critic's path of his own choosing, a deeply respected and frequently honored figure in the intellectual world.

Yet in the music of Trilling's professional life between the ages of forty-five and seventy, there is a jangling discord, a puzzle in its harmony. Before he entered college, he had aspirations as a novelist, and the handful of short stories that he published between 1925 and 1945 showed both talent and a mastery of craft. Why was *The Middle of the Journey* the only novel by a man who was "always surprised [to] hear myself referred to as a critic"? "After some thirty years of having been called by that name, the role and the function it designates seem odd to me . . . being a critic was not, in Wordsworth's phrase, part of the plan that pleased my boyish thought, or my adolescent thought, or even my thought as a young man. The plan that did please my thought was certainly literary, but what it envisaged was the career of a novelist." Something moving, something that hints of a sense of failure in a person whom the world judged so successful, pervades a statement from the same source: "This isn't the occasion on which I might appropriately attempt to say why I did not pursue, or not beyond a certain point, the career of a writer of prose fiction, and perhaps such an occasion will not ever present itself."[35]

The mystery is deepened by two other observations. First, a story called "The Lesson and the Secret," which appeared in *Harper's Bazaar* in 1945, was conceived as a chapter for a novel that was never completed. Second, in an interview occasioned by the publication of *The Opposing Self* in 1955, Trilling remarked, "I think we have to let it stand that I am a critic, but it was kind of an accident." Surprisingly, when we recall his agonies over his doctoral work on Matthew Arnold, he continued, "In 1939 I did a critical dissertation on Matthew Arnold, and I found it was a good deal easier to write criticism than fiction." Then, putting his critical efforts in the past tense and making public his future plans, he said, "One essay led to another, but it was never actually a program—like writing fiction. From now on I plan to give a good deal of time to that. I'm writing a second novel at the moment."[36] He was nearing fifty. Few men exceeded him in self-knowledge, and, although he had achieved (*ad astra per aspera*) a considerable degree of self-esteem, he was never brash and never one to ignore commitments, including commitments made to himself. A jarring chord sounds in this disjunction between his comments here and the complete dearth of fiction from his pen after *The Liberal Imagination* brought him fame and security.

Perhaps a clue presents itself through Trilling's perception of the reactions evoked by *The Middle of the Journey*. In the introduction to the reissue of the book in 1975, he refers to it as an "obscure novel" and reports that it "was not warmly received upon its publication or widely read."[37] More revealingly, discussing his friendship with Robert Warshow, who had reviewed *The Middle of the Journey* in *Commentary*, he says, "I was uneasy about the book, being aware of all sorts of things that were wrong with it, and of course it was my uneasiness that made me especially sensitive to adverse criticism, but I thought that Warshow was captious and inaccurate in the particular objections he made—I still think so—and I took his review personally. My resentment apparently went quite deep."[38] Because this frank statement is the only one publicly available in which Trilling records his reactions to the reviews of his novel, and because Warshow's judgment of the book is both the harshest of those evaluations and quite representative of the doubts expressed by many, it is important to note his "particular objections."

In essence, he makes six charges.[39] First, *The Middle of the Journey* owes a debt to E. M. Forster, especially to *Howards End*, but Forster "has a complex sense of character and a richness of wit that Mr. Trilling lacks." Second, the book makes its major appeal to the intelligence; it is highly cerebral. As a consequence, Trilling as a novelist "is removed from experience *as*

experience; the problem of feeling—and thus the problem of art—is not faced." Third, in his treatment of the
character of Gifford Maxim, whose guilt-ridden conver-
sion from Stalinism to a kind of born-again Christianity
must be motored by powerful and deep-seated psychological drives, Trilling pays little attention to the matter
of motives. Indeed, "one of the underlying implications
of the book's thesis [is] that motivations do not really
'count.' But . . . such a thesis and such an approach to
character rest ultimately on the assumption that the
most fruitful way of dealing with experience is to pass
judgment on it—and this is not the assumption of a
novelist." Fourth, in the development of Duck Caldwell, a drunken and vicious representative of the lower
class, Trilling shows naiveté: "If it was a sentimental
error to credit the working class with a virtue and an
innocence that it never possessed, it is only another
kind of sentimentality to make too much of correcting
the error." Fifth, the author's clear identification with
John Laskell, the novel's protagonist, violates a fundamental novelistic rule—no character should obviously
define the writer's "mouthpiece." And finally, Trilling
reduces the experience of his characters to a conflict
between two orthodoxies, Stalinism and Christianity,
and the problem of how to discover the "right opinion"
that can be derived from them. In taking this reductive
approach to the people and the circumstances of his
book, Trilling fails "to detach himself from the cultural
atmosphere he seeks to transcend," thus displaying a
lack of that "Olympian disinterestedness (not neutrality) which enables Forster to encompass all the complexities and impurities of experience without strain or
shock." It also requires him to "convince his reader
that some characters are 'right' and others 'wrong' (although 'rightness' and 'wrongness' are qualities not of
human beings but only of ideas); whereas the true novelist tries only to make his characters and their behavior 'convincing,' which is something entirely differ-

ent." Warshow concludes not only that Trilling "is not
a great novelist" but that he has "not yet solved the
problem of being a novelist at all."

These strictures and the final judgment to which
they lead are severe, and one can readily understand
the sense of being wounded that an author might experience on reading them. Nor is their sting much mod-
erated by Warshow's quite genuine acknowledgment of
Trilling's "intelligence and honesty" and his warm
tribute to his style: "Parts of this novel . . . are written
with beauty, imagination, and intensity." But two considerations pose an important question. On the one
hand, Warshow's concerns reflect typical reactions to
The Middle of the Journey at the time of its first appearance. Richard Cordell, for instance, commented on
how the "characters are more interesting than credible"
and observed that, "To some readers the novel will be
too chill and intellectual."[40] Similarly, the anonymous
reviewer in *Time* for October 20, 1947, found Trilling
to be "not yet a finished novelist," felt that he "mis-
handles the Dostoevskian character of Maxim," and
charged that "A good deal of the book frays out in thin,
earnest psychologizing." On the other hand, Warshow's
condemnation stands quite alone in its intensity and in
its almost unrelievedly negative tone. If the appraisals
by Cordell and in *Time* were quite in keeping with the
central negative features of the reviews, they also represent the positive emphasis that ran regularly through
them. The piece in *Time* refers to the book as a "good
and honest novel," in which Trilling "writes beautifully
about children and sometimes with gently dazzling insight about their elders," and it indicates that he can
'rival E. M. Forster in the manipulation of surprise and
anticlimax." Cordell calls *The Middle of the Journey* a
"mature and intelligent novel . . . of ideas," marked by
writing of "consistent excellence," and his final opinion
is that "Trilling has chosen to write of the modern man
whose dilemma is intellectual as well as emotional, and

has done so with acumen and compassionate understanding."

In short, the book may have been a good bit less
than a smashing success; but its critical reception—
Warshow's attack aside—was actually generous and respectful, with a fair share of praise outweighing the
expressed reservations. The reservations, however,
tended to be widely shared and to fall into the categories of Warshow's distinctive denunciation.

The question to which these two considerations
bring us is clear: Did Trilling respond in his hurt and
resentful manner *only* to Warshow's "captious and inaccurate objections"? Or was he disturbed by interaction between his own confessed awareness that "all
sorts of things were wrong" with *The Middle of the
Journey* and his perception of the consistency of the
negative comments about it? If the latter was the case,
then Warshow's dismissal of Trilling as a novelist may
have appeared as far more than a "captious and inaccurate" judgment. It may have sounded like an alarm
bell, warning him away from danger.

At age forty-two, Trilling had realized for the first
time his dream since boyhood of writing a novel. He
had his own doubts about it; and one reviewer, speaking with a special animosity but also speaking for most
other commentators on the book, sent him back for
another try. During four dark years, Emery Neff had
sent him back to try again as his dissertation chapters
failed to pass muster. Warshow, without Neff's spirit of
helpfulness, had touched a nerve still raw. Worse, his
objections probably seemed quite congruent to Trilling's own. Passionate as he was, he was devoted to
ideas and managed his life, both personally and profes-
sionally, by thought, by a rather severe reliance on cognitive and intellectual processes rather than by spontaneously translating his feelings into action. If his first
novel proved a highly cerebral form of art, it was what
one would expect, given its author's strong tendency to

live so fully through his brain. Was he *capable* of writing an extended work of fiction in which the visceral life, the life of feeling and emotion, could play a more central and authentic part? Moreover, his short stories all have an autobiographical cast. Their protagonists at least share striking resemblances to Trilling, if they are not straightforwardly his fictional doubles. ("The Other Margaret" may be an exception. Yet even here the similarities between central character and creator show straightforwardly. Elwin, for example, the story's protagonist, like Trilling, is too young to have served in the military during the first of the world wars and too old for service during the second.) This kind of identification makes for little doubt about which character speaks with the writer's voice. Was Trilling *able* to create a fictional world inhabited by convincing and authentic people, no one of whom was really himself? Involved as he was with ideas and principles, could he *novelistically* come to grips with the motives of his characters, capitalizing artistically on his interest in Freud and his rich comprehension of psychoanalysis? Or could he subdue, in an aesthetically appropriate fashion, his disposition to focus on tensions between ideas and world views rather than between persons? Was he, in short, characterologically fit to function as a novelist?

Such questions meshed all too closely with his intimate and protracted encounter, only ten years before, with failure—failure that had threatened his livelihood, his career, and his self-respect. Trilling's dismissal from his instructorship in 1936 had capped at least four years of unproductive wretchedness. He had not only drunk deeply of the gall of insecurity; he had experienced acute depression and, in his own eyes, had accomplished virtually nothing. He had had occasion to brood on the contrast between his mother's bright and hopeful aspirations for him and his father's lifelong sense of shame and of *being*, not merely experiencing, a failure, a sense essentially confirmed by his disastrously changing his occupation from that of a tailor to a furrier. When Trilling paid his startlingly uncharacteristic visits to the senior members of the English department, he had determined to avoid at all costs his father's unhappy destiny, and he had made a promise: If given the necessary opportunity, he would bring distinction to the department and add to its eminence.

If he had kept that promise in his own way, he had left no room to doubt the shining quality of his achievements. When *The Middle of the Journey* appeared in 1947, he was already known as a superb teacher. *Matthew Arnold* and *E. M. Forster* had won considerable praise, and a kind of respectful excitement had greeted eleven published essays that he was to collect with five others in 1950 as *The Liberal Imagination*. Criticism was proving a special and congenial *métier* for him. The short stories added a fillip and a dimension to both his intellectual contribution and to his image as a literary figure, but they were few in number and seemed peripheral to his primary commitments.

Against these rewarding developments, novels in which "all sorts of things were wrong" did not represent a fulfillment of his promise, nor were they in keeping with his anxiety-driven determination to avoid his father's immersion in failure. Indeed, the shift from successful critic and teacher to doubtfully regarded novelist may have seemed dimly but significantly akin to David Trilling's fateful shift from tailor to furrier. The recognition and admiration that teaching and criticism evoked were not only intrinsically pleasing. They discharged the debt that Trilling's promise imposed upon him; they vindicated the graduate student who had shown so little talent and who had so nearly failed to earn his doctorate, and they legitimized and justified the deep-seated but often beleaguered self-esteem on which he relied in crises. In contrast, his foray into novel-writing had engendered an "uneasiness" in him—

an uneasiness that began with his father, that was intensified by his experience as a Jew during the twenties and thirties in a heartlessly anti-Semitic America, and that had become intimately familiar between 1932 and 1936, when he had come perilously close to personal disaster. Warshow's uniquely damning review, given force by the much more mildly voiced but similar substance in other judgments of *The Middle of the Journey*, had raised the ghosts of the dark years between his return to New York from Wisconsin and his desperate confrontation of his departmental mentors in 1936.

Writing fiction after 1947, then, posed for Trilling an intense psychological threat. Even a person of his moral courage might well quail before the risks of failure that his experience with his first novel had unleashed. But his novelistic ambition had not only taken form early in his life, it was an "abiding" one.[41] As an abiding component of himself, it could be suppressed by the fears of failure associated with it, but it could not be completely dissipated. An understanding of this state of affairs may help in accounting for a secondary puzzle, a curiously fallow period in his productivity between 1956, when he declared in a public interview that he was busy with a second novel, and 1965, when *Beyond Culture* was published.

As we have seen, when his novel appeared in print, Trilling had completed eleven of the sixteen essays in *The Liberal Imagination*, which he published in 1950. That enthusiastically hailed book consolidated his critical reputation. Five years later, he published *The Opposing Self*, and in the following year, he brought out *A Gathering of Fugitives*, a charming compilation of seventeen relatively short pieces written between 1949 and 1956, eleven of them prepared originally for *The Griffin*, the magazine of the Readers' Subscription book club. Along with Jacques Barzun and Wystan Auden, he had served as an editor with the monthly task of selecting a book and reviewing it for the club's members. Some of these reviews combine a relaxed manner and a comfortable tone with a wit and a level of intellectual penetration that make them especially noteworthy. The present point, however, is that the time from the disturbance over *The Middle of the Journey* through *A Gathering of Fugitives* was richly productive. It was a time, too, when he became even more popular and in greater demand as a teacher. Part of his response to the anxiety that his novel's reception had elicited was to intensify his already impressive instructional and critical energies, and his doing so reassured him and restored his self-confidence.

But his next book, *Beyond Culture*, did not appear for almost a decade. Although a work of immense solidity and striking range, it contains only eight essays. Two of them are *pièces d'occasion*: the Freud Anniversary Lecture, delivered before the New York Psychoanalytic Society and the New York Psychoanalytic Institute in May of 1955; and the Henry Sidgwick Memorial Lecture, presented at Newnham College, Cambridge University, in February of 1965. It seems improbable that a man so intensely committed to his work should have done, by his own standards, so little in that nine-year span. The improbability is heightened by his having announced to the world in the interview of 1956 that he was occupied with a second novel. Because Trilling was hardly a man to renege on his commitments, it seems highly likely that he struggled for a considerable portion of that period with a fictional work that he longed to complete but could not bring himself to publish. The disappointments entangled with *The Middle of the Journey* had left him vulnerable, and the risks were simply too great even for him. In the light of his history, there can be little doubt that, beneath that splendid layer of public success, his private demons continued to harry him, and they at least played a major part in denying him the joyous satisfaction of realizing his long-dreamed-of career as a novelist.

That denial is intensified by a fateful irony. The American sales of *The Middle of the Journey* when it first appeared in 1947 approximated 5,000 copies. Nearly thirty years later, in 1975, it was reissued in paperback with Trilling's introduction, recounting the manner in which he had used Whittaker Chambers as the prototype for the novel's Gifford Maxim. Because Trilling died in November of that year, that piece may have been the last from his pen that he saw through the process of publication. In the five years following its author's death, *The Middle of the Journey* sold nearly 50,000 copies. Posthumously, Trilling achieved his boyhood ambition of becoming a successful writer of fiction, and his artistic aspirations won a significant degree of vindication.

Unaware, of course, of the vindicative but bitterly ironic destiny of his one novel, Trilling emerged, as he always did, a somewhat battered but authentic victor from his battles with his internal devils. After 1965, when he published *Beyond Culture* at the age of sixty, he edited the comprehensive anthologies, *The Experience of Literature* and *Literary Criticism*, the former with a remarkably insightful set of commentaries to accompany his selections. With his colleague Steven Marcus, he abridged Ernest Jones's three-volume *Life and Work of Sigmund Freud* into a more accessible one-volume edition. He served as coeditor of *The Oxford Anthology of English Literature* and as a member of the Planning Committee for the National Humanities Center. He received the first Thomas Jefferson Award from the National Endowment for the Humanities and gave the first Jefferson lecture, published as *Mind in the Modern World*.[42] In 1969 and 1970, he was Charles Eliot Norton Professor of Poetry at Harvard, and in 1972 and 1973, he was a Visiting Fellow at All Souls College at Oxford. Above all, he wrote what Irving Howe has called that "wonderful book,"[43] *Sincerity and Authenticity*. Even at the moment of his death, he remained in intellectual harness as the holder of a Guggenheim Fellowship.

Over the course of the precise half-century that elapsed between the publication of "Impediments" in *The Menorah Journal* in 1925 and his death, Trilling richly elaborated but never fundamentally altered his point of view or his preoccupation with four central human themes. His deepest and recurrent concerns centered on the struggle between the individual, striving for self-realization, and the culture that simultaneously nurtures him and ruthlessly bends him to its impersonal and corporate will; the precarious balance in our experience of freedom and necessity, the tension between personal will and the recognition of the world's intransigeance; the perils of Utopian dreams, of fanaticism, of the damage that can be done by decent people who have no doubts about their own ideas, their own ideals, or their own commitments; and the uses of the imagination in dealing with reality, especially social reality—the reality of politics and of our cultural experience. In making these concerns articulate in relation to a variety of specific topics and as a means of illuminating a wide range of literature, his achievement permits us to say of him what R. H. Super has said of Trilling's most important, except perhaps for Sigmund Freud, intellectual and spiritual model—Matthew Arnold:

in an age when the moral desperadoes might look to a past that could never be retrieved, when the liberals might lose sight of reality in claptrap and machinery, he perceived that . . . though the modern spirit was necessarily liberal, yet [that] liberalism was hopelessly inadequate to the demands of humanity. . . . By perceiving what elements of . . . liberalism gave promise for the [future], he became, not only what he called Emerson, "the friend and aider of those who would live in the spirit," but the best representative . . . of the modern spirit.[44]

2

7777777777777777777777777777777777777777777777

Civilization
and Its Discontents

No set of ideas so consistently, so dominantly, preoccupied Lionel Trilling throughout his career as those formulated by Sigmund Freud in *Civilization and Its Discontents*.[1] From the time of its first appearance in English in 1930, Trilling frequently reread and pondered this little book. He taught it often in his classes at Columbia University, and it formed a significant and fundamental component of the background of thought out of which his lectures, essays, and judgments of literary and social affairs emerged. Our comprehension of Trilling is enriched by an understanding of Freud's view of how individuals develop in the cultures of which they are inevitably a part.

Developed as a psychoanalytic theory of culture, Freud's basic notions and primary thesis in *Civilization and Its Discontents* are surprisingly independent of the corpus of psychoanalytic thought.[2] One needn't be an orthodox Freudian or belong to one of the derivative but closely related psychological movements to find a moving cogency in this reading of the human condition. It begins with the observation that, from an evolutionary point of view, humankind has specialized in neither strength nor speed nor adaptive camouflage. The grizzly bear, the deer, and the chameleon are among our many masters in these capacities. *Homo sapiens* survives and thrives by virtue of being *homo faber*, the only member of the animal kingdom who creates—who uses tools, including weapons, who manipulates symbols and ideas, who *makes* the conditions that permit his living anywhere on earth, rather than being confined to a particular ecological niche. What enables our species to conceive of and to manufacture everything from surgical instruments to cyclotrons, from fur garments to air conditioning, from statutes and constitutions to songs and paintings, is essentially our complex nervous system, our big and highly convoluted brains.

That large and intricately folded brain of ours requires the birth of an extraordinarily incomplete organism. In contrast to kittens or puppies, or even to the offspring of monkeys and apes, all of which enjoy a reasonable chance of survival as independent organisms within a few short weeks after birth, the human baby enters the world much too soon. Yet the alternative, given the mammalian nature of the human species, would be mothers of gigantic size—much too large to function with necessary efficiency in a terrestrial environment, and quite lacking in earthly survival value. The open fontanels in the infant's skull are only one of the provisions in the evolutionary scheme for a nervous system that does not reach full maturity until about the eighteenth year of extrauterine life. The entailment of this peculiar neural specialization in the biological, evolutionary sense that gives humankind its distinctiveness is the uniquely long period that we know as infancy and childhood.

The price, then, of our remarkable nervous systems is an extended experience of virtually complete helplessness and dependency, during which our well-being and our very survival rest on the mediation of our needs by others. Perhaps even more importantly, all of us go through a stage of infantile omnipotence in which the world is simply an extension of ourselves, responding to our cries with food, warmth, tactile support, stroking and gentle stimulation, and similar ministrations. But, as we begin to recognize the external world as quite independent of us, we acquire the frightening knowledge that, far from being omnipotent, we are powerless—small, weak, ignorant, and quite literally dependent on adults over whom we can exercise no controls at all. Still later, as young children, as we begin in more autonomous ways to direct our energies and to interact with our environments, we learn to model our behavior on that of the adults whose presence remains indispensable to us and whose will, potency, and authority impress us as irresistible.

Simultaneously, however, the same evolutionary process that has made a long dependency and helplessness a part of our neural specialization has also endowed us with what Cannon[3] called "emergency reactions." These are the tendencies to flee or to do battle—the famous capacities for "fight or flight"—that become prepotent when we are threatened. These physiologically grounded propensities, which have a high survival value under primitive conditions but which have probably been untouched by evolutionary change for ten millennia or more,[4] prepare us for essentially violent activity and set up the internal conditions that we quickly learn to recognize as fear and anger, terror and hostility or hatred. Similarly, our biological endowment includes the raw sexual impulse that insures the continuation of the species but that, in itself, has little inherent connection to love, the qualities of intimacy in human relationships, or the experiences of affection that clothe survival with distinctively human value.

Quickly sketched, these circumstances set the stage on which the dramas of our individual lives must be played. On the one hand, we are clearly and definitely *cultural* beings. Inescapably, our initial survival and our later realization of at least some of the major potentials inherent in our nervous systems depend on our membership in a group and on our acceptance to some significant degree of the folkways and norms of that group. Even more critically, much of what we are

we learn from participating—first as a helpless dependent and later as a more or less full-fledged citizen—in
the affairs of the group. In short, we begin early to form
rudimentary concepts of right and wrong, good and
bad, desirable and undesirable, and to attach to these
dimly conceived ideas our feelings of security and acceptance by the people on whom we are dependent and
with whose destiny our own fate is somehow bound up.
This process defines the beginnings of our moral sense,
our perception of a moral order in the corporate life on
which we, willy-nilly, rely, regardless of how reluctantly, for our personal survival and growth. Out of
these beginnings develop both our awareness of the
moral bond that ties us to our society and our unconscious connection with the moral order that at once
protects and restrains us. If that involvement in the
moral dynamics of the culture is always tenuous, it
remains implacable, inevitable, and, to greater or lesser
degree, we incorporate into ourselves the norms and
values of our cultural context. On the other hand, we
are ineluctably *selves*. Inherently, we are self-protec-
tively drive-ridden animals, strongly inclined to take
what we desire, to destroy whatever frustrates us, and
to behave as amoral egoists under the control of biolog-
ically motored wishes.

Human life consists, then, in an endless encounter
between the impulse-dominated individual and the nay-
saying, regulatory culture. Without the supports of culture, we fail at even rudimentary levels to achieve the
attributes that we identify as distinctively those of *persons*, or to attain the security, the capacity for delight,
or the kinds of relationships that underlie our prizing of
life itself, and that permit us to behave in reasonably
rewarding and effective ways. But the culture exacts a
price: We may act on our impulses only under pre-
scribed conditions; otherwise, the probability of punishment is high. In consequence, no matter how highly
socialized we may be, no matter how fully we have

interiorized the manners and morals of our society, we are not infrequently likely to feel trapped and thwarted by the network of regulations and commandments our society has woven around us, to experience alienation and loneliness by virtue of our "otherness" from that ruling social context in which we are inevitably imbedded, and to find all too familiar the pangs of conflict as we struggle to enhance our sense of selfhood against the constraints and restrictions of the culture in which we nevertheless live and move and have our being.

It is against this background that we can understand Trilling's insistence that the idea that "preoccupies . . . literature and is central to it" is the idea of the self. Although his reference here is to literary works of the nineteenth and twentieth centures, his incisive commentaries in *The Experience of Literature*, an anthology of fiction, drama, and poetry from Sophocles to Bernard Malamud and Robert Lowell, make it clear that he hardly regarded earlier works as discontinuous from later ones in this respect. What he perceived as distinctive about *modern* literature, however, was "its intense and adverse imagination of the culture" of which it is a part.[5] When Thomas Mann once indicated that all his work represented an effort to free himself from the middle class, he was articulating this yearning to realize self more fully by slipping the shackles of the determining culture. Trilling responded sympathetically and positively to that impulse toward selfhood, that assertion of individuality against the cabining influences of traditional values, that imagination of a socially unmediated commerce between the person and his distinctive experience.

But he also perceived that the longing to break the bonds of the middle class engaged a still deeper desire to escape society generally, to divorce the self from a culture conceived as alien and repressive. Without romanticizing it, Trilling would have found at once the moving significance in the story of Willy Wolfe.[6] Willy began his life as the favored son of a well-to-do physician in Litchfield, Connecticut, one of New England's most advantaged, beautiful, and tradition-steeped villages. He ended it at age twenty-three as Cujo the Unconquerable, the last guerrilla of the sordid Symbionese Liberation Army, firing futilely at police and FBI agents from the crawl space under a seedy little frame house in Los Angeles, until the burning structure fell on him. That journey from conventionally happy beginnings to a darkly nihilistic death symbolizes action in obedience to the modern voices that tempt and lure and urge beneath the surface and under the forms of modern art. Although, obviously, Yeats and Eliot, Joyce and Proust and Kafka, Lawrence, Mann, and Gide did not directly incite Willy Wolfe to his frightening and destructive quest, they embody and make articulate some of the same drives, some of the same sensed discontent with the culture, to which Willy responded in so fatal a fashion.

For Trilling, literature, which he took as the central diagnostic index of a society, always invites its audience to new perceptions and new ideas, always recruits readers to changed behavior and to changed styles of living and of participating in the community. The invitations and the recruiting efforts of the modern writers to whom he was most committed stem from an enhancement of the self over culture, from a condemning analysis of the moral chaos and the often brutal coerciveness of Western society, from the rejection of our inherited verities as deceptive and hypocritical, and from a critical questioning of the largely institutionalized values of our industrial age. The works of the moderns emanating from these oppositional concerns are "manifestly contrived to be not static and commemorative but mobile and aggressive, and one does not describe a quinquereme or a howitzer or a tank without estimating how much *damage* it can do."[7] In the warfare between self and culture, the self may prove the casualty. One doubts, for example, that Cujo the Unconquerable attained, even privately, a sufficient degree of self-actualization to warrant his wholesale, hostile, and finally self-defeating disavowal of his culture. And in that warfare, culture may lose much of its facilitative and developmental powers along with some of its nay-saying oppressiveness.

Recognizing this potential for damage aroused in Trilling a counter-sense of the human condition that conferred on Freud and the Judaeo-Christian legacy a validity that the modern prophets, despite his sympathetic admiration of them, could not dissolve. For him, Freud's view of the nature of humanity preserved "something—much—of the stratum of hardness that runs through the Jewish and Christian traditions as they respond to the hardness of human destiny. Like the Book of Job, it propounds and accepts the mystery and the naturalness—the natural mystery, the mysterious naturalness—of suffering." In formulating his essentially austere vision, Freud "had the intention of sustaining the authenticity of human existence that formerly had been ratified by God."[8] Within himself, and therefore in his criticism and in his fiction, Trilling joined the issue. On the one hand, he found value in the massively liberating thrust of the moderns and supported their aggressive advocacy of a more richly realized self; on the other, he found in culture the very groundwork of humanity and defended it on historic principles. Although secular in conviction and outlook, he invested an informed seriousness in the moral traditions of both Jewish and Christian faith and theology. Although very much a modern, he adhered to classical ideals in his understanding of the antique maxims of "the middle way" and "nothing in excess" as entailing a measure of self-restraint[9] and often a personal and somewhat precarious balancing and management of unresolved and perhaps unresolvable tensions—like the tension between self and culture. And, although one of the least doctrinaire of men, he maintained a profound commitment to psychoanalytic ideas because he found compelling Freud's tragic view of the human condition.

This complex point of view—perhaps, more accurately, this complex and informed sensibility—found special nourishment in Trilling's encounter with Matthew Arnold. Concerned initially with Arnold as a poet "whose melancholy spoke to me in an especially personal way,"[10] Trilling's long immersion in the writer whom he came to identify as "the first literary intellectual in the English-speaking world" deepened and enriched his understanding of the modern era's special conflicts between self and culture. The experience of loneliness and the barriers to effective, durable, and mutually satisfying interpersonal relationships, the relationships of friendship and of love, came into clearer focus for him. His analysis of the well-known "Dover Beach" is illustrative. In that poem Arnold characterizes "the world"—that is, the human world, the culture —despite its seeming "To lie before us like a land of dreams, / So various, so beautiful, so new," as really affording

> neither joy, nor love, nor light,
> Nor certitude, nor peace, nor help for pain;
> And we are here as on a darkling plain
> Swept with confused alarms of struggle and flight,
> Where ignorant armies clash by night.

The reason for this disjunction between appearance and reality is that the "Sea of Faith," which once "round earth's shore / Lay like the folds of a bright girdle furl'd," now only howls

> Its melancholy, long, withdrawing roar,
> Retreating, to the breath
> Of the night-wind, down the vast edges drear
> And naked shingles of the world.

As an antidote to this state of sad and joyless uncertainty in the lot of humanity, the poet can only plead,

"Ah, love, let us be true / To one another!" He can only offer and ask for loyalty in intimacy—not pleasure, erotic excitement, a warm sharing of experience, a confidence in mutual understanding, but only loyalty. As Trilling notes,

perhaps never before in literature has a lover given a reason for love, and a reason, which, while asserting its necessity, denies its delight. It is believed by all lovers that love has the power not only of making the world various and beautiful and new, but also of maintaining it in variety, beauty, and novelty. But the lover of "Dover Beach" denies love's efficacy. . . .[11]

But there is more. Arnold comments that "Sophocles long ago" also heard the ocean's

> grating roar
> Of pebbles which the waves draw back, and fling,
> At their return, up the high strand,
> Begin, and cease, and then again begin,
> With tremulous cadence slow, and bring
> The eternal note of sadness in,

and his hearing this melancholy sound "brought / Into his mind the turbid ebb and flow / Of human misery." Although Arnold is responding in part to the ebbing of the sea of Christian faith under the impact of Darwin and the rising science of the latter half of the nineteenth century, his direct reference to Sophocles makes it clear that a waning Christianity fails to account by itself for his bleak reading of the human situation. Trilling makes two points. First, Arnold interpreted a lessening of religious faith as symptomatic of a general diminution in personal zest and vital self-confidence, in that delighted and essentially hopeful and optimistic involvement in life that William James called "animal faith." It is the erosion of that basic *feeling* that humanity enjoys a proud destiny that so deeply distresses him.

Second, Arnold almost certainly had in mind the third chorus of Sophocles's *Antigone*: "Blest are they whose days have not tasted of evil. For when a house hath once been shaken from heaven, there the curse fails nevermore, passing [from generation to generation] even as, when the surge is driven over the darkness of the deep by . . . Thracian sea-winds, it rolls up the black sand from the depths, and there is a sullen roar from the wind-vexed headlands that front the blows of the storm." Although the chorus speaks only of the dreadful and inescapable fate of the members of certain families under a curse, and not of human misery universally, "the generalization," as Trilling says, "can of course be made." Making it, we strongly suspect that Arnold thought further of the difference between this passage from the play and the tone of *Antigone's* second chorus, which opens "Wonders are many, and none is more wonderful than man," and then proceeds to sing of man's achievements and glories. The contrast underscores the vulnerability of both human pride and human security. Fate can deal harshly with that confident relish for life that lies at the heart of animal faith. When we perceive, in all their power, these harsh, uncaring, destructive forces in the universe, then we lose our rejuvenative wonder at the triumphant qualities of our species; the world seems suffused with uncertainties and dangers, and love is robbed of its joys and of its invigorating, revitalizing potentials.

This theme recurs often in Arnold, but if, in "Dover Beach," it reflects primarily a commentary on a disheartening, alienating culture, in the Marguerite poems, as Trilling observes, it cuts closer to the bone of personality itself. A love affair, as love affairs sometimes will, fails. Out of his heartache, and taking the ending of the relationship as the symbol of human separateness, the poet perceives that "in the sea of life enisled, / . . . We mortal millions live *alone*." Between person and person there surges an "unplumb'd, salt, estranging sea" that forces a grim recognition of a fundamental truth: "Thou hast been, shalt be, art, alone." If driven by loneliness, one asks, "And what heart

knows another?" then the answer, simultaneously cold
and touching, suggests itself at once: "Ah! who knows
his own?" But if one turns from the world of culture to
the world of nature, seeking both for self-knowledge
and for the calm and composure that the sea and the
stars seem to possess, the response tends to prove a bit
Olympian for a member of the mortal millions. An "air-
born voice" says, "Wouldst thou be as these are? Live
as they." The forces of nature "demand not that the
things without them / Yield them love, amusement,
sympathy . . . /self-poised they live, nor pine with
noting / All the fever of some differing soul." Although
the poet hears in his heart an echoing and affirmative
cry—"Resolve to be thyself; and know that he, / Who
finds himself, loses his misery"—he cannot escape an
awareness of the terrible entailments. If being oneself
means absolute self-dependence, and if absolute self-
dependence is the one means of escaping misery, then
one remains forever cut off from the love, regard, and
companionship of others. Of equal importance, it implies that one must achieve a complete indifference
to others; one must be forever unmoved by their suffering, unattracted by their laughter or beauty. And we are
back, as individuals, enisled within the unplumb'd, salt,
estranging sea.

For Trilling (as for others), beyond the articulation here of the universal human vulnerability to loneliness, two ideas in this context have particular significance. One is Arnold's affirmation of the validity and
centrality of *feeling* in human affairs. The fear of the
loss of the power to feel defines one of the major and
repeated themes of literature at least since the industrial
revolution. D. H. Lawrence springs at once to mind,
but Nietzsche, Kafka, and a host of others, including so
current and so popular a writer as Philip Roth,[12]
crowd close behind. For all his prizing of the intellect
and of intellectual values, Arnold's concern with the
desiccating effects of rationalism—the rationalism

bound up with an increasingly scientific industrial and economic life—was profound. He saw this kind of rationalism as smothering the instinctual processes and narrowing the imaginative capacities of individuals, and Trilling, extending this view into the twentieth century, shared Arnold's alarm and with him looked largely to literature as a corrective. It is elements in the culture, not hardship or sorrow or old age, that threaten to dry up the wellsprings of emotion and imagination:

> we may suffer deeply, yet retain
> Power to be moved and soothed, for all our pain . . .
> No: 'tis the gradual furnace of the world,
> In whose hot air our spirits are upcurled
> Until they crumble, or else grow like steel—
> Which kills in us the bloom, the youth, the spring—
> Which leaves the fierce necessity to feel,
> But takes away the power . . .

The restricting, the hardening, the withering of the *power* to feel may be a function of a culture that sets a premium on a preeminent and narrow concept of reason. But what is the source of that *fierce necessity* that so obdurately remains? As much as did Freud, Arnold saw the self as taking shape under the molding influence of culture, as quite literally determined by it. But like Freud, he also thought of the self as in continuing opposition to the culture, as locked in a continuing struggle with it. Much of the energizing force, the motivating vigor, for that struggle stems from that fierce necessity to feel. If that emotional impetus lacks both direction and content until experience and reflection have colored it, it nevertheless operates as one of the inherent engines of human conduct and finds its seat not in the cultural surround but in the biology, the fundamental evolutionary nature, of humanity. Although this notion was deeply rooted in Arnold's thought, he never—Victorian literary intellectual that he was—discussed the biological groundwork of the

idea. Freud, of course, made much of it. Trilling,
steeped in Arnold, comments,

> . . . Freud may be right or he may be wrong in the place he
> gives to biology in human fate, but I think we must stop
> to consider whether this emphasis on biology, correct or
> incorrect, is not so far from being a reactionary idea that it
> is actually a liberating idea. It proposes to us that culture
> is not all-powerful. It suggests that there is a residue of
> human quality beyond the reach of cultural control, and
> that this residue of human quality, elemental as it may be,
> serves to bring culture itself under criticism and keeps it
> from being absolute . . . somewhere in the child, some-
> where in the adult, there is a hard, irreducible, stubborn
> core of biological urgency, and biological necessity, and bio-
> logical *reason*, that culture cannot reach and that reserves
> the right, which sooner or later it will exercise, to judge the
> culture and resist and revise it.[13]

To that form of reason and to that basis for the self's
resistance to culture, Trilling unswervingly gave his allegiance. In significant part, his commitment to biologi-
cally grounded *feeling* as at least a fundamental datum
in the human condition stemmed from Arnold's persuasiveness about the nature of emotion, of animal
faith.

But Arnold's second idea carries rather different
implications. If the gradual furnace of the world, the
culture, burns away our power to feel, the cultivation of
that power—the cultivation of the self in its distinctiveness—necessarily sets us increasingly apart from
our fellows. The more richly we develop and diversify
our private, inner lives, the more different we become
from those from whom we expect love, amusement, and
sympathy; and the greater that difference becomes, the
more difficult and the more subject to misunderstanding
the chancy process of communication grows:

> Are even lovers powerless to reveal
> To one another what indeed they feel?
> I knew the mass of men conceal'd

Their thoughts, for fear that if reveal'd
They would by other men be met
With blank indifference, or with blame reproved;
I knew they lived and moved
Trick'd in disguises, alien to the rest
Of men, and alien to themselves . . .
But we, my love!—doth a like spell benumb
Our hearts, our voices—must we too be dumb?

Arnold's answer is, in Trilling's phrase, an acknowledgment of "the general inability of human atoms to meet:"[14]

Why each is striving, from of old,
To love more deeply than he can?
Still would be true, yet still grows cold?
—Ask of the Powers that sport with man!

They yok'd in him, for endless strife,
A heart of ice, a soul of fire;
And hurl'd him on the Field of Life,
An aimless unallay'd Desire.

The result is an unwitting, frequent, damaging flaw in our relationships with one another—our relationships as friends, lovers, parents, and children. It was familiar to Freud; it was to Trilling. "No writer of his time," he says, "understood in terms as clear and straightforward as Arnold's this psychological phenomenon of the distortion of purpose and self and the assumption of a manner to meet the world."[15] The divorce between the reality of self and its appearance permeates our interpersonal transactions. In order to cope with the exigencies of the moment, to defend ourselves against some immediate threat or to serve some short-range objective, we play a role. While satisfying, through role-playing, the demands of these social impingements on our selfhood, we come to the rather bewildered and guilty realization that "what we say and do / Is eloquent, is well—but 'tis not true." Alienation from self may be intimately related to alienation from culture, but the two aspects of modern experience are far from identical.

For Trilling, it was Arnold the poet who made this distinction both humanly crucial and relevant to literature, that centrally important criticism of life that permits persons to keep alive their aspiration to be at once uniquely individual and corporately civilized. This insight of Arnold's, blending with Freud's perceptions, deeply affected Trilling. His understanding of it prevented his taking fashionable stands with those who account for all human ills on the grounds of oversimplified conceptions of cultural deficiencies and cultural oppression. It heightened his sense of complexity in human affairs while deepening his respect for the individual's limited but real capacity to influence his own destiny. And it provided him with a perspective from which he illuminated in a remarkably distinctive way much of the literature and many of the issues with which he so influentially concerned himself.

He exemplifies this perspective and its value in his treatment of Jane Austen. In agreement with F. R. Leavis that she is "the first truly modern novelist of England,"[16] Trilling speaks of her as requiring a reader "to make no mere literary judgment but a decision about his own character and personality, and about his relation to society and all of life." This kind of challenge most deeply commands his respect. It is the challenge of Yeats and Eliot, of Joyce and Proust and Kafka, of Lawrence, Mann, and Gide, who insistently ask "if we are content with ourselves, if we are saved or damned"; here is the radical criticism of life that excites his commitment, his fear, and his ambivalence.[17] Nowhere does Jane Austen throw down her gauntlet in a more complex or imperious fashion than in *Mansfield Park*.

Although its original publication evoked more admiration than any of the other five novels in her canon, Trilling notes that this book goes curiously against the modern grain. Austen's devotees, he says, find it an embarrassment; her detractors point to it as full justification for their animosity. Unlike the sprightly, responsive, and interestingly strong-minded heroines of the other stories, Fanny Price is sickly, priggish, and colorless. Worse, she is self-consciously virtuous and reaps, in an outlandish way, material benefits from her practice of self-righteousness. In contrast to the cosmic expansiveness and the generosity of spirit that pervade the other novels, *Mansfield Park* speaks as "no other work of genius has ever spoken . . . for cautiousness and constraint, even for dullness. No other great novel has so anxiously asserted the need to find security, to establish a refuge from the dangers of openness and chance." It seems to prefer stillness over action, withdrawal over involvement, in a manner that today strikes us initially as not only impracticable but irresponsible. And yet, Trilling argues, "it is a great novel, its greatness being commensurate with its power to offend."

One of the issues that preoccupies the characters in *Mansfield Park* has to do with whether Edmund Bertram shall become a clergyman—with, that is, the nature of his commitment to a profession. The idea of a profession had a peculiar importance for Jane Austen as it did for nineteenth-century England generally. As the earlier ideal of the gentleman lost its force, a considerable portion of its moral prestige descended on the professions. Daniel Doyce, the engineer in Dickens's *Little Dorritt*, and Dr. Lydgate, the physician in George Eliot's *Middlemarch*, illustrate the strongly emergent belief that one's moral life is deeply connected with one's devotion to the discipline of one's vocation. This belief, in turn, reflected a central concept in English ethical and spiritual life, the concept of duty. Edmund's consideration of the Anglican priesthood as a career was entirely consonant with this view of the professions. In 1814, when *Mansfield Park* first appeared, the

church functioned in a fashion quite congruent to that
of secular institutions: Its objective centered far less on
salvation than on the performance of duty.

That notion of duty, for us on the eve of 1984,
seems quaintly and even a bit harshly old-fashioned.
Our contemporary locutions—"cooperation," "responsible action," "accepting group consensus," etc.—imply
doing what one should do without subjecting the self to
pain or even to serious inconvenience. Duty, on the
other hand, suggests a self in which impulses and desires powerfully assert themselves but, by unremitting
and uncomfortable effort, are offset by a willingness to
subordinate them to some external and essentially abstract value. Matthew Arnold found it necessary to
remind himself daily of his duty; he insisted that the
impulses had to be "bridled" and "chained down," and
he spoke eloquently of the "strain and labour and suffering" of the moral life. Trilling recounts a telling
anecdote of F. W. H. Myers. He was walking one evening in Cambridge with George Eliot. Their talk turned
on God, immortality, and duty; and she spoke of how
inconceivable was the first, how unbelievable the second, "yet how peremptory and absolute the third."
Myers continues, "Never, perhaps, have sterner accents
affirmed the sovereignty of impersonal and unrecom-
pensing Law. I listened, and night fell; her grave majes-
tic countenance turned towards me like a sybil's in the
gloom; it was as though she withdrew from my grasp,
one by one, the two scrolls of promise, and left me the
third scroll only, awful with inevitable fate."

Aware of the puzzlement that this psychological
state of affairs characteristically evokes in readers verg-
ing on the twenty-first century, and knowing the un-
familiarity now attendant on this moral position, Trilling appeals to Wordsworth, as he often does, for a
clarifying bridge across the years. He takes for granted
some remembrance of the "Ode to Duty," in which that
stern daughter of the voice of God is invoked as "a

light to guide," and as a power that "From vain temptations dost set free; / And calm'st the weary strife of frail
humanity." Personified (even deified to a degree), duty
is portrayed as having "saving arms" and a "smile upon
thy face," and as the giver of support and serenity. If
the discipline of duty proves severe, the rewards of
practicing it include serenity and a sure and uninter-
rupted sense of identity in which one can take a quiet
pride.

Against this background, we can understand the
use to which Trilling puts "Resolution and Independence." Wordsworth there poses the problem of how
the self can preserve itself from its own nature, how it
can protect itself from "the very sensibility and volatil-
ity that define it." Wordsworth is quite clear: "As high
as we have mounted in delight / In our dejection do we
sink as low"; and in the cultivation of self—of perceptiveness, of talent, of reputation, through aspiration
and achievement—we recognize an inherent potential
in ourselves (not in society or in circumstance, but in
ourselves) for anxiety and depression, for "despon-
dency and madness." An intercessor appears in the
person of a poor leech-gatherer ("The oldest man he
seemed that ever wore grey hairs"), a figure "not all
alive nor dead, / Nor all asleep." Although he obviously
"had many hardships to endure," the old man speaks
with a courteous gravity, and he is first seen "As a huge
stone is sometimes seen to lie / Couched on the bald top
of an eminence." Trilling characterizes the leech-gatherer as "rocklike in endurance, rocklike in insensibility,
annealed by a simple, rigorous religion, preserved in
life and in virtue by the 'anti-vital element' and trans-
figured by that element." The poet recognizes him as
what we would presently call a "model."[18] What he
embodies—and the point has the same validity today as
in 1802, when "Resolution and Independence" was
composed—is the perception "that the self may destroy the self by the very energies that define its being,

that the self may be preserved by the negation of its own energies. . . . Much of the nineteenth century preoccupation with duty was not a love of law for its own sake, but rather a concern with the hygiene of the self."

This "hygiene of the self" constitutes the substance of *Mansfield Park*. A recognition of this conception is essential to our understanding of a seemingly absurd but central scene in the novel where a great and ostensibly pointless debate occurs over the amateur production of a play as a means of amusement in a relatively isolated country house. What is decisively at issue here is a rather primitive feeling about dramatic impersonation, a feeling that Jane Austen turns to pointed account. That feeling entails, as Trilling puts it, "the fear that the impersonation of a bad or inferior character will have a harmful effect upon the impersonator, that the impersonation of any other self will diminish the integrity of the real self."

The notion of role-playing, in which all of us as moderns are heavily and inescapably implicated, suddenly acquires a certain brittleness and confronts a surprising challenge. We hear here a resonant echo of Arnold's "what we say and do / Is eloquent, is well— but 'tis not true," and the contrast between Wordsworth's mercurial poet, troubled by anxieties and fearing madness, and the massively permanent and imperturbable identity of the leech-gatherer comes sharply into focus. In such context, the question of Edmund Bertram's choice of the clergy as a profession takes on new meaning. The election of a career can be primarily an assumption of a role, or it can be a commitment that contributes to a fixing of the nature of the self. Is the "impersonation" of a parson to be a permanent one that enlarges the true self and establishes Edmund's personal integrity, or is it to be a bit of role-playing that may serve momentarily to solve an external exigency but that carries him further from a sense

of who, in a fundamental sense, he is? Is it, in other
words, an act of sincerity?

Critical as it is for Edmund, the problem of sincerity takes crucial form—for the first time in the history
of the novel in English—in the character of Mary
Crawford. At first blush, Mary seems to be a kind of
reprise on the engagingly attractive Elizabeth Bennet of
Pride and Prejudice, an active and handsome woman of
great charm, gaiety, and wit. As we become acquainted
with her, however, we begin to realize a quality in her
that is as disagreeable as it is familiar. She is not, as
Trilling points out, a hypocrite; her intention is not to
deceive the world. Rather, her aim—her necessity—is
"to comfort herself; she impersonates the woman she
thinks she ought to be. . . . In Mary Crawford we have
the first brilliant example of a distinctively modern
type, the person who cultivates the *style* of sensitivity,
virtue, and intelligence. . . . Style, which expresses the
innermost truth of any creation or action, can also hide
the truth. . . . *Mansfield Park* proposes to us the possibility of this deception." In other words, Mary is a
role-player, far from a true self. Disliking the clergy, for
example, she justifies her aversion to Edmund by saying, "I speak what appears to me the general opinion;
and when an opinion is general, it is usually correct."
Although she looks upon marriage as a "maneuvering
business" in which people are "taken in," she still recommends it wholesale: "I would have every body marry
if they can do it properly; I do not like to have people
throw themselves away; but every body should marry
as soon as they can do it to advantage." When her
brother involves himself in a loveless affair in London,
Mary attaches no moral importance to it; as he himself
says, "She saw it only as folly, and that folly stamped
only by exposure." Trilling, knowing that Jane Austen
was no prude, is quick with a clarification: It is not
"sexuality that is being condemned, but precisely that

form of asexuality that incurred D. H. Lawrence's
greatest scorn . . . sexuality as a game, or as a drama,
sexuality as an expression of mere will or mere personality, as a sign of power, or prestige, or autonomy; as,
in short, an impersonation and an insincerity."

Lack of principle, the absence of a moral and psychological core—of *character*—creates no barrier to
social respectability. Far from disrupting the social
order, the busy, role-playing self can live harmoniously
with virtually any society that requires only the outward and visible signs of conformity. In this sense,
Mansfield Park is a brilliantly modern study of what
David Riesman has called the other-directed personality.[19] As such, it insightfully contrasts character with
personality and moral principle with moral style, and it
documents the ways in which moral choice tends to be
influenced not by the norm most applicable to the situation, but by the kind of selfhood that the moral agent
wishes to "assume" or to "project." Painstakingly examining the operations of selfhood grounded neither
in a viable tradition nor in explicit ideals of personal
worth—with no leech-gatherer on the moral horizon—
Jane Austen reveals to us the "ubiquitous anonymous
judgment" that largely shapes the impersonations that
make up much of our lives. To the extent that role-
playing is a dominant motif in the dynamics of the
contemporary self, we ironically learn from her, Trilling says, "what our lives should be and by what subtle
and fierce criteria they will be judged, and how to pass
upon the lives of our friends and fellows. Once we have
comprehended her mode of judgment, the moral and
spiritual lessons of contemporary literature are easy . . .
Lawrence and Joyce, Yeats and Eliot, Proust and Gide,
have but little to add save in the way of contemporary
and abstruse examples." Simultaneously, however, she
demonstrates, through Edmund, who finally makes a
firm commitment to the clergy, and most of all through
frail, quiet Fanny Price, that genuine heroine in spite of

herself, that "the path to the wholeness of the self which is peace" lies not through adeptness in impersonation or the cultivation of personal style but through the sanctions of principle. Arnold's elegiac quest for the "best self" and Wordsworth's oddly sunny invocation of duty emerge as protectors of personhood.

But personhood stands always in need of protection, not least from the culture which, while giving individuals their very being, yet straitjackets them and forces them into molds. Arnold's reference to "the gradual furnace of the world" is developed in his thesis that "Most men in a brazen prison live," and Wordsworth's idea that "Shades of the prison-house begin to close / Upon the growing boy" reflects the spirit of Rousseau's "Man is born free, and everywhere he is in chains." These widespread feelings that culture imprisons, that it chains the human spirit and padlocks humanity's heart, define what Trilling called the "historic sense" of modern literature. That historic sense, he says, emerges from

a long *excess of civilization* [italics added] to which may be ascribed the bitterness and bloodshed both of the past and of the present and of which the peaceful aspects are to be thought of as mainly contemptible—its order achieved at the cost of extravagant personal repression, either that of coercion or that of acquiescence; its repose otiose; its tolerance either flaccid or capricious; its material comfort corrupt and corrupting; its taste a manifestation either of timidity or of pride; its rationality attained only at the price of energy and passion.[20]

Trilling's insistent emphasis here is the diagnosis, not the symptoms, however horrifying the catalogue of pathological indicators may be. As we read his statement (written in 1961) today, we think inevitably of events that range from the First World War through Hitler and Auschwitz to My Lai and the Iranian substitution for the Shah's repressive cruelty of the vengeful fanataicism of the Ayatollah Khomeini; of the repressive measures associated with the Red Raids of 1920, the fears that numbed the era of Senator Joe Mc-Carthy, the feelings of threat and betrayal bound up with Watergate and its "list of enemies"; of the figures on deaths from starvation, on political imprisonings, on crimes against persons in the world's great cities; of the slow, reluctant, and sullen responsiveness of both corporations and institutions of the state to consumers and legitimate petitioners; of the number of people who hate their unrewarding jobs, who find their marriages joyless and their children sources of anxiety, who seek for surcease or for the semblance of delight in alcohol or other drugs; of the ways in which advertising and television capture, corrode, and corrupt our most creative talent. We are not bound—nor did Trilling intend for us to be bound—by the illustrative events about which he offered his commentary. His central point is that the appalling terror of whatever particulars that we contemplate pales before the judgment of modern literature: The disease lies in the nature of society itself, in an *excess of civilization*.

Although this diagnosis carries important political implications, it is not fundamentally a political matter. Reasonably well-educated persons of good will are consistently preoccupied with the elements of civilization's excess—with the issues that emerge from that root-deep malaise—and seek political redress for them. These preoccupations and meliorative efforts have clear virtue and specify the decencies of liberalism—that valuable but indefinable point of view that loosely comprises "a ready if mild suspiciousness of the profit motive, a belief in progress, science, social legislation, planning, and international cooperation" ("perhaps," Trilling added in 1940, "especially where Russia is in question"). What astonishes us is "that not a single first-rate writer has emerged to deal with these ideas, and the emotions that are consonant with them, in a great literary way." For Proust and Joyce and Lawrence, for Yeats and Pound and Eliot, for Mann and Gide (at least as novelists), and for Dostoevski, Rilke, and Kafka, "the liberal ideology has been at best a matter of indifference." They certainly have a commitment to justice and to a notion of a humanly fulfilling way of life, but "in not one of them does it take the form of a love of the ideas and emotions which liberal democracy, as known by our educated class, has declared respectable . . . no connection exists between . . . the political ideas of our educated class and the deep places of the imagination."[21] Some great writers, Trilling continues, "have in their work given utterance or credence to conservative and even reactionary ideas, and . . . some in their personal lives have maintained a settled indifference to all political issues, or a disdain of them. No reader is likely to derive political light from either the works or the table talk of a modern literary genius, and some readers (of weak mind) might even be led into bad political ways."[22]

Beyond politics, the passionate hostility to civilization in the foremost literature of almost two centuries focuses on society's basic nature, questioning not its particular forms and aspects but its very essence. To this depth and to this extremity, has literature, as a criticism of life, extended itself. Neither dismay nor regret, neither disbelief nor denial, constitutes a fruitful response to this massive cultural phenomenon. The serious puzzle consists in the extent to which this intensely held idea of an excess of civilization represents a sign of the decline and probable fall of the culture of the West, as against the extent to which it reflects the still critical energies of that culture—"the effort of society to identify in itself that which is but speciously good, the effort to understand afresh the nature of the life it is designed to foster."[23] The task of criticism may generate few specific resolutions to so large an issue, but its socially important functions are clear: to examine—sensitively, carefully, and unremittingly—

that fierce opposition to civilization for its human, personal significance, and to formulate the best judgments possible to help narrow the gap between our immediate political ideas and "the deep places of the imagination," to contribute to that informed struggle for a more widely distributed dignity that is the proper commitment of the liberal spirit.

In his own practice of the critic's responsibilities, Trilling's consideration of Dickens's *Little Dorritt* makes telling use of that image of the prison that haunts so much of modern literature. Its symbolic force derives from its prior actuality; the prison is the practical instrument by which society neutralizes and negates the individual will. As a result, Dickens's indictment of society as an overweening and cruel constraint on the personal variability and diversity that give both challenge and delight to individual life, and as a constraint on the range and depth of love and generosity as they can be expressed in a variety of human relationships, achieves power from the way that,

The story opens in a prison in Marseilles. It goes on to the Marshalsea, which in effect it never leaves. The second of the two parts of the novel begins in what we are urged to think of as a sort of prison, the monastery of the Great St. Bernard. The Circumlocution Office is the prison of the creative mind of England. Mr. Merdle is shown habitually holding himself by the wrist, taking himself into custody, and in a score of ways the theme of incarceration is carried out, persons and classes being imprisoned by their notions of their predestined fate or their religious duty, or by their occupations, their life schemes, their ideas of themselves, their very habits of language.[24]

Our comprehension of the richness and penetration of these metaphors and emblematic devices is deepened by Trilling's gloss on them. He recalls "a certain German picture of the time":

It represents a man lying in a medieval dungeon; he is asleep, his head pillowed on straw, and we know that he dreams of freedom because the bars on his window are shown being sawed by gnomes. This picture serves as the frontispiece of Freud's *Introductory Lectures on Psychoanalysis*—Freud used it to make plain one of the more elementary ideas of his psychology, the idea of the fulfillment in dream or fantasy of impulses of the will that cannot be fulfilled in actuality. His choice of this particular picture is not fortuitous . . . [his] general conception of the mind does indeed make the prison image peculiarly appropriate . . . [Mind] is based upon the primacy of the will, and . . . the organization of the internal life is in the form, often fantastically parodic, of a criminal process in which the mind is at once the criminal, the victim, the police, the judge, and the executioner. And this is a fair description of Dickens' own view of the mind, as, having received the social impress, it becomes in turn the matrix of society.[25]

Dickens's anticipation and social application of Freud's notion is central to *Little Dorritt*. The story turns essentially on Arthur Clennam's obsession with the thought that his family's fortune was amassed by virtue of an unjust injury to William Dorritt, who has been imprisoned for twenty years in the Marshalsea. He is correct in that his mother has indeed damaged a member of the Dorritt family, although Dorritt himself was locked up neither at the instigation nor under the wish of Mrs. Clennam. Arthur comes to his only partially right conclusion by reflecting on his mother's years of invalidism. While entirely active mentally, she has for a long time been confined through illness to a single room of her house, her movement completely restricted to exchanging her bed for her chair. "A swift thought shot into [Arthur's] mind. In [Mr. Dorritt's] long imprisonment . . . and in her long confinement to her room, did his mother find a balance to be struck? I admit that I was accessory to that man's captivity. I have suffered it in kind. He has decayed in his prison; I in mine. I have paid the penalty."

Yet Dickens understands human complexity far too well to argue that prisons are merely instruments of

social or psychological injustice. The character of
Blandois represents the kind of depressing, frightening
evil that our newspapers daily report. Blandois is
among those, as Trilling phrases it, in whom "the social
causes of their badness lie so far back that they can
scarcely be reached, and in any case causation pales
into irrelevance before the effects of their actions; our
effort to 'understand' them becomes a mere *form* of
thought." So long as a Blandois exists, prisons remain
necessities. A kind of exemplar of the observation in
King Lear that "The prince of darkness is a gentleman," Blandois is a forerunner of both Smerdyakov
and the shabby-genteel devil of Dostoevski's *The
Brothers Karamazov*, and he performs the same function for Dickens as his descendants do for the great
Russian. As the man who acknowledges no social imperatives and seems quite without conscience, he owns
no citizenship but is, in a vaguely cosmoplitan fashion,
"French"—that is, Blandois behaves as a supreme ra-
tionalist and logically disdains all of society's protective
and supportive regulations. He presents himself as "nature's gentleman dispossessed of his rightful place . . .
the natural genius against whom the philistine world
closes its dull ranks. And when the disguise, which de-
ceives no one, is off, he makes use of the classic social
rationalization: Society has made him what he is; he
does in his own person only what society does in its
corporate form and with its corporate self-justifica-
tion." With Dickens, Trilling recognizes the hard actuality of the world's Blandoises; with Dickens, he insists,
good Arnoldian that he is, on seeing the object as in
itself it really is, and he refuses to be taken in by the
typical Blandoisian self-justifications.

But if the sad and terrifying imperfections of humanity render prisons necessary, prisons still function
as the great inhibitors of humanity positively realized.
Part of the complex subtlety with which Dickens uses
the prison metaphor reveals itself in his application of it

to parenthood. At the very heart of *Little Dorritt* is Mrs. Clennam. A false mother in more ways than one, she does not deny love. She does, however, distort it and dull its effects by withholding the nourishment of love. She neither encourages liberty nor expresses tenderness; she shows no pleasure in companionship, and she provides no exposure to those arts that evoke and nurture the power to feel. Because of her harsh upbringing of her son, Arthur has reason to say of himself in his fortieth year, "I have no will." Trilling is prompt to point out that a person whose will is deficient and weak, who has no elements of selfhood that he is moved zestfully to assert in the arena of his relationships and in his commerce with the larger society, lives inevitably in a prison. Like Mary Crawford in *Mansfield Park*, he can only play roles dictated by others or by circumstance, or subject himself in a manner devoid of intrinsic rewards or enduring satisfactions to wills stronger than his own. "With Dickens as with Blake," Trilling says, "the perfect image of injustice is the unhappy child, and, like the historian Burckhardt, he connects the fate of nations with the treatment of children." Not least among the harms that prisons do is the stunting of childhood wills, leaving us as adults confined to a chamber of insecurities, a self-protective parochialism of outlook and imagination, and an inability to assert ourselves effectively in our interplay as persons with society. The best that remains is the futile stubbornness, to which Trilling often refers, of Melville's Bartleby the Scrivener: "I prefer not to."

Trilling persuasively argues that as it is with Dickens, so it is with Dostoevski, Gide, Joyce, and Eliot: Modern culture is a kind of prison. In opposition to it, the modern self seeks fulfillment through the experience of alienation. Alienation is a painful condition that entails the defining of one's society as "other," as a context hostilely foreign to the development of the person, and that commits the individual to strategies of avoidance, evasion, and subversion. The accompanying emotions are those of anger and anxiety, and the setting of oneself against one's culture represents a dangerous commitment against great odds. The story is told that Josef Stalin, when once told that the Pope had publicly disapproved of one of his actions, responded by asking, "How many divisions does the Pope command?" Against the alienated individual, society commands too many divisions for him to live without the heavy burdens of disruptive inconvenience, frustration, and fear. As a consequence, the dynamics of alienation characteristically include an element of ambivalence, an occasional wistful longing for a culture in which one's faith could find repose and from whose powers one could draw one's own strength. Although this component of alienation contributes to the pain of the experience, it also contains a kind of redeeming element. The great risk in alienation, according to Marx, especially the young Marx of the *Economic and Philosophical Manuscripts*, lies in the possibility of transforming the self into something not quite human. The person who would eject himself from his own civilization and maintain himself outside it must cope with this most serious of all hazards.[26]

For this reason, Joseph Conrad's *Heart of Darkness* troubles us in a peculiar and important fashion. For Trilling, this brilliant novella "contains in sum the whole of the radical critique of European civilization that has been made by literature in the years since its publication"[27] in 1899. It provides the template in relation to which the later moderns have shaped their ideas and their sensibilities.

The story significantly finds its base in what we would call today one of the nastiest racist imperialisms ever launched, the hegemony of Leopold II, the Belgian king, over the so-called Congo Free State. Begun in 1885, Leopold's rule concentrated on the lucrative extraction of African ivory through means that were ruthlessly exploitative and cruel. Nevertheless, the Belgian monarch readily convinced the Western world that he was shedding the light of Europe over those who had previously lived in darkness. When Marlow, Conrad's narrator, first lands in the Congo, he sees at once and experiences a deep revulsion over the contrast between these claims of humane benignity and the dreadful reality of oppression. On the other hand, Kurtz, the central character, who represents one of the great Belgian trading companies, works in the belief that he not only is promoting Africa economically, but advancing it culturally. Nowhere in the tale does he ever seem to realize the terrible discrepancy between Belgium's rationalizing claims and its ugly practices. Marlow first learns of Kurtz, however, as a gifted man whose perceptiveness and character inspire from other agents both respect and jealousy. He is astounded, as we are, to discover that Kurtz, who has gone alone to collect ivory up the far reaches of the Congo River, has established himself as the chief and essentially as the god of a local tribe. It becomes obvious that his command of the natives involves a cruelty remarkable even in the context of institutionalized Belgian heartlessness.

Kurtz harbors no illusions about the "noble savage."[28] Primitive life appalls him. In one of his high-minded reports on Congolese tribes that Marlow reads after his death, he has broken off his account to scrawl violently, "Exterminate all the brutes!" Comparably, Marlow can feel the fascination of tribal life and admire the virile grace of the natives, but he regards the culture that supports and impels them as sordid and revolting, as evil in its own fashion as the European culture that so demeaningly and harshly exploits it. Nor does Marlow believe that Kurtz, by electing the life of savagery, has achieved any sort of moral purification. He clearly has rid himself of none of the European vices, including personal greed. Yet, as Trilling points out, "By his regression to savagery, Kurtz has reached as far down beneath the constructs of civilization as it was possible to go, to the irreducible truth of man, the innermost core of his nature, his heart of darkness." From that complete rejection of the values of civilization comes a light

cast not only on the souls of the Belgian business agents, servants of what Marlow calls a "flabby, pretending, weak-eyed devil," but also on the soul of Kurtz's dedicated fiancée, who embodies all the self-cherishing, self-deceiving idealism of Europe . . . monumental in her bereavement, appalling to Marlow in her certitude that her lost lover had been the reproachless knight of altruism.[29]

But if, in the illumination shed by Kurtz's incredible career and death, Marlow understands civilization as fraudulent and shameful, he retains a passionate commitment to civilization—so long, as Trilling makes clear, that that civilization is English. Trilling characterizes the opening scene of *Heart of Darkness*, set on a yawl in the estuary of the Thames, as "a hymn . . . to the Englishness of the river," and he tellingly quotes Marlow:

The conquest of the earth, which mostly means the taking it away from those who have a different complexion or slightly flatter noses than ourselves, is not a pretty thing when you look at it too much. What redeems it is the idea only. An idea at the back of it; not a sentimental pretence but an idea; and an unselfish belief in the idea—something you can set up, and bow down before, and offer a sacrifice to.

"Marlow does not doubt," says Trilling, "that it is the English alone who have such an idea."

In Trilling's interpretation, then, Conrad's novella moves simultaneously toward quite opposite poles. On the one hand, it advances powerfully the idea that "civilization is of its nature so inauthentic that personal integrity can be wrested from it only by the inversion of all its avowed principles." On the other hand, it asserts that "civilization can and does fulfill its announced purposes, not universally, indeed, but at least in the significant instance of one particular nation."

Aside from noting it, we need not consider here Trilling's treatment of the ironies in Marlow's celebration of English society and its values that must strike any reader in the 1980s. What is important for our present purpose is his perception of the importance of a faith in *some* civilization, a belief that civilization *can* assume the institutional forms and embody the animating ideas that further human decency and that facilitate the positive potentials of humanity. That kind of animal faith, entirely compatible with a clear-eyed perception of the dark side and the failings of culture, provides a basis for investing hopeful energies in the improvement of civilization and in the quality of life lived in it. It also reduces the risks of alienation; the belief that, through some process of discovery or creation, an idea can be identified that "you can set up, and bow down before, and offer a sacrifice to" is a safeguard against the dehumanizing entailments of setting oneself outside society and in fundamental opposition to it.

That hazard compounds itself complexly when, in the interest of the self's greater autonomy of perception and judgment, the alienated come together to form, however loosely, a functional *adversary* culture. When an adversary culture, like that of artists, writers, and intellectuals in the West, becomes reasonably well-established, it "shares something of the character of the larger culture to which it was—to which it still is—adversary, and . . . it generates its own assumptions and preconceptions, and contrives its own sanctions to protect them."[30] No matter how radical its origins, no matter how antagonistically it may criticize and struggle against the traditional society, the established adversary culture transmutes itself, willy-nilly, into a constraint on the individuals who adhere to it and into an environmental force that the autonomy-seeking self must

resist. Even in a climate of radical opposition to tradition and convention, the old struggle between the assertive self and a nay-saying world takes its ineluctable
and uneasy course.

For these reasons, and because of his concern with
these complexities, Trilling took his stand, gravely, a
little grimly, and a bit unfashionably, with the Freud
whose most encompassing vision found expression in
Civilization and Its Discontents. In that small but enduringly insightful book, Freud

puts to us the question of whether or not we want to *accept*
civilization . . . [not as] a divagation from a state of innocence. Freud had no illusions about primitive innocence . . .
[but] with all its contradictions, with all its pains. . . . He
had his own answer to the question—his tragic, or stoic,
sense of life dictated it: We do well to accept it, although
we also do well to cast a cold eye on the fate that makes it
our better part to accept it.[31]

But that cold-eyed acceptance hardly does justice
to the zest that it releases. Helped by Matthew Arnold,
Trilling discovered early what fortunate men and
women repeatedly and beneficially discover: "it is the
strange power of art that it can give Joy through sadness." Although art in general and literature in particular "can settle no questions, give no directives . . . it
can . . . cultivate what is best in the reader—his moral
poise," and it can bring "relief to the reader's own
moments of philosophic despair, naming and ordering
his own incoherent emotions, taking them beyond the
special misery of privacy."[32] That shared and public
sense of humanity's struggle, the quality of moral poise,
and—most of all—a pervasive tone of joy are not the
least of the gifts that Trilling's ambivalent (which can
be a synonym for "balanced") self has bestowed on
modern culture.

3

Freedom vs. Necessity

From the point of view that Lionel Trilling distinctively crafted out of the ideas of Sigmund Freud and Matthew Arnold, the egoistically assertive self, which is the "subject" of literature, engages the culture that both nurtures it and constricts it in a lifelong battle. This inevitable struggle between self and society is the stuff of tragedy and inevitably raises the question of whether we as persons want to accept the civilization that provides our human matrix. With Freud and with Arnold, Trilling concluded that "we do well to accept it."

For all the price that the acceptance of civilization exacts, what makes it our better part is the larger range of choices that civilized life presents to individuals. The power of persons to avail themselves of those options that civilization makes possible is what defines freedom, and the functions of the liberal imagination are to envision the "variousness and possibility" that increase the scope of choice, and to give voice to the sentiments and yearnings that energize the great human quest for freedom. Because, as Charles Péguy put it, *"Tout commence en mystique et finit en politique,"* the liberal outlook entails a political posture and an involvement in political affairs. That posture and that involvement, however, although they must direct themselves toward some organizational and corporate end, concern themselves most fundamentally with "the modification of sentiments, which is to say, the quality of human life."[1] For this reason, art and literature are deeply bound up with political considerations, especially those political considerations that bear on the auton-omy of the self in relation to the growing network of social controls—the politics of freedom. Since the late eighteenth century, Trilling notes,

Of the writers . . . who command our continuing attention, the very large majority have in one way or another turned their passions, their adverse, critical, and very intense pas-sions, upon the condition of the polity. The preoccupation with the research into the self that has marked this liter-ature, and the revival of the concepts of religion that has marked a notable part of it, do not controvert but rather support the statement about its essential commitment to politics.[2]

Three considerations become central here to an under-standing of Trilling's perceptions and of his position.

First, politics as a literary motif—at times, and in some great writers, a literary compulsion—only occa-sionally entails the politics of party or of ideology. As we have seen, the widespread judgment, powerfully registered by Lawrence, Yeats, Mann, and others, that modern life suffers from an "excess of civilization" lies beyond politics in its typical forms, but it certainly is not without political implications. Trilling illustrates the point by Lear's agonized reflections during the vio-lent storm in Shakespeare's play. Reviewing his own record as a ruler (and pressing us to review our experi-ence generally of the state and of political authority), the king cries out,

> Poor naked wretches, whereso'er you are,
> That bide the pelting of this pitiless storm,
> How shall your houseless heads and unfed sides,
> Your loop'd and window'd raggedness, defend you
> From seasons such as this? O, I have ta'en
> Too little care of this: Take physic, pomp;
> Expose thyself to feel what wretches feel,

> That thou mayst shake the superflux to them,
> And show the heavens more just.

If there is little here that translates easily into parties, doctrines, and the electoral process, there is, Trilling insists,[3] much that bears on the moral basis for a humane politics—a new consciousness of justice and a sense of *caritas*, a concern or caring for the well-being of the individuals whom society comprises. Indeed, the play underscores this crucial idea, Trilling says, by the very act out of which the terrors of *King Lear* arise, Lear's division of his kingdom among his daughters. His taking this step violates the unity of the state, the organic relationships among the parts of a polity; to portion out a realm, to deal with it as if it were less than a whole and living thing, not only marks a failure in prudence but a transgression of a moral norm fundamental to both political decency and political effectiveness. Despite the despairing references to the gods ("As flies to wanton boys, are we to the gods,/They kill us for their sport"), the horrors and misfortunes here do not issue from a divinely engineered fate. They are the consequences of willful acts by men and women, rich in political significance despite their apparent remoteness from the next election.

Second, Trilling took with great seriousness the political propositions of literature, whether of the implicative type that *Lear* illustrates or of the more direct kind exemplified in Robert Lowell's "For the Union Dead"[4] or Virgil Gheorghiu's *The Twenty-Fifth Hour*.[5] For him, art always functions under motives that are more than aesthetic and demands responses from those who attend to it. Art, like ideas, has consequences, including political consequences, and Trilling never failed to communicate his conviction, often to share it compellingly, that, because of their consequences, the writers and the issues that he discussed are *important*, that they figure among the things that matter most. He frequently commented, in his classroom and over luncheon tables, on the influential power of art gener- ally and of literature in particular, and on how political dictators understood this kind of potency that arises from the imaginative reason. From their point of view, they are quite correct in looking to censorship and to the control or banishment of poets as among the safe- guards of their authoritarian regimes. In Trilling's eyes, politics is a means of coping with the endless tension between the individual's yearning for unconditioned freedom and the nay-saying culture's insistence on order as one of the necessities of social life. As a focus of literary concern, in either what we are here calling its implicative or its direct mode, politics becomes the evaluation of that tension by the powers of mind and imagination.

Third, conceiving in this fashion of politics as an intrinsic literary concern, Trilling confronted the para- dox of the freedom-affirming liberalism to which he was drawn. The liberal spirit puts a special premium on human emotions, witness the way in which a notion of happiness occupies the center of its thought. The liberal mission is essentially to envision the "variousness and possibility" with which such affects as joy, love, curi- osity and interest, and positive excitement can be more firmly established and given wider play in our experi- ence as persons. When John Stuart Mill, despite his massive and sharp disagreement with Coleridge, ex- horted his liberal confreres in the nineteenth century to become acquainted with Coleridge's powerful conserva- tive mind, he did so for two reasons. He hoped that Coleridge's intellectual and imaginative pressure would force liberals to examine their own position for its weaknesses, and he hoped that the poetic vision within which Coleridge cast his political and metaphysical views would stimulate and buttress the liberal commit- ment to a freer emotional life. For, in spite of liberal- ism's premium on the emotions, the politicizing of the liberal spirit seems to chill its conception of humanity and to yield what Mill called a "prosaic" formulation of its purposes. This transformation occurs partly because the political impulse necessarily expresses itself through organization, and, as Trilling puts it, organization

means delegation, and agencies, and bureaus, and technicians, and that the ideas that can survive delegation, that can be passed on to agencies and bureaus and technicians, incline to be ideas of a certain kind and of a certain simplicity; they give up something of their largeness and modulation and complexity in order to survive. The lively sense of contingency and possibility, and of those exceptions to the rule which may be the beginning of the end of the rule—this sense does not suit well with the impulse to organization . . . we have to expect that there will be a discrepancy between what I have called the primal imagination of liberalism and its . . . particular manifestations.[6]

The dream of freedom, in other words, collides with reality's necessities. The liberal spirit encounters the mundane but ineluctable requirements of organizational life. The self faces its own dependency on the culture. The quest for an unlimited range of choices must contend with the intractable elements in our own nature, in the external world, and in our social and corporate experience of one another. If literature is the activity that takes most richly into account variousness and possibility, it also, at its finest and most serious, attends with comparable vigor to complexity and difficulty; and if the job of criticism is to recall liberalism "to its first essential imagination of variousness and possibility," that task inherently implies an awareness of the complexity and difficulty that lie always before it. Perceived in such terms, the zestfully carried burden of complexity and difficulty rode on Trilling's shoulders throughout his career.

That burden is managed with a firm delicacy in one of his best short stories, "The Other Margaret," published in 1945.[7] Its dramatis personae includes

Lucy and Stephen Elwin and their thirteen-year-old daughter, Margaret, the members of a decent, affection-ate, comfortable middle-class family; the title character, who has the same name as the Elwins' daughter, is a maid of disagreeable temper, contemptuous manner, and a penchant for "accidentally" breaking valuable objects like pieces of the Elwins' china. The first com-plexity, the first difficulty, stems from the fact that "the other Margaret" is black.

Presiding over the relationships among these four people is a portrait, a print of Rouault's king, holding a spray of flowers, that Elwin has just bought and brought home. "A person looking at it for the first time might find it repellent, even brutal or cruel. . . . The king, blackbearded and crowned . . . had a fierce quality that had modulated, but not softened, to authority . . . He had passed beyond ordinary matters of personality and was worthy of the crown. . . . Yet he was human and tragic." While buying the picture, Elwin meets a young and newly commissioned second lieutenant who, he learns, has "said he did not want to miss sharing the experience of his generation"—which is, of course, the Second World War. Elwin never hears this com-monplace comment of the time without a twinge of envy and a touch of guilt. In this instance, in the pres-ence of Rouault's king, he is comforted by the notion "that this man with the black beard and the flowers had done his fighting without any remarks about experience and generations." The portrait projects a "tragic au-thority" that rests on its more fundamental projection of a capacity for *being*. The king seems to know who he is and what he is, and out of that knowledge he can both do what must be done and refrain from doing what must not be done quite independent of fashion, public opinion, or sheer considerations of role.

This preoccupation with being, with questions of personal identity, was pervasive in Trilling's thought. It is peculiarly fitting in a critic who regards the self as the central subject matter of literature, and it is still more fitting in a man who explicitly strove to make his work accessible to a general public and not just to a community of literary scholars.[8] It accounts for his rare invocation of Walt Whitman: "There is, in sanest hours, a consciousness, a thought that rises, independent, lifted out from all else, calm, like the stars, shining eternal. This is the thought of identity—yours for you, whoever you are, as mine for me. Miracle of miracles, beyond statement, most spiritual and vaguest of earth's dreams, yet hardest basic fact and only entrance to all facts." This passage appealed to Trilling because it is "boldly explicit" about "the sentiment of being," and because Whitman "goes on to speak of this 'hardest basic fact' as a political fact, as the basis, and the criterion, of democracy."[9]

Most of all, the preoccupation with the nature of personal identity accounts for Trilling's admiration of Wordsworth, one of the very few poets to whom he repeatedly devoted his critical attention.[10] And the Wordsworth he frequently appealed to is the reflective artist and observer of the human condition who was "contented" only when

> I felt the sentiment of Being spread
> O'er all that moves and all that seemeth still;
> O'er all that, lost beyond the reach of thought
> And human knowledge, to the human eye
> Invisible, yet liveth to the heart.

That weighty "sentiment of Being" has intimate connections with the will, with aspiration, with the energies of selfhood. Responding to the beauty and the ruggedness of the Alps, Wordsworth avows that

> Whether we be young or old,
> Our destiny, our being's heart and home,
> Is with infinitude, and only there;
> With hope it is, hope that can never die,

> Effort, and expectation, and desire,
> And something evermore about to be.

But that affirmation of the will takes a sudden and distinctive turn:

> Under such banners militant, the soul
> Seeks for no trophies, struggles for no spoils
> That may attest her prowess, blest in thoughts
> That are their own perfection and reward,
> Strong in herself and in beatitude . . .

The energies of the self serve properly only to enlarge the self and to refine its perceptiveness, not to assert the self's dominion over others or to engage in conquest. When fully conscious of the sentiment of being, the self is "unsubdued . . . by the regular action of the world." It can be "Rebellious, acting in a devious mood," and constitute "A local spirit of its own, at war / With general tendency," but by its welcome and beneficent discipline, it remains "Subservient strictly to external things" with which it communes. What Trilling calls this "unassailable intuition" represents, for him, our "entrance [to] . . . social and political life—it is through our conscious certitude of our personal self-hood that we reach our knowledge of others."[11] In this notion of how we construct social reality, Trilling echoes William James.

The world of living realities as contrasted with unrealities is ↓ . . anchored in the Ego, considered as an active and emotional term. That is the hook from which the rest dangles, the absolute support . . . *Whatever things have intimate and continuous connection with my life are things of whose reality I cannot doubt.* Whatever things fail to establish this connection are things which are practically no better for me than if they existed not at all. (Italics in original.)[12]

It is against this background that we can best understand the Elwins in relation to "The Other Margaret" as their little drama unfolds under the shadow of Rouault's king.

Margaret, the daughter, has absorbed from a much adored teacher at a modern progressive school the feeling and the principle that black people cannot be blamed for what they do; they are the victims of a cruel and prejudicial society. Hearing her parents comment in irritated and condemnatory ways about the other Margaret, the perpetually angry black maid, she can hardly bear it. She reminds them that the maid "has a handicap. . . . She has to struggle so hard—against prejudice. It's so *hard* for her." She seeks refuge in "her own world of sure right reason. In that world one knew where one was, one knew that to say things about Jews was bad and that working men were good. And *therefore*." Are not these the "obvious" imperatives under which civilized people live? Victims cannot be justly held accountable; they can only be compassionately understood.

Her father also shares the civilized imperatives, but Elwin, by the explicit effort of thought, brings himself to transcend the reflex pieties of liberalism. Black or otherwise, he reflects, the other Margaret probably is, as his wife Lucy has characterized her, "a nasty, mean person." She also is a genuine victim of a culture riddled with prejudice. But she remains responsible; she is inherently responsible for what she does, including the deliberate breaking of the Elwins' Wedgwood. Who, however, has the authority to hold her responsible, to require her, for example, to pay for the smashed valuables? If the will cannot resist an ineluctable fact when it presents itself to a reasonably responsive intelligence, neither can the will attack an ineluctable reality in the service of a principle that the reality refuses to acknowledge. Dealing with Margaret illustrates the burden of actual living in the contemporary world. She exemplifies an all-too-familiar kind of personality that baffles almost daily our interpersonal understanding. She is a prototype of that often-encountered figure who defeats our hopes, frustrates our best and most sincerely held intentions, and mocks our ideals of warmth and sympathy. For Trilling, Margaret sums up a frequently experienced form of social reality in the presence of which we lose faith in our capacity to translate concepts of decency and humane aspirations into effective concrete action. She cherishes her anger and claims her desire for revenge as a right. In doing so, she establishes a link—she defines a downright and frightening similarity—between victims and aggressors in the reality of our corporate life.

Unlike Elwin, daughter Margaret, unable to realize the import of these sad and alarming reflections, explains away the maid's breakage as accidents: "She didn't mean to." But at the end of the story, the other Margaret knocks off a table a ceramic lamb that the little girl has made and given that afternoon to her mother as an early birthday present. Her creative investment in fashioning the clay piece had been considerable, and she had enjoyed enormously her mother's delighted reception of the gift. Seeing the lamb in fragments, the daughter's liberal sentiments dissolve in copious tears, and she sobs repeatedly, "She *meant* to do it." Her parents, knowing what a "foolish and weak thing" it is to say, can only murmur, "It's all right, Margaret. Don't worry . . . it just happened." But beyond the impotence there is insight. As his child weeps passionately on the sofa—"She meant to. She didn't like me. She hated me."—Elwin becomes aware that "it was not because the other Margaret hated her that his Margaret wept, but because she had with her own eyes seen the actual possibility of what she herself might do, the insupportable fact of her own moral life." The connections between victim and aggressor, between hatred and self-pity, between envy and guilt, between fear and vengefulness, have all come full circle. Trying to com-

fort his shattered daughter, Elwin's eyes fall on Rouault's king; "at the moment he seemed only quaint,
extravagant and beside the point."

The theme of "The Other Margaret," then, is the
world's intractability. It is not absolute, not completely
impervious to meliorative effort, but the complexity and
obstinacy of social reality repeatedly defeat consciousness and good will. The translation of knowledgable
awareness into effective action meets the fate of frustration a good deal of the time, largely because of what
Trilling calls "the inextricable tangle of good and evil."
For this reason, he praises E. M. Forster for his clear-
eyed concern with "moral realism, which is not the
awareness of morality itself but of the contradictions,
paradoxes and dangers of living the moral life," and he
quotes from Milton's *Areopagitica*, "one of the charter-
documents of liberalism":

Good and evil we know in the field of this world grow up
together almost inseparably; and the knowledge of good is
so involved and interwoven with the knowledge of evil,
and in so many cunning resemblances hardly to be dis-
cerned, that those confused seeds which were imposed upon
Psyche as an incessant labor to cull out, and sort asunder,
were not more intermixed. It was from out the rind of one
apple tasted, that the knowledge of good and evil, as two
twins cleaving together, leaped forth into the world. And
perhaps this is that doom which Adam fell into of knowing
good and evil, that is to say, of knowing good by evil.[13]

The "mystery of the twins" inevitably conditions
the quest for freedom in the world of the real—that is,
in the world, the only world that we know, inhabited by
"other Margarets." The freedom that matters is likely
to be found through cultivating the sentiment of being,
which may be ". . . at times Rebellious . . . / A local
spirit of his own, at war / With general tendency, but
for the most, / Subservient strictly to external things."
When we cope with the world's intractability, as we
inevitably must, we are not likely to enjoy sufficient

success sufficiently often to feel proudly satisfied. Rouault's king is "human and tragic," because he knows,
out of his fiercely won authority, what he must refrain
from doing as well as what he must do, and that knowledge derives from his keen sense of his own being. Yet
clarity about one's own identity implies clarity about
one's own limitations, especially the limits on one's
capacity to turn perception and comprehension into social action. It is not so much illegitimate as futile for
the soul to seek for trophies or to struggle for spoils
that may attest her prowess.

The function of that necessity defined by the
"mystery of the twins" and apprehended by what
Forster identified as "not the knowledge of good and
evil, but the knowledge of good-and-evil" occupies
Trilling in his analysis of William Morris's *News from
Nowhere*.[14] When Morris died in 1896 at the age of
sixty-two, one of his physicians diagnosed his illness as
"simply being William Morris and having done more
work than most men."[15] Poet and writer of prose ro-
mances, first-rate businessman and outstanding printer,
translator of Icelandic legends, and the most influential
designer and theorist of design in his time, Morris was a
passionate socialist, strongly responsive to Marx, and a
devoted and energetic participant in the radical politics
of Victorian England. In the generation following his
own, both William Butler Yeats and George Bernard
Shaw, profoundly dissimilar though they were, acknowledged his massive impact on their thought and on their
imagination of possibility. As Trilling points out, "The
young Yeats was encouraged in his dreams of an authentic existence by Morris's celebrations of the old
cultures of Northern Europe. In the socialism which
was the central concern of Morris's later years, Shaw
found confirmation of his own vision of a society that
would be the perfection of rational order and peace."
Here was a man cut to generous scale, and uncom-
monly joyous in his fulfillment of it. As Trilling ob-

serves, "His thought was large, was ultimate; its informing idea was the goodness of life, and its end in
view was nothing less than making that goodness universally apparent and universally accessible."

Nowhere is a Utopia in which both private property and factory-based industry have been abolished. In
Trilling's summary, the natural environment, which
meant a great deal to Morris, is clean, lush, and lovely.
Money has disappeared; because there is plenty of
everything, distribution follows the principle of to each
according to not just his needs but his desires and even
his whims, which can be counted on not to run counter
to the corporate good. With economic necessity no
longer either a driving force or a grinding condition in
experience, people display a relaxed beauty and a cooperative friendliness that make easy the love of one's
neighbor. Because the future entails no anxieties, the
present fully occupies individual consciousness, and
consciousness focuses primarily on two sources of rich
satisfaction—an awareness of one's own adequacy of
being and of one's own innocent appetites and their
gratification, and an awareness of one's fellows, a sense
of community and a high confidence in the positive
regard of others. Work in *Nowhere* provides particular
satisfactions. "Everyone does some sort of physical
work; no one does work he does not like; hopelessly
unpleasant and dehumanizing work is relegated to a
certain few highly sophisticated machines which have a
kind of secret existence, and there is no residual necessary work that someone does not find pleasure in
doing." Harvesting the fields and building roads illustrate a category of "easy-hard" work that is looked
upon in much the way that we regard athletics. Erotic
love involves the only complexity. Essentially uninhibited, it entails intense emotions; when love goes un-
requited, it is one of the few sources of deep and painful disappointment and frustration in *Nowhere*. In Trilling's phrase, "in the general felicity it is the only source

of pain." It is also the only source of aggression. When a jealous man kills a rival in love, as infrequently but occasionally happens, the social response is one of comprehending grief, as great for the murderer as for the victim and his surviving family and friends. There is no retaliation, because the perpetrator of the murderous act, as we would call it, will surely be moved to shattering remorse for the rest of his days and never behave again with such disruptive violence.

Nowhere, then, is, for Trilling, a world in which

The state having withered away, there are no politics with their inevitable implications of present aggressivity. Such questions of policy as do exist—for instance, where a bridge shall be built—may arouse debate, but never a passionate commitment to one's own views. Although conversation is not in short supply, there is no intellectual activity as we would define it; the world is an aesthetic object to be delighted in and not speculated about or investigated; the nature and destiny of man raise no questions, being now wholly manifest . . . the judgment having once been made that grandiosity in art is not conformable with happiness and that Sir Christopher Wren has exemplified radical error in designing St. Paul's, the race has settled upon a style for all its artifacts that is simple and modestly elegant, and no one undertakes to surprise or shock or impress by stylistic invention.

Felicity in *Nowhere*, while entirely genuine, entails, in short, the expense of high art, of science, of philosophy —indeed, of all that we would subsume under the name of achievement. The poignant element in this state of affairs emerges quietly in a remark by one of Morris's characters: "I wish that we were interesting enough to be written about or painted about."

This rather touching observation lies close to the heart of the point that Trilling underscores. If felicity in *Nowhere* is won at the cost of achievement, of being interesting, then it finds its foundations in the virtual extinction of all aggressive impulses. War, imperialistic ambitions, interpersonal hostility (except in the noted rare cases of sexual frustration), and such self-destructive behavior as suicide not only do not occur, they neither tempt nor threaten, because they have been literally uprooted through the massive and systematic reinforcement of contrary tendencies. The term *reinforcement* suggests affinities between *News from Nowhere* and B. F. Skinner's notions of human engineering and social control, as expressed in his *Beyond Freedom and Dignity* and in his own earlier Utopian novel, *Walden Two*. Trilling had these affinities clearly in mind—witness his skeptical and critical reference at the end of his essay to *Beyond Freedom and Dignity* as evidence for the probability of "a new and clandestine mode of aggression," rather than a "regenerate peaceableness" as the outcome of deliberate efforts to fashion a culture unmarked and unmarred by aggressivity. His main business, however, lay elsewhere.

First, Trilling is at pains to demonstrate that Morris knew explicitly what he was doing in bringing us the *News*. What Morris says of his Utopian dispensation is that it is the regaining of childhood and the epoch of man's rest. "Not maturity and activity but childhood and rest are represented as making the ideal condition of man." This conception not only repudiates the ethos of capitalism but the entire humanistic tradition of what constitutes self-esteem; it jettisons, Trilling points out, the fundamental assumption in Western culture that

man's nature and destiny are fulfilled not through his success in achieving pleasure but through setting himself goals which are beyond pleasure—though not, of course, beyond gratification—and pursuing them with unremitting energy, with ceaseless devotion in the face of defeat and frustration. It is from this "effort and expectation and desire"—the phrase is Wordsworth's—that man's highest value to himself is commonly thought to derive, that is to say, his sense of his largeness of spirit, his dignity, his transcendent significance. . . . Morris's social creed . . . is overtly hostile to conceptions of largeness and dignity. It rejects the line of thought which connects transcendence with the putting forth of superlative effort and with the risk of defeat and frustration. . . . Its conception of man's nature and destiny is informed by . . . a calculated modesty.

Trilling is not arguing Pollyanna's case for the blessings of adversity. He is calling attention to the intractable *fact* of adversity in all known human experience and to the moral implications of our response to it. He is also at least raising a question about an important distinction. In the humanistic tradition, he says, the aggressive energies, "even when they are defeated, constitute the ground of man's . . . projection of himself into the permanence of the future, into what he calls 'immortality' and 'glory' or at least 'dignity,' which is to say 'worth.'" He couples a quotation from Keats with his favorite, and much invoked, one from William James. "Though a quarrel in the streets," reads a passage in one of Keats's letters, "is a thing to be hated, the energies displayed in it are fine; the commonest Man shows a grace in his quarrel. . . . This is the very thing in which consists poetry." And James declares himself, "If this life be not a real fight in which something is eternally gained for the universe by success, it is no better than a game of private theatricals from which one may withdraw at will. But it *feels* like a fight."

The reference to James, whose search for a moral equivalent of war commanded much admiration but little following, underscores the distinction with which Trilling concerns himself. In our own time, on the eve of 1984, a deep animus has established itself in our culture and in our selves against the humanistic values of disciplined persistence in the pursuit of prized ends, of the uncomplaining sacrifice of one good in order to attain another, of the maintenance of effort in the face of failure and frustration. Trilling draws the parallel:

"By something of the same logic that moved Morris,"
he says,

hostile aggression, the aggression of one man against his
fellow, has been assimilated (perhaps not without reason)
to that manifestation of aggression which presumably goes
into creative achievement. . . . That special kind of fighting
in which, as Keats puts it, consists poetry—in which consists high art in general—is now looked at with a skeptical
eye; the preeminent genius is less likely to be thought of
as having gained something for the universe and is now
open to the charge of having sequestered for his own purposes the creative forces of the race, of being an illicitly
dominating figure . . . there is . . . a tendency to identify
with the aggression imputed to nationalism and capitalism
that element of "fighting" which, in the cultural tradition
of the West, has been thought essential to the artistic life,
the intellectual life, and the moral life, and thus to repro-
bate and reject it.

Here is vintage Trilling. While a clear moral passion warms his words, his courtesy never flags; his
sense of complexity and difficulty never falters. The
parenthesis indicates his acceptance of the possibility
that hostile aggression and creative aggression are separated, if they are separated at all, by too thin a mem-
brane to make the distinction that he seeks a persuasive
one. Although his liberal disposition aligns him with the
judgment that nationalism, capitalism, and imperialism
entail hostilities that are destructive of selves—that
limit the individual's sentiment of being—he uses the
term "imputed," acknowledging a complicated matter
that cannot be dealt with adequately in a line or a
paragraph and about which there is always room for
honest debate. Despite his own yearning for "regenerate peaceableness," he puts himself clearly on record:
The price is high art, serious intellectual achievement,
and—perhaps most of all—moral commitments of a
kind tested by a long and distinguished tradition. He

will not pay it; but while he makes his argument with the full force of his mind and with genuine emotional intensity, he attempts only to raise the issue for others of whether the outcome merits the expense. The echo of Paul Elmer More's "law of costingness"[16] lends iron to Trilling's formulation and specifies a necessity that human experience cannot escape.

This position entails a dislike and a mistrust of Utopian literature, Utopian thought, and Utopian politics. The long line of ideal societies, from Plato's *Republic* through Sir Thomas More's *Utopia* to Edward Bellamy's *Looking Backward* and Aldous Huxley's *Island*, do indeed represent the envisionings of human variousness and possibility that Trilling prized. But, with rare exceptions, they also express that fundamental and tragically self-defeating human desire to get something for nothing, to enjoy an enhanced freedom without regard for necessity, for the intractability of the world, which refuses to disappear merely because it is unrecognized.

The redeeming contrast lies with More, who treats his ideal society with skeptical irony. It was Sir Thomas who invented the term Utopia, as a pun on two Greek words meaning "good place" and "no place," and it seems clear that he believed that the good place that was no place could exist nowhere else. In his book, which was first published in 1516, he gives the description of the ideal society under consideration to a character named Hythloday, the Greek word for "babbler," and against Hythloday's enthusiastic recommendations that England at once adopt the forms and procedures of Utopia, he opposes careful arguments for introducing such social and political novelties gradually, with adequate determinations of their suitability for the English people. The English people, after all, do not exist "no place" but in a realm that is concrete and definite not only in its geography but in its culture, its history, and its distinctive range of personal temperaments. Like

Lear's kingdom, it constitutes an organic whole, constantly changing but equally constantly unitary. Just as dividing it arbitrarily—as in Shakespeare's play—sets in train a series of fatal disruptions and disasters, so imposing upon it the dreams of political idealists risks a comparable chaos through its reckless denial of the world's intractability, of the tenuousness of the ties between social reality and the sentiment of being. Utopian dreams have their genuine uses; but their usefulness depends heavily on the degree to which those who dream and those who respond to dreams realize, in Yeats's phrase, that "in dreams begin responsibilities."

His mistrust of Utopias and his heeding of the Yeatsian warning underlie Trilling's insightful evaluations of writers as poles apart as Rudyard Kipling and Scott Fitzgerald. Because he admires Fitzgerald,[17] he presses a bold, even a startling, comparison and makes it hold: "between Goethe, at twenty-four the author of *Werther*, and Fitzgerald, at twenty-four the author of *This Side of Paradise*, there is not really so entire a difference as piety and textbooks might make us think; both the young men so handsome, both winning immediate and notorious success, both rather more interested in life than in art, each the spokesman and symbol of his own restless generation." This involvement of Fitzgerald with one of the greatest names in Western culture takes fully into account Fitzgerald's lack of prudence, his having been, in his own language, "only a mediocre caretaker . . . of my talent," his too frequent carelessness of style. Its justification rests, for Trilling, on two characteristics of his fiction and the stance that it reflects.

The first of these qualities Trilling calls "the delicate tension" that Fitzgerald "maintained between his idea of personal free will and his idea of circumstance," the seriousness with which he took the responsibility that begins in dreams. Quite aware of the multitude of ways in which society is flawed and at fault, he knew

that social realities define the field of personal tragedy,
but his novels never make the case that his heroes
(whom he called his "brothers" in his meticulously
kept notebooks) suffer tragic destinies by virtue of the
world's imposition, and he never presented himself as
the victim of the social order. This sense of a personal
directorship over one's own fate contrasts, as Trilling
notes, with the fashion of the 'twenties and 'thirties (as
of now) to lay all personal difficulties at the door of the
culture. It also lies at the root of Fitzgerald's moral
outlook and of his politics. As we cannot feel of all
moralists, we feel of him, in Trilling's words, that "he
did not attach himself to the good because this attachment would sanction his fierceness toward the bad—his
first impulse was to love the good . . . " He was not, as
was the case with so many of the splintered peace
movements during the war in Vietnam, seeking moral
sanctions for drubbing the villains and assaulting the
varmints of the social world; his moral goals were positive, loving without sentimentality. Free of self-righteousness, he was also free of rancorous hostility and
hatred. This complex of factors gives a "tone and pitch
to [his] sentences which suggest his warmth and tenderness, and, what is rare nowadays and not likely to
be admired, his gentleness without softness."

Fitzgerald's moral position is related to the second
of the qualities in his work that Trilling valued. His
books combine a detailed and accurate representation
of contemporary manners—his novels provide a remarkable sociological record of the mores of the jazz
age—with an awareness of how any given historical
moment embodies enduring human concerns. *The
Great Gatsby*, for example, can be read not only as a
documentary of the 1920s; as a literary work, it remains
"as fresh as when it first appeared; it has even gained in
weight and relevance, which can be said of very few
American books of its time." This achievement results

basically from the conception of Gatsby as its hero. Although he remains largely undeveloped, growing only in the understanding of the narrator, Gatsby acquires enormous significance. Trilling perceives him, "divided between power and dream," as "coming to represent America itself . . . the only nation that prides itself upon a dream and gives its name to one, 'the American dream.'" He continues, "To the world it is anomalous in America, just as in the novel it is anomalous in Gatsby, that so much raw power should be haunted by envisioned romance. Yet in that anomaly lies, for good or bad, much of the truth of our national life."

In other words, Gatsby as a personality and Gatsby's society are deeply examined in the light of an active and serious sense of the past and of the demands that the past levies on the present. That clear awareness of a complex human continuity gives authenticity to Fitzgerald's voice:

I became aware of the old island here that flowered once for Dutch sailors' eyes—a fresh green breast of the new world. Its vanished trees, the trees that had made way for Gatsby's house, had once pandered in whispers to the last and greatest of all human dreams; for a transitory and enchanted moment man must have held his breath in the presence of this continent, compelled into an aesthetic contemplation he neither understood nor desired, face to face for the last time in history with something commensurate to his capacity for wonder.

Trilling speaks of this well-known passage as illustrating "the habitual music of Fitzgerald's seriousness." That habitual music of seriousness, together with his dream-born sense of personal responsibility, earns for Fitzgerald, despite the grief and humiliation of his last years, the "exemplary role" of a tragic hero among the writers who have contributed most to our understanding of the American experience. More successful

than many, he ranks in Trilling's eyes among the few
who have attempted to bridge the dangerous chasm between liberal politics and the liberal imagination.

With Kipling,[18] the poet of the white man's
burden, of prototypical imperialism, and of a concept
of nation contaminated by "swagger and swank . . .
bullying ruthlessness, and self-righteousness," Trilling
deals with a much more complicated nest of issues. T.
S. Eliot has argued that Kipling was not a fascist but
simply a Tory. While Trilling agrees that Kipling was
not a fascist, he balks at ordering him to a class that
includes Dr. Johnson, Edmund Burke, and Walter
Scott. The complications of judgment arise from primarily three sources: Kipling's considerable assets as
both poet and novelist, his almost paradoxical "anthropological" point of view, and his massive influence
as the perceived spokesman for British imperial ambitions and the "callousness, arrogance, and brutality"
attached to them.

Kipling's literary capabilities, Trilling acknowledges, remain undeniable if short of greatness. Few
treatments of animal life have been more exquisitely
imagined than *The Jungle Book*. Beyond "the marvelous but credible abilities of Mowgli," it embodies "a
whole council of strength and wisdom which was as benign as it was dangerous" and communicates a comfortable sense of the integrity and "benignity of the
feral world." The Pack and its Law encompass a highly
generalized idea of society, deeply in tune with the processes of socialization that every viable culture must
rely upon for its continuity.[19] The Law is persuasively
presented as "mysterious, firm, certain, noble, in every
way admirable." Kipling's admiration of craft and special competence, his keen ear for speech and his attentiveness to dialects and accents, and his powers as an
observer of terrain and atmosphere and behavior are
illustrated richly in the poetry and in such fiction as
Plain Tales from the Hills, The Light that Failed,

Stalky & Co., and *Kim*, his best book. Only when his enthusiasms are insufficiently restrained does he become vulgar or silly. If he seldom fully involves an adult reader, he just as seldom bores or wearies him, and he is often informative and sometimes movingly admirable.

Moreover, in what Trilling perceptively identifies as his "anthropological view," Kipling clearly and strongly holds to the "perception that another man's idea of virtue and honor may be different from one's own, but quite to be respected." The dominant emotions in *Kim*, despite the dislike it has always evoked in India, "are love and respect for the aspects of Indian life that the ethos of the West does not usually regard even with leniency." And *Kim*, like much of the verse and many of the stories, suggests a merit in "the rank, greasy, over-rich things, the life that was valuable outside the notions of orderliness, success and gentility." Kipling shows genuine sympathy toward not only a wide variety of ways of life, but also toward a wide vairety of modes of thought, and it is essential that we "remember this when we condemn his mindless imperialism."

Yet his mindless imperialism remains, and it has a context. Kipling continues to occupy, although with diminishing force, the odd status of a popular villain. His writings originally commanded a wide audience, and his influence seems somehow to maintain itself in significant measure through the conservative, expansionist, somewhat jingoistic spirit that he so wholeheartedly represented. It is not too much to say that he hated liberal intellectuals, and liberal intellectuals "responded by hating everything that Kipling loved, even when it had its element of virtue and enlightenment." For this reason, Trilling calls him "one of liberalism's major intellectual misfortunes." Mill urged his fellow liberals to study Coleridge as an "enemy who would make us worthy of ourselves." Kipling, says Trilling, was "an enemy who had the opposite effect. He tempted liberals to be content with easy victories of right feeling and with moral self-congratulation." On two issues, this "opposite effect" proved crucially important.

First, one of the great divisions between conservatives and liberals has centered in the conservative's reliance on administration and executive authority, as opposed to the liberal's faith in legislation. Kipling constantly supported the administrator, and just as constantly viewed the legislator with an almost paranoid suspicion. After observing that one of the weaknesses of liberalism is "a fogginess about administration (or, when the fog clears away a little, a fancy and absolute notion of administration such as Wells and Shaw gave way to)," Trilling commits himself. "This [attitude of Kipling's] is foolish, but . . . it is a prejudice which, in the hands of an intelligent man, say a man like Walter Bagehot or like Fitzjames Stephen, might make clear to the man of principled theory, to the liberal, what the difficulties not merely of government but of *governing* really are." Such seems to have been Kipling's original intention, but he so colored his effort with ill temper, with contempt and caste feeling, with an impatient dismissal of intellect, "that he simply could not be listened to or believed, he could only be reacted against." In that capacity to elicit reactions nearly as mindless as his own positions lay his strangely great influence, and it sealed his fate as an artist. Trilling's judgment embodies both his values and his sublety of perception: Kipling's work, for all its considered virtues, "is unloved and unlovable not by reason of his beliefs but by reason of the temperament that gave them literary expression."

Second, Kipling, Trilling charges, "did more than any writer of our time to bring the national idea into discredit." People tend less and less to give their loyalty to their country or to find the concept of their nation intellectually or emotionally compelling. The exceptions are those countries where at least the forms of patriotism are enforced by powerful tyrannies, or those where nationalism of a kind finds nourishment in active threats from other governments or in actual domination by a foreign authority. Otherwise, men and women increasingly tie their interests and their affiliative longings "to their class, or to the idea of a social organization more comprehensive than that of the nation, or to a cultural ideal or a spiritual fatherland.[20] True enough, a part of this disposition appears associated with "the modern impulse to say that politics is not really a proper human activity at all; the reluctance to give loyalty to any social organization which falls short of some ideal organization of the future may imply a disgust not so much with the merely national life as with civic life itself." Such ideas, which are partially descendants of the unthinking reactions that Kipling evoked, are anathema to Trilling. Politics, for all its imperfections and the vices to which it is susceptible, is the properly limited means for a people's dealing corporately with the world's intractability; and Trilling directs his sharpest scorn against those who seek for apolitical ways of coping with the inherent tensions in society. When, for example, Virgil Gheorghiu argues, in *The Twenty-Fifth Hour*, "the total rejection of the political life in favor of the individual life of the spirit," he draws this reply:

Mr. Gheorghiu is not checked in his triumphant exposition of this dull and inaccurate idea by any historical recollection, although a native of Rumania, a nation whose history is peculiarly marked by cruelty, should have recalled that, say, Vlad the Impaler reigned in an age of faith . . . when, by the bloodiest means, the masses of Rumanian people were kept in the most extreme subjection. Yet in the face of such obvious considerations, Mr. Gheorghiu goes on to tell us that modern men have sunk to the level of *citizens*, and the citizen, we are told, is "the most dangerous wild beast" that has appeared on the face of the earth since the cross be-

tween man and the mechanical slave." Political ideas as
feeble as these . . .[21]

appeal not at all to the imaginative reason but only
to thoughtless despair.

It is the feebleness, far more than the content, of
Kipling's political ideas that evokes Trilling's final
harsh assessment. Reluctantly, he accepts Eliot's notion
of Kipling as a Tory rather than a fascist, but the contrast with Samuel Johnson and Johnson's tradition
mocks the classification. Kipling had nothing of Johnson's comprehension of nationhood in Shakespearean
terms—as an organic unity with its serious limitations
and its considerable dangers, but with the potential for
drawing people together in their loneliness and for providing them with the mechanism for recognizing and for
resolving their shared problems, and for identifying and
attaining their shared aspirations. He had nothing of
Johnson's respect for citizenship as the condition of the
"individualism [that is] morally prepotent and [of] the
freedom of the individual [that] is the first criterion of
social good."[22] He lacked Johnson's generosity and
displayed none of his largeness of mind. Quite unlike
Johnson's, Kipling's toryism was too often marked by
"a lower-middle-class snarl of defeated gentility," and
his mindless imperialism offends and is self-defeating
less because of its imperial commitments than because
of its thoughtless ignoring of their costs and consequences in the contexts of modern social reality.

Trilling's judgment of Kipling, contrasting so
sharply with his evaluation of Fitzgerald, explains in
large part his obdurate opposition to "the degraded version of Marxism known as Stalinism."[23] During the
1930s and 1940s, a large segment of the intelligentsia
of the West became persuaded that the Soviet Union
"had resolved all social and political contradictions and
was well on the way toward realizing the highest possibilities of human life." For Trilling, this persuasion

did not represent a political position at all; rather, it
reflected "a settled disgust with politics, or at least
with what politics entails of contingency, vigilance, and
effort." Stalinist intellectuals perceived in an imposed
and monolithic state "the promise of rest from the particular acts of will which are needed to meet the many,
often clashing requirements of democratic society . . .
they cherished the idea of revolution as the final, all-
embracing act of will which would forever end the ex-
ertions of our individual wills." Impatient with politics,
they rejected the responsibilities that their dreams of
freedom demanded.

For Trilling, this Utopian animus against individual wills in conflict leads to a devaluing of thought and
feeling, of art, and of "all such energies of the human
spirit as are marked by spontaneity, complexity, and
variety." When human variousness and human possibilities rank among the highest human values, absolutism
in any form is their dangerous enemy; and their price is
an honest grappling with the complexities and difficulties that are inherently a part of the world's intractability. To subject oneself to an absolute or to deny that
cost amounts to stunting growth in the sentiment of
being that is the essence of selfhood and of personal
freedom.

Trilling's battle with the Stalinist mentality obviously did not end with the death of the Russian dictator
from whom its identity was derived. The China of Mao
Tse-tung and the Cuba of Fidel Castro became for
many the symbols of political arrangements that rendered unnecessary that unremitting engagement of the
will in social experience. Even the regime of North
Vietnam was invested with virtue that it did not possess,
as an expression of the longing for relief from the exigencies of the human condition.[24] In the hippie movements and the counterculture of the 1960s, "hostility,
authoritarianism, perversity, and mindless paranoia"[25]
clearly dominated freedom of choice and left little room

for even the costly felicity of Morris's *News from No-wothere*. While condemning the violence of the war in Indochina and of police oppression, the counterculture admired third-world revolutionaries, Black Panthers, and motorcycle gangs like Hell's Angels. While deploring the materialism of contemporary civilization, it devoted itself to motorcycles, stereo sets, and electronic guitars. Although an extreme example, the "family" of Charles Manson illustrates in a particularly ugly and sypmtomatic fashion the persistence and the pervasiveness of Stalinism in guises quite different from its original form. Its essence consists always in the substitution of apolitical processes for that engagement—known as politics—of the imaginative reason, powered by will, in the endless human effort to resolve the issues of corporate life in ways that maximize freedom while taking account of necessity.

If freedom, which is another word for human variousness and possibility, consists in a wide range of choices, then each choice entails an expense, demands a negation. In education, in the election of a career, in the establishment of a family, Trilling reminds us,

If you set yourself to shaping a self, a life, you limit yourself to that self and that life. You preclude any other kind of selfhood remaining available to you. . . . Such limitation, once acceptable, now goes against the cultural grain—it is almost as if the fluidity of the contemporary world demands an analogous limitlessness in our personal perspective. Any doctrine, that of the family, religion, the school, that does not sustain this increasingly felt need for a multiplicity of options and instead offers an ideal of a shaped life, a formed life, has the sign on it of a retrograde and depriving authority, which, it is felt, must be resisted.[26]

The politics of such a resistance is not a liberal politics, a politics of the extended choices that constitute freedom; it is a politics of Utopia, of *Nowhere*, of the resignation of the individual will that is no-choice.

To be significant, both for the development of

self and for the development of a more humane culture, choice must entail commitment and a coming to terms with the law of costingness, with necessity. When Joseph Frank charges Trilling with conceiving his task as "to defend not freedom but the virtues of acknowl- edging necessity,"[27] he is only partially correct; given our modern circumstances, the "charge" implies more than a measure of homage, and what Frank fails to understand is that the acknowledgement of necessity is a *condition* of freedom.

4

Decent People
Who Have No Doubts

The dominant focus in Lionel Trilling's thought lies in his strong tendency "to see literary situations as cultural situations, and cultural situations as great elaborate fights about moral issues, and moral issues as having something to do with . . . images of personal being, and images of personal being as having something to do with literary style."[1] In the often embattled interplay between the struggles of the self and conceptions of the moral life, between literary values and the quality of the larger culture, Trilling found the basic stuff of modern human experience. Characteristically, his insistence on complexity and difficulty led him to the contradictions and the conflicts in that experience.

Central among those contradictions and conflicts is the frequent and soul-rending gap between our "good impulses" and the outcome of our actions. In the mirror held up to life by books as different as E. M. Forster's *The Longest Journey* and Henry James's *The Princess Casamassima*, richly developed characters passionately and articulately concern themselves with social injustice; their taking up arms in such a cause has the ring of rightness and even nobility about it, and their valiant, well-intentioned efforts, rather than solving social problems, generate new ones of peculiar complication and intensity. The moral outcome, in an all-too-familiar fashion, lacks congruence to the manifest moral intention.[2]

Trilling introduces his argument gently. He quotes from a publicity release from a publisher:

Blank & Company reports that the current interest in horror stories has attracted a great number of readers to John Dash's novel . . . because of its depiction of Nazi brutality. Critics and readers alike have commented on the stark realism of Dash's handling of the torture scenes in the book. The publishers, who originally envisaged a woman's market because of the love story, now find men reading the book because of the other angle . . . I cite the example only to suggest that something may indeed lie behind our sober intelligent interest in moral politics. In this instance the pleasure in the cruelty is licensed by moral indignation. In other instances moral indignation . . . may be in itself an exquisite pleasure. To understand this does not invalidate moral indignation but only sets up the conditions on which it ought to be entertained, only says when it is legitimate and when not.[3]

But the gentle, amusing approach pulls us into a daring enterprise—the examination of the seamy side of the laudable drive, inherent to the liberal spirit, to create an atmosphere in which injustice finds it harder to flourish. Trilling anticipates his opposition: "Life presses us so hard, time is so short, the suffering of the world is so huge, simple, unendurable—anything that complicates our moral fervor in dealing with reality as we immediately see it and wish to drive headlong upon it must be regarded with some impatience."[4] But if the power of the moral passions, the welling up of self-righteousness, at least matches the urgent potency of the self-seeking drives, "All history is at one in telling us that their tendency is to be not only liberating but also restrictive." The conclusion cuts close to the bone of both our individual and collective experience:

Some paradox of our nature leads us, when once we have made our fellow men the objects of our enlightened interest . . . to make them the objects of our pity, then of our wisdom, ultimately of our coercion. It is to prevent this corruption, the most ironic and tragic that man knows, that we stand in need of the moral realism which is the product of the free play of the moral imagination.[5]

This eloquently phrased observation not only reminds us of our personal experience of well-intentioned people "who live for others": You can tell the "others" by the hunted look in their eyes. It takes us to the heart of the Inquisition, of the terror that followed the French Revolution, of the purges and liquidations in Stalin's Russia and Mao's China. It carries disturbing echoes of the impulses on which Kipling played with his urgent admonition to "take up the white man's burden," and it anticipates the continuation of torture and summary executions in Iran after the overthrow of the Shah in the name of justice and equity.

A Richard Sennett has aptly noted,[6] Trilling perceived that "the most destructive acts are committed by decent people who have no doubts," by those whose ideas, ideals, and moral commitments are "presided over by an impassioned longing to believe."[7] The positions that we take, and from which we act, are not patterned abstractions, susceptible only to the criteria of pure reason; they implicate us as needful, striving, willing (and willful) selves. If we fail to take this circumstance into account, then our formulated intentions overlook, at best, determinative components in our actual aims, and our moral objections, distorted and partially hidden, can only be linked in a tenuous way with the often disappointing and distressing surprises that are the outcomes of our conduct.

This concern focuses on what, in old-fashioned terms, we would call the roots of evil. Preoccupied with it throughout his career, although never heavy-handedly, Trilling examined it in special detail and with special penetration in two books. One is his novel, *The Middle of the Journey*, published in 1947; the other is *Sincerity and Authenticity*, which appeared in 1972.

For all its author's doubts about it, and despite his

painful overreaction to what he regarded as its reception,[8] *The Middle of the Journey* is a firmly conceived and handsomely written piece of fiction that may most fully represent the general cast of Trilling's mind. Set in the 1930s, when Stalinist Communism was central to the intellectual *Zeitgeist*, the novel brings together five principal characters, each distinctly individual, but exemplifying different tendencies within the liberal community of informed and thoughtful people.

The protagonist is John Laskell, "a fortunate young man of the middle class," for whom the world "might perhaps have absorbing doubts but certainly not any fears." His recently published *Theories of Housing* has established him as an expert on urban affairs; he is untroubled by economic adversity, and his outlook is that of a generous and sensible man, who shares the dreams of a more just and decent world, while still discriminating between the aspirations of dreams and the demands of reality. Mature and skeptical, Laskell has been shaken by two brushes with death. His fiancee has recently died, and he himself, when the story opens, is convalescent from an illness that has nearly proved fatal. At thirty-three, he finds himself particularly alert to the press of fate against the contours of his self and at that point at which *The Divine Comedy* begins—*nel mezzo del cammin*—where crucial orientations must be developed.

Laskell's most deeply loved friends are Nancy and Arthur Croom, with whom he spends a few weeks recovering from his illness, at their summer place in Connecticut. Arthur, a professor of economics, has just won considerable recognition by a book on business cycles and anticipates a call to Washington to serve the New Deal. He also writes occasionally for liberal magazines, and he and Nancy live more or less on the fringe of radical politics. Pregnant with her second child, Nancy has charm and warmth and shares with her husband a "passionate expectation of the future" as a time

when justice will be more generously distributed and
when reason will prevail in the large affairs of the nation and the world. As bright, industrious, good-hearted
people, the Crooms occupy a place in Laskell's heart as
something of a "justification of human existence."

Kermit Simpson, a relatively minor but necessary
figure, enjoys a friendship with both Laskell and the
Crooms. A man of inherited wealth, Simpson has a
genuine interest in liberal causes, but he also is rather
touchingly driven by a need to prove his personal worth
in the face of the great advantages that the luck of his
birth has conferred upon him. He publishes, at his own
expense, *The New Era*, "a rather sad liberal monthly,"
that provides a forum for leftist ideas and programs.

Finally, there is Gifford Maxim, known to both
the Crooms and to Laskell. He has long worked as an
underground agent for the Communists, and his ascetic
devotion to realizing the Marxist vision of a good society has marked him for Laskell as "a man of the far
future, the bloody, moral, apocalyptic future that was
sure to come." In Laskell's and the Crooms' eyes, Maxim's dedication, self-sacrifice, and the willingness to
take major personal risks make him the measure—by
which they are consistently a bit embarrassed—of their
own more prudent, less hazardous, and more conventional political involvements and loyalties. This special
status that Maxim occupies deeply influences the nature
of the relationships involved. Although friendly, Maxim
and Laskell, for example, are not quite friends:

Laskell saw him flanked by two great watching figures. They
were abstracted and motionless, having the air that figures
in a mural have. . . . On one side of Maxim stood the figure
of the huge, sad, stern morality of all the suffering and
exploited men in the world, all of them, without distinction
of color or creed. On the other side of Maxim stood the
figure of power, noble, fierce, indomitable. . . . The face
of the one was old and tragic, the face of the other was
young and proud. Yet both had that brooding blind look

that is given by men to the abstractions they admire, in the belief that a lack of personal being is the mark of all great and admirable things. Behind Maxim and his two great flanking figures were the infinite dim vistas of History, which was not the past but the future.

If Maxim is very much a person, he is also a symbol and a moral force. If his presence is always compelling, he rarely seems likeable, and he is seldom available for those shared intimacies that are one of the foundations on which friendship rests.

Although the matter has little bearing on the quality of *The Middle of the Journey* as a work of art, at least one aspect of the novel's significance, its realistic connection with history, gains clarity through the realization that the prototype for Gifford Maxim was Whittaker Chambers.[9] Chambers won his minor but visible part on the American public record by instigating and serving as chief witness in the case of Alger Hiss, an official in the Department of State, whom he charged with transmitting government documents to the Soviet Union. Accused of treason, Hiss was found guilty in 1950 of perjury and served a five-year prison term, always and consistently protesting his innocence. At least three elements of the litigation make it memorable. First, it established the reputation of a member of the House of Representatives who functioned as an avid prosecutor. In 1952, Richard Nixon became Dwight D. Eisenhower's vice-president, largely on the strength of the impression he made in the Hiss case, and, in 1968, he was elected to the presidency of the United States. Second, Hiss's protracted and bitter hearings and his trial carried the dramatic freight of intense moral issues, as well as of the politics of national security. Chambers and Hiss had once been fast friends, and the betrayal of that relationship put Chambers as much on trial as the man whom he had brought to the bar. And the revelations by persons who had once belonged either to the American Communist Party or to the Soviet espionage apparatus in the United States—the two were far from synonymous—both alarmed and divided the country. Prior to that time, there had been little public awareness of the extent of the Russian underground in America, and the notion of its reaching to the high post that Hiss had held, and to people as distinguished and as trusted as he had been, shook national confidence.

At the same time, the whole legal process seemed to many to be overblown and contrived, an effort to promote political support for anti-Communists more than a serious investigation of treason. The lack of convincing evidence that Hiss had indeed given government documents to the Soviets, and the settlement of the case by a conviction for perjury, struck large numbers as a demonstration of the rigged nature of the affair. For others, however—also in large numbers— that outcome appeared a miscarriage of justice, the punishment of a profound violation of American security by little more than a slap on the wrist. Finally, the Hiss case conferred a kind of legitimacy and prominence on Communists who had recanted; in generating widespread public interest and sympathy for their accounts of life in the subterranean reaches of Russian intelligence, it did much to usher in the age of suspicion and witch-hunting associated with the name of Senator Joseph McCarthy.

Among the recanting Communists, Chambers found himself most sharply in the limelight. He had joined the Party in 1925. In 1932, he was drafted from the editorship of the *New Masses* to serve in the Soviet underground. By 1936, he had become disenchanted with Communism as a theory of government and with the Russian translation of that theory into practices that included overseas political infiltration and espionage. Searching for a way out of his secret involvements, he confronted the crucial distinction. To break with the American Communist Party—legally constituted, the publisher of low-subscription periodicals like the *Daily Worker* and *New Masses*, the parent of large numbers of more or less impotent committees, and the distributor of petitions—meant little more than outrage from one's associates and a period of condemnation in the Communist press. But to break with the secret organization that ultimately took its orders from Moscow entailed the risk of one's life. To protect himself, he enlisted his acquaintances in establishing for himself a socially recognized identity and public existence marked by routines and by formalized and steady relationships with others. If he could regularly be seen by people who could testify that he had been alive on a given day, then he would enjoy some measure of safety from the reprisals that his defection would evoke.

In a remote fashion, Trilling was acquainted with Chambers when they both were undergraduates at Columbia College. They were never friends, although, if there was something about Chambers that repelled, there was also something that commanded interest and respect. Solemn and seeming never to have been young, Chambers exercised a moral authority rare among students, enjoyed a degree of prestige because of his talent as a writer, and made his commitment to radical politics the controlling core of his personal being. With a number of his friends, Trilling had been tenuously involved with the Communist Party in 1932 and 1933. After Hitler came to power in the latter year, that involvement deteriorated rapidly and became mistrustful and hostile.

Trilling knew of Chambers's going underground; and in a peripheral way, he was among those who, in 1936, helped him to a degree of security when he left the espionage apparatus. When one of Hiss's attorneys in 1948, well after the publication of *The Middle of the Journey*, asked that he speak against Chambers in court, Trilling refused. "Whittaker Chambers had been engaged in espionage against his own country; when a change of heart and principle led to his defecting from his apparatus, he had eventually not only confessed his own treason but named the comrades who shared it, including one whom for a time he had cherished as a friend. I hold that when this has been said of him, it is still possible to say that he was a man of honor."[10] One of the questions that *The Middle of the Journey* poses bears on the extent to which honor protects a person from that disjunction between his good impulses and the outcome of his acting on them, which is the "most ironic and tragic" experience of corruption that we know. Another asks about the character of the functional differences between extreme moral and political points of view; like his prototype Chambers, Maxim adopts an essentially dialectical version of Christianity when he defects from Communism.

The novel opens in the quiet heat of late summer. Laskell, having escaped death by a narrow margin from a raging febrile illness is closing his apartment in New York to spend a few weeks of convalescence with his friends the Crooms in the Connecticut countryside. A frightened Maxim appears, announcing his break with the Party. To lessen the likelihood of assassination, he asks Laskell to persuade Kermit Simpson to give him a job on the staff of *The New Era*; neither the nature of the work nor the pay matters, but the appearance of his name on the masthead and his having an office to go to every day are crucial. Shocked by Maxim's political turnabout, Laskell reluctantly telephones Simpson and wins from him an agreement to talk with Maxim the next day at his Westport summer house. At Maxim's instigation, which, despite his distaste, Laskell is still too weak to resist, the two men arrange to take the train together as far as Westport. The next morning, Maxim presents himself in need of a bath and a shave; for the sake of his safety, he has spent the night on Laskell's roof. The two depart, Maxim's fear of being murdered for political reasons serving as a counterpoint to Laskell's intense but objectless anxiety, born of his recent intimacy with death, about the short trip by rail from New York to the Crooms' country place.

Although experiencing something like horrified disgust at Maxim's forsaking his political ideals, Laskell finds himself in a similar situation; he also must take new bearings and find new directions. During his long illness, one of his nurses commented on the "great love affair" that he was having with a tawny pink rose on his bedside table. Recalling his fascination with the beautiful flower, he is startled by the realization that its evanescent perfection symbolized the peace of eternity and that in becoming preoccupied with it, he was accepting his own death. The episode strikes him as momentous, but once with the Crooms, settled with a nearby family in whose house they have arranged for him to stay, he discovers that he cannot discuss the event with his friends. Deeply concerned about him and warmly welcoming, they simply refuse to admit serious illness and death into their optimistic and rational world of thought and discourse. Indeed, they look upon death, with its implied denial of a bright, reasonable, and egalitarian future, to be achieved through political effort, as a reactionary idea. Though they treat him with affectionate tenderness, whenever Laskell tries to talk about what it was like to be seriously ill and to come so close to dying, the Crooms disengage themselves "in a polite, intelligent, concerted way . . . as if they were the parents of a little boy and were following the line of giving no heed to the obscenities their son picked up on the street and insisted on bringing to the dinner table. . . . They simply, in a sensible modern way, paid no attention at all."

This refusal to recognize the importance of Laskell's experience is joined in a complex but comprehensible manner with the Crooms' perception of Duck Caldwell, their handyman. Duck drinks too much, cannot be relied on, is a womanizer of the coarsest sort,

and escapes indigence by unwillingly taking odd jobs in
the town. The support he provides for his wife and
daughter barely exceeds subsistence; and while he
hardly represents a large-scale source of evil, he dully
and irritatingly exemplifies "the pure will of nothingness."

Emily, his wife, however, seems cut from quite a
different cloth. On the one hand, she behaves in a
mildly absurd way that is sometimes touching, sometimes embarrassing. She affects a bohemianism that is a
bit out of date; her intellectual pretensions leave her
looking foolish, as when she talks about "doom" re-
sounding through Spengler's *Decline of the West*,
which she has borrowed from the Crooms, and "vague
gentilities" mark her speech, her dress, and her manner.
But as the sensitive and responsible mother of her vivacious little girl, Susan, in "her worry about Susan's
education, in her function as a housekeeper with her
little prides in the midst of poverty, in her not at all
striking talk about ordinary things," she has, Laskell
learns, "a womanly dignity that (does) . . . not depend
on intellect—a kind of biological intelligence."

Because the Crooms' attitude toward the lower
class is determined essentially by political principle and
not by familiarity, because their benevolence is abstract
and not a matter of immediate sympathy, Nancy and
Arthur perceive the Caldwells not as distinctive persons
but as examples of their kind. Emily's ingrained integrity and fundamental common sense levies less on their
generosity than Duck's shiftlessness and untrustworthy
habits. They consequently respond with malice to Emily's awkwardness and sometimes silly ideas and com-
portment. On the other hand, they refer often and
romantically to Duck as "a high manifestation of ordinary life," as a kind of noble savage. Duck, Arthur
rather admiringly tells Laskell, "has his own way of
doing things and . . . can't be hurried." Laskell reacts to
this characteristic observation by wondering why his

progressive friends, so eager to hurry other reconstructions of reality, extend an exemption to their unsavory handyman while subjecting his wife to a kind of courteous scorn.

Dimly perceiving the association between the Crooms' judgment of his experience of intimacy with death as somehow politically reactionary and their peculiarly principled exclusion from their consciousness of the ugly actuality that Duck presents, Laskell puts off telling Nancy and Arthur about Maxim's break with the Party. Finally, knowing that they will regard his withholding of this news as a sort of betrayal, he recounts for them the story of Maxim's visit in New York, his declaration of his defection, his overwhelming fears of being murdered in reprisal, and his plea for a job with Kermit Simpson as a means of establishing a protective public identity. Predictably, the Crooms react with angry shock. Maxim has abdicated the heroic role of the radical activist in which they had cast him; he has proved disloyal to the basic tenets of radical politics, and he cannot, in their view, be justified in his fear of retaliation, which impresses them as paranoid. Furiously, they pronounce him mad, and they express displeasure with Laskell for his failure to dissuade Maxim from his unforgivably insane course.

A few days later, the latest issue of *The New Era* arrives in the mail. Maxim's name occupies a place on its masthead, and an article under his by-line makes evident that he has not only rejected Communism but that he has embraced a relatively extreme form of Christian theology. Entitled "Spirit and Law," Maxim's piece analyzes Melville's *Billy Budd*. The argument holds that the character of Claggart represents Evil in the world and that Billy, while not absolutely pure, stands for Spirit. Captain Vere embodies the principle of Law or of Necessity in human affairs. Because Claggart or Evil exists, Vere or Law must rule to insure the safety and orderliness on which bearable social interactions depend. Vere's judgment against Billy Budd, Maxim writes, is therefore both ineluctably correct and quite incomprehensible to modern liberals. Insisting that "Spirit should find its complete expression at once," liberals find Captain Vere culpable because of his refusal to acquit Billy in defiance of Law. Melville's perception, the essay continues, is quite different. So long as Evil inhabits the world, Law rather than Spirit must dominate, and Vere's tragic choice as judge is that of "God the Father, who must condemn his own Son," although the condemnation represents "not the familiar transaction of . . . a sacrifice and an atonement" but must be enforced "for the sake of the Son himself, for the sake of Spirit in humanity."

Maxim is quite right. His meditation on the problem of evil, for which *Billy Budd* is the point of departure, both offends and lies beyond the comprehension of the Crooms. This new creed of an ex-Communist appears to them as reactionary and disgustingly obscurantist. Even for Laskell, it carries no meaning beyond "the odor of corruption." But the intellectual and ideological stage has been set. With all the moral force and personal dedication that he once gave to Communism, Maxim has been established as the proponent of conventional law and societal necessity, sanctified by religious considerations. Nancy and Arthur Croom, energized by angry disappointment and their aroused need for a radical hero, become his antagonists, the spokesmen for the thesis that he once so largely stood for and to which he now opposes an antithesis.

Into this tense air, Maxim emerges. He and Simpson have formed a surprisingly easy relationship, and in Simpson's shiny new camper-trailer, the two of them are taking a brief holiday through New England that includes a visit for a few days with the Crooms and Laskell. The visit coincides with the village's annual church bazaar. This event traditionally concludes with an entertainment involving both local residents and the "summer people." As a part of the entertainment, Susan, Emily and Duck Caldwell's daughter, is to give a recitation of Blake's "Jerusalem." Laskell, feeling considerable affection for the little girl and having won her trust, has been hearing her practice. To his not entirely comfortable amusement, she declaims the poem in an old-fashioned elocutionary manner, stamping her foot in passionate refusal at the line, "I will *not* cease from mental fight." He gently recommends that the stresses might better be evenly distributed: "*I will not cease . . .*" Her readiness to be persuaded gives him some qualms, but the presentation does become less ludicrous when she makes the suggested modification. On the afternoon of the performance, however, she unthinkingly reads the line after her original fashion, stamping her foot. Her dismay at her mistake leaves her unable to continue, until Laskell, seated near the stage, softly supplies her with the necessary words. Her little girl's poise recovered, Susan winds up with a gallant flourish and wins a friendly and approving ovation from the spectators.

But during her recitation, Duck, freshly shaved for the occasion but dead drunk, has come into the church. As his daughter leaves the stage in triumph, he stumbles toward her, saying, "A fine one you are. A disgrace." He slaps her twice. She falls, and when she is picked up, she is dead; her heart has failed. Laskell has earlier learned from Emily that she has never told her husband of Susan's serious cardiac disorder for fear that, in his arrogant virility, he would not "respect" their child. Although no question of murder arises, a winsome little girl has still died as a consequence of her father's insensitive and careless brutishness.

This devastating and grief-producing event becomes the background for the inevitable confrontation between Maxim and the Crooms. Sitting before the fireplace on a day when the weather has turned rainy and

cold, the five principals of *The Middle of the Journey*,
all of them deeply touched by the sadness of Susan's
death and its mindless manner, try to sort out what
requires resolution and judgment. The Crooms do not
hold Duck responsible. When Nancy insists passionately that "It's not his fault," Arthur explains, a little
professorially, that "social causes, environment, education or lack of education, economic pressure, the
character-pattern imposed by society, in this case a dis-
organized society, all . . . account for any given individual's actions." Nancy agrees fully but imposes a
distressed condition: "We can't say he's to blame personally, individually. But I can't stand the idea of having him around me. Not that I'd be afraid, but I'd
always be thinking that this man killed his child."

At this point, Maxim states the issue from his
newfound Christian perspective:

Nancy's dilemma is an inevitable one. She refuses to say
that Caldwell has any responsibility, any blame or guilt.
And then she refuses to allow him to come near her . . . I
reverse your whole process. I believe that Duck Caldwell—
like you or me or any of us—is wholly responsible for his
acts. Wholly. And for eternity, for everlasting. That is what
gives him value in my eyes—his eternal, everlasting responsibility. . . . Yet in my system there is one thing that yours
lacks. In my system, although there is never-ending responsibility, there is such a thing as mercy. . . . Duck can be forgiven. I can personally forgive him because I believe that
God can forgive him. . . . I think his will is a bad one, but
not much worse, not different in kind, from other wills.
And so you and I stand opposed. For you—no responsibility
for the individual, but no forgiveness. For me—ultimate,
absolute responsibility for the individual, but mercy. Absolute responsibility: it is the only way that men can keep
their value, can be thought of as other than mere *things* . . .
social causes, environment, education—do you think they
really make a difference between one human soul and another? In the eyes of God are such differences of any meaning at all?

In the silence that ensues, Simpson turns to Laskell to ask, "John, what is your feeling about this?" Trilling's interposed comment is wryly important: "To Kermit a difference of opinion was a difference of opinion and showed that liberalism still flourished." Laskell, called upon, has a response: "An absolute freedom from responsibility—that much of a child none of us can be. An absolute responsibility—that much of a divine or metaphysical essence none of us is." And he explains: "I cannot absolve the world or society or God or my parents or nature from all blame from what I am or do. I didn't make myself and I don't dare cut my connection with all the things in the world that made me. I cannot hold myself free of these things. I will blame them when they injure and reduce me, as they do every moment of the day. And for that matter, I cannot avoid my gratitude to them."

Both Maxim and the Crooms react with anger to Laskell's position. "Neither beast nor angel!" Maxim sneers, "Pascal said it long ago." Nancy snaps, "Certainly there's a good deal of shilly-shally in what you've just said, John." And Arthur adds, "And a good deal of name-calling and motive-attributing." Trilling's commentary is explicit. Laskell

knew why they were angry at him. It was the anger of the masked will at the appearance of an idea in modulation. The open will does not show that anger, only the will masked in virtue shows it. His idea . . . had affronted them. They were staring at him as silently as the great mural figures that once had flanked Gifford Maxim when he talked of politics and the future.

Maxim reveals something of the nature of "the masked will" by an invasion of Laskell's privacy, and he forcefully poses the great issue that is the novel's central business. Perceptive observer that he is, Maxim has correctly inferred that Laskell has had an affair with Emily Caldwell. Their sexual union, and the man-

ner of Emily's participation in it, has contributed to
Laskell's return to life after his intense encounter with
illness and death. Without loving her, feeling "no community of passion with her," he nevertheless realizes
that "in that moment, in all the empty world, she was
the one person who existed for him in love." Not long
before the interchanges that have just culminated in
Laskell's becoming the object of anger from both the
Crooms and Maxim, Laskell and Emily have met for
the last time. With great dignity and simple honesty,
making no demands, Emily tells him, against his pro-
tests, "you have been very good"—to Susan, to her,
even to Duck, and she lightly kisses his cheek in good-
bye. Maxim has seen the episode and uses it both as a
weapon and to make a point.

"You spoke," he says, "as a forgiven man, because of what happened on the road this afternoon
between you and Emily Caldwell." He drives on:

"You spoke with courage and the intelligence of courage
because you felt forgiven. It was a frightening thing to be,
wasn't it? . . . What a blow—to be kissed on the cheek and
forgiven! . . . You were freed from guilt—from the immediate guilt of not having loved Emily Caldwell, though
you had made love to her, for having valued her low,
though you liked her and got pleasure and help from her.
And from the general guilt of other people's sins, or of
their suffering, or of their death. Perhaps you were freed
from your guilt of your own death. . . . I think we do not
fear extinction, not extinction of our whole being but the
part of our being that keeps everything else in check. As if
we feared the death of conscience in ourselves, or the death
of the State, or as if we were killing our parents—whatever
it is that keeps in check every filthy impulse in our selves
that would overwhelm us . . . this afternoon poor Emily
Caldwell gave you what you think was forgiveness, and
now you feel that being human is permissible. That's why
you spoke out of the old knowledge of what the human
fate is. . . . It is too late for that . . . the day for being
human in the way you feel now is over. Gone. Done for.

Finished. Maybe it will come again. But . . . not until the Crooms and I have won and established ourselves against the anarchy of the world. . . . [The Crooms] will preach the law for the masses. I will preach the law for the leaders. For the masses, rights and the freedom from blame. For the leaders, duties and nothing but blame, from without and from within. We will hate each other and we will make the new world."

Kermit Simpson reacts to Maxim's speech by exclaiming, "Giff, I swear I think you're crazy," and Nancy says, "He is crazy. He's insane." But Laskell responds, "No, he's not." And Maxim leaps, almost gaily, for the kill: "Remember it! . . . The supreme act of the humanistic critical intelligence—it perceives the cogency of the argument and acquiesces in the fact of its own extinction." Holding to his conception of "the human being in maturity, at once responsible and conditioned," Laskell replies, "I do not acquiesce."

To digest *The Middle of the Journey* in this fashion violates the book's carefully constructed architecture, its subtlety, and its insights into the interplay of character and ideological commitments. Explicitly conceived as a novel of ideas, it may have limited appeal, but few works of fiction from the 1940s retain the cogency, the provocative power, or the perceptiveness into the contemporary human heart that this one does. It embodies three major themes.

First, Trilling himself, commenting on the "polemical" element in his story, indicates that his aim was to illuminate "the clandestine negation of the political life which Stalinist Communism had fostered among the intellectuals of the West. This negation was one aspect of an ever more imperious and bitter refusal to consent to the conditioned nature of human existence."[11] When that consent is withheld, then absolutism and its twin, the conviction that ends justify means, become dominant. Both inhibit the ability of the imaginative reason to conceive of human variousness and possibility in

novel ways and to explore the means of facilitating
their attainment. Licensed by good intentions and given
the dream of a successful method by ideology, human
beings aspire to the status of angels, stimultaneously
just, loving, and rational in a world to be achieved. In
pursuit of that achievement, they risk becoming beasts.
With only minor regrets, both the Maxims and the
Crooms willingly liquidate the John Laskells—the
"humanistic critical intelligence"—to usher in a social
order presided over by rational authority and marked
somehow by both equality and excellence. If the appeal
of Stalinism to Western intellectuals in the 1930s illustrates this kind of corruption of the liberal spirit, its
significance lies more in the susceptibility of intellectuals to this kind of corrosion than in Stalinism as the
specific corrosive. In the years since *The Middle of the
Journey's* first publication, readers have needed only to
substitute the names of different ideologies and to perceive the striking similarities among different concrete
circumstances to find the book a penetrating gloss on
widely shared human tendencies and on the vulnerability of the civilized self to "the dangers which lie in our
most generous wishes."[12]

The second theme illuminates the first. Its vehicle
is Nancy Croom, whose brightness, warmth, and personal decency lie beyond doubt. Her politics, which
includes a fellow traveler's commitment to Communism,
expresses a personal demand that the world fulfill "the
promises" that have been made to "the well-loved
child" of modern, middle-class society. Beneath her
liberal rhetoric, she has transformed a deeply felt insecurity of her own into a sense of destiny, projecting her
own wish and will in political form onto the future. In
consequence, she is capable of striking cruelty. The
flippant symbol of her destructiveness is her order to
Laskell when he inadvertently steps into her flowerbed:
"Step out of the cosmos, John." The lighthearted pun
only emphasizes by contrast Nancy's willingness to re-

move from the larger cosmos virtually anyone who
seems to stand in the way of her realizing the politicized
actualization of her inner longings. When, for example,
Laskell tells her and her husband about Maxim's defection, she attacks him as a "romantic" who cannot grow
beyond old-fashioned ideas and who has allowed himself to become a little addled by the death of his fiancee. Shocked, Laskell becomes aware that whether
Maxim is or is not in the danger that he has claimed, it
is clear that emotions at least compatible with political
murder are easily aroused among Communists and
Communist sympathizers. Profoundly invested in Communism as an idea, Nancy has no appreciation for the
need to modulate that idea in relation to the passions
associated with it or to the actions that it instigates. For
all her pleasant ways and her capacity for tenderness,
Nancy is dangerous because she lives in what Wordsworth called that "Tempting region . . . / For Zeal to
enter and refresh herself, / Where passions had the privilege to work / Without ever hearing the sound of their
own names." What Trilling calls "the masked will" involves, in part, the exclusion from awareness of the
feelings, the personal impulses, and the private wishes
that cling like barnacles to political concepts and political commitments. Zeal suffers no hindrance from the
healthy doubts that only self-knowledge provides.

Finally, there is the theme of John Laskell's re-
affirming return to life. In the course of his near-mortal
illness, he had "taken a fancy" to an experienced state
"just short of extinction. It was the removal of all the
adverse conditions of the self, the personality living in
nothing but delight in itself." From this intimate intim-
ation of mortality, he derives the insight to oppose a
quiet knowledge against Nancy Croom's insistence that
"History shows that man is dialectically developing and
improving himself all the time." Suffering cannot be
"improved." An immunity to death cannot be "developed." The ultimate finiteness of human beings can

confront anyone at any time. In the middle of his
journey, Laskell has learned from his close encounter
with death that ripeness indeed is all, that "maturity"
brings the future and present together, "that you lived
your life *now* instead of preparing and committing
yourself to some better day to come." This awareness
derives not at all from self-indulgence or immediate
gratification. Rather, it has its roots in Pascal:

. . . the present is generally painful to us. We conceal it
from our sight, because it troubles us; and if it be delightful
to us, we regret to see it pass away. We try to sustain it by
the future, and think of arranging matters which are not in
our power, for a time which we have no certainty of reaching. . . . The present is never our end. The past and the
present are our means, the future alone is our end. So we
never live, but we hope to live; and, as we are always preparing to be happy, it is inevitable we should never be so.[18]

But to live, to achieve some semblance of happiness, entails three requirements. One is the cultivation
of the sentiment of being, self-knowledge that includes
"the adverse conditions of . . . the personality" as well
as the bases for self-esteem. The second is a willingness
to acknowledge and grapple with exigency and contingency as inherent components of the world and of culture. Because, as imperfect beings, we always imperfectly perceive our environment, our experience is
necessarily colored by surprises, not all of them pleasant. And third, there is the discrimination between wish
and world, between the character and direction of our
will and wish, and the character of the external world,
including the external world of other persons. Not as
adages or imposed prescriptions, but as qualities of his
perception and his personhood, these comprehensions
have been achieved by Laskell as a consequence of his
confrontation first with death and then with the Crooms
and Maxim during his convalescence. It is a tribute to
Trilling's novelistic powers that *The Middle of the
Journey* displays this kind of human growth with a min-

imum of sheer conceptualization and with no preaching. Very much a novel of ideas, it makes its intellectual point through the interplay of circumstance and character.

Twenty-five years later, with still greater firmness, Trilling was again dealing with similar themes. *Sincerity and Authenticity*, although far from a study in politics, concentrates on the bases for stability and an appropriately conditioned quality in our political intelligence. Significantly, except for *Matthew Arnold*, it is Trilling's only critical book conceived as a whole and prepared as a self-contained unit. All his other volumes are collections of essays, unified by the concerns that focused his thought and engaged his sensibility as he responded to the shifting patterns of culture at particular periods in his life. Developed originally as the Charles Eliot Norton Lectures at Harvard in 1971, *Sincerity and Authenticity* incorporates Trilling's experience of the 1960s. True to his Arnoldian distinction between the realm of ideas and ideals and the realm of practical politics, he does not deal with the specfic issues of that harried decade in American history. Rather, he reviews nearly 400 years of cultural changes to provide a perspective for those issues. In the course of his analysis, Trilling examines the sea-changes that beset human purposes, as they move from intention and impulse to actual consequences both in society and in the formation of the self.

That examination demonstrates that, repeatedly, in the interplay between persons and their culture, the corruption of goodwill emerges as a danger against which eternal vigilance remains the tenuous but only available protection. Trilling perceived the sixties as an era that began in great goodwill. Through a failure of vigilance, of exigent self-monitoring, goodwill soured into egocentricity and nihilism. What he saw as the hallmarks of the decade—ugliness, violence, incivility, self-indulgence—amounted to the expressions of a degenerate egocentricity and nihilism turned pointless and self-defeating. The central issues of the time were those of civil rights and the war in Vietnam. Neither, in Trilling's judgment, was resolved or meliorated through the actions that emerged from the dynamics of egocentricity and nihilism, the dynamics of the masked will. As was *The Middle of the Journey, Sincerity and Authenticity* is, in a very real sense, a lament over the human tendency to corrupt goodwill as it moves into practical action. The self-centered rejection of compromise, the refusal to accept the conditioned nature of striving humankind, replaces benign intentions with destructive combat that loses sight of generous purposes. Such was the pattern, as Trilling understood it, of the 1960s.

But it is also a human pattern that has displayed itself before. Continuing his faith in the power of people to rearrange their patterns of life if they will look honestly into the mirror of their cultural and personal histories, Trilling holds up that mirror, in *Sincerity and Authenticity*, for our not always comfortable examination. He begins by indicating that, as a central element in the moral life, the notion of sincerity rose to prominence in the sixteenth century. We can hardly discuss the patriarch Abraham in terms of his sincerity, and the extent to which Achilles or Beowulf were sincere is a clear irrelevancy. But when Polonius says to Laertes,

> This above all: to thine own self be true
> And it doth follow, as the night the day,
> Thou canst not then be false to any man,

we face something novel. We cannot even accommodate the lines to our perception of Polonius as a near-senile, bumbling self-server, such is their "lucid moral lyricism."

The central idea of sincerity involves two components, both touched on in Polonius's speech. One has to do with the degree of congruence between avowal and actual feeling (to thine own self be true); the other stresses the social consequences of that congruence (thou canst not then be false to any man). If sincerity demands a kind of private classical practice of the examined life—a considerable measure of self-knowledge —it also requires a public pattern of accurate self-disclosure, of not representing oneself socially as one is not, of honesty not only about events but about the self.

The difficulties here, however, seem predictable. Trilling resorts to one of his principal teachers, Matthew Arnold ("The poets," Freud remarked, "not I, discovered the unconscious"), to make them manifest:

Below the surface-stream, shallow and light,
Of what we say we feel—below the stream,
As light, of what we *think* we feel—there flows
With noiseless current strong, obscure, and deep,
The central stream of what we feel indeed.

Locating the "own self," to which we can and must be true, is and remains far from a simple matter. "And yet at a certain point in history certain men and classes of men conceived that the making of [the] effort [to do so] was of supreme importance in the moral life, and the value they attached to the enterprise of sincerity became a salient, perhaps definitive, characteristic of Western culture for some four hundred years."

Despite that saliency, the difficulties of being sincere have always included, of course, discrepancies between the intentions clustered about the effort at sincerity and the social consequences engendered by the effort. Trilling finds in Molière's *Le Misanthrope* a fitting example. The character of Alceste persuasively claims that "My chief talent is to be frank and sincere"; his chief pride derives from his sincerity, from his remorseless dedication to truth. But, as Trilling observes,

"The obsessiveness and obduracy of his sincerity amount to *hubris*, that state of being in which truth is obscured through the ascendancy of self-regarding will over intelligence. It is to his will and not, as he persuades himself, to truth that Alceste gives his stern allegiance." Although Moliere handles Alceste's absolutism gently, by questioning it and teasing it, he makes it contrast sharply with quite a different idea of right conduct. That idea, so much more difficult to live by and to realize in a life-style, requires the testing of behavior by the touchstones of good sense and realism, by judgments of the quality of inevitable compromises between idealized conceptions of the truth and both one's own internal inconsistencies and the outright defects of the society in which persons always hold membership. For Alceste, however, his experience of disappointment, disillusion, and despair arises not from the fact

that first one and then another of the members of his immediate circle, and then still another and at last almost all of them, out of vanity or for material advantage, make avowals which are not in accord with what they feel or believe, but rather that the life of man in a developed community must inevitably be a corruption of truth. When in the end Alceste vows himself to solitude, it is not out of mere personal disappointment in the entrancing Celimene but out of disgust with society, an entity whose nature is not to be exactly defined by the nature of the individuals who constitute it.

Unclear about the character of his "own self," Alceste has projected onto abstract society (after the fashion of Nancy Croom) the requirement that it conform to those qualities in himself to which his pride is most intimately attached and from which the strivings of his will take their direction. As is typical when societies are conceived as abstractions and not as complicated patterns of individual wills contending together under culturally established rules, Alceste really cares not a fig for his commitment to truth. In reality, his commitment is to the imposition of his will on others. As a result, he produces effects far different from those that he intends, and he himself suffers pain, helplessness, and impotent anger as an outcome of this incongruity that he cannot understand.

In many ways, Trilling's treatment of sincerity both as a state of being and as a social virtue amounts to an elaboration of a comment in his "Of This Time, Of That Place," a short story that he published in 1943. At the opening of an academic year, the protagonist, Dr. Howe, a college professor of literature and a published poet, finds pleasure in "a busy and official day of cards and sheets, arrangements and small decisions. Even when it was time to attend the first of the weekly Convocations he felt the charm of the beginning of things, when intention is still innocent and uncorrupted by effort."[14] Whatever other impediments that it may encounter, does sincerity depend in some measure on the "innocence" associated with "the beginning of things"? And to what extent is sincerity inherently eroded by the corruptions of effort—that is, by the entailment of working with very different others toward goals that, because of those very differences, can only be partially shared, partially held in common? The raising of these movingly central questions echoes the concern in *The Liberal Imagination*—the way in which opportunities for the realization in society of liberal ideas and liberal ideals confer "value and necessity" on the organizational impulse of liberalism, but the organizational impulse "means delegation, and agencies, and bureaus . . . and . . . the ideas that can survive delegation . . . give up something of their largeness and modulation and complexity in order to survive."[15]

In what Trilling calls an "old and merely fanciful etymology," the word "sincere" stems from *sine cera*, without wax; it implies an object that has not been patched up, that is not passed off as sound when it has been broken and cunningly repaired. In that sense, pure

ideas become necessarily less sincere when they un-
dergo the effort demanded by their translation into reality, when they are exposed to the contending and quite
different wills that compose society and the social process, when they are acted on by the organizational impulse. In a way that may be paradoxical, and in a
manner that may occasion deeply felt regret, their becoming less sincere seems to become a condition of
their effectiveness.[16]

If this observation is anathema to the absolutist,
an outrageous disappointment to the passionate idealist, it reflects once again Trilling's insistence on human
limitation, on the acknowledgment of necessity, on consenting to the conditioned nature of human life. This
insistence, which lies at the base of his humanism,
undergirds his liberal position, gives him flexibility in
coping with particular issues, and permits his breadth
and generosity of perspective. Grounding himself in his
fundamental views and capitalizing on the powers that
they make possible, he achieves a special sharpness and
a rare intensity in his analysis of authenticity as a modern idea that has superceded sincerity as a moral quality and that has become chic, a kind of modish if
self-destructive instrument in the warfare of self with
culture. From these same moral emplacements, he
directs his heaviest fire against those who argue that
"madness" represents a legitimate and even desirable
route to authenticity in a culture that is corruptly and
decadently inauthentic or phony.

Trilling accepts authenticity as "suggesting a more
strenuous moral experience than 'sincerity' does, a
more exigent conception of the self and of what being
true to it consists in, a wider reference to the universe
and man's place in it, and a less acceptant and genial
view of the social circumstances of life." As the concept of authenticity has come to supplant that of sincerity, many cultural attributes—traditional and conven-

tional belief systems and institutions, the structures of interpersonal courtesy, the dominant mores—have lost much of their value. They appear increasingly as fantasies, empty rituals, or sheer shams. On the other hand, much that the culture has directly disapproved or outlawed has seemed to acquire a peculiar moral authority by virtue of the authenticity, somehow, sometimes mysteriously, invested in it—cultivated disorder in dress and conduct, destructive violence against both property and persons, the elevation (not infrequently with the help of various drugs) of the instinctual, the intuitive, and the emotional over the rational.

With his lasting concern for the power to feel, with his intimate knowledge of the inevitability of relationships that sorely try the individual spirit, Trilling does not lack appreciation for this tendency. Among other things, he notes that although authenticity can deny art, it can also figure prominently as the "dark source" of art. He quotes Yeats, writing at the moment "when all his performances seemed to him of no account and he had to discover how to devise new ones":

> Those masterful images because complete
> Grew in pure mind, but out of what began?
> A mound of refuse or the sweepings of a street,
> Old kettles, old bottles, and a broken can,
> Old iron, old bones, old rags, that raving slut
> Who kept the till. Now that my ladder's gone
> I must lie down where all the ladders start,
> In the foul rag-and-bone shop of the heart.

Moved as he is by Yeats's clear-eyed fusion of desperation and determination, Trilling still recalls, in contrast, Sir Philip Sidney's admonition through the Muse to poets: "Look in thy heart and write!" And his dryly impassioned comment is, "There is no foul rag-and-bone shop in *that* heart."

Diderot's *Rameau's Nephew* provides Trilling with

the vehicle for demonstrating the breakdown in the eighteenth century of the social values of sincerity before the rising allure of authenticity's private and internal attractions. Diderot's novel articulated a strengthening sense that the "own self" to which one's being true permitted one to relate to others in socially approved ways was, at bottom, merely a role. Who and what one *really* is cannot be communicated through social forms. It becomes lost in the tissue of cultural expectancies, and it loses its validity when burdened by the normative requirements of one's neighborhood, class, or nation. Because society demands "impersonations," obedient role-playing, dancing in minutely choreographed patterns, it crushes personal integrity and deprives individuals of the dignity that resides in their selfhood. The moral judgment that the perceptive person must make of society, therefore, is one of condemnation—absolute, unremitting, and implacably hostile, even when the tactics of opposition entail a superficial and entirely cynical conformity.

But Trilling emphasizes a second element in *Rameau's Nephew*. Rather gaily, that element suggests that the moral categories of society are "not ultimate, that man's nature and destiny are not wholly comprehended within the narrow space between virtue and vice." Whatever must be said about the reprehensible character of culture, the Nephew transcends society's restrictions and the adverse judgments that they generate. Regarding himself "as an aspect of humanity . . . as the liberty that we wish to believe is inherent in the human spirit, in its energy of effort, expectation, and desire, in its consciousness of itself and its limitless contradictions," the Nephew invokes the moral categories at the same time that he violates and exposes them. This second component in Diderot's work gives it a lasting charm and worth. It stands as one of the great studies in the delicate balance between self and culture that is not only one of the dominant and persistent themes of literature but the condition of reasonable serenity and decent competence in life. But, through the history of ideas, this aspect of *Rameau's Nephew* has consistently lost ground to the first, the exhibition of socially expressed forms of selfhood as merely imposed social roles. Through Rousseau and others, this idea gave impetus to the exponents of authenticity who look upon "madness" as an appropriate and even commendable means of negating an unendurable culture.

In our own day, these exponents comprise a not inconsiderable group—Herbert Marcuse, Norman O. Brown, Michel Foucault, R. D. Laing, and David Cooper. Marcuse evokes from Trilling an assault tempered by a cordial and discriminating understanding. Although he casts himself as the prophet of "the virtual end of necessity," Marcuse "discovers in it a perverse beneficence—upon its harsh imperatives depends the authenticity of the individual and his experience." Besides, Trilling observes in a vein of sly geniality, Marcuse "*likes* people to have 'character,' cost what it may in frustration. He holds fast to the belief that the right quality of human life, its intensity, its creativity, its felt actuality, its weightiness, requires the stimulus of exigence." Because he acknowledges the intransigeance of much of our social experience, because he honors the concept of character as a component of selfhood that is derived from the culture, Marcuse enjoys a degree of gentle respect that is a bit surprising; his radical outlook embraces a number of features that Trilling strongly objected to.[17] With the others, however, Trilling permitted himself a measure of severity to which he rarely gave public voice.

In general, the position occupied by Brown and Foucault, Laing and Cooper, holds that "madness," insanity, is a state of human existence that commands esteem and admiration for two basic reasons. First, it is a "direct and appropriate response to the coercive inauthenticity of society." It is not only a condition en-

gendered by the culture, passively but somewhat heroi-
cally endured; it is also an effort to meet and to
overcome the immoral coercion that figures centrally in
the etiology of psychosis. Further, madness is a critical
act: It makes public the nature of society, exposing it
as the heartless and demeaning force that it is. Second,
madness denies the general limitations on human nature. It provides a form of existence in which "power is
assured by self-sufficiency," and it represents a distinctive and profound way of knowing, of penetrating in
perception to the outermost fringes of human capability
and potential.

Having accurately summarized in this fashion the
posture of his opponents, Trilling first restates the humane passion that energized his entire career:

Who that has had experience of our social reality will doubt
its alienated condition? And who that has thought of his
experience in the light of certain momentous speculations
made over the last two centuries . . . will not be disposed to
find some seed of cogency in a view that proposes an anti-
nomian reversal of all accepted values, of all received
realities?

But once he has established his comprehension of the
proponents of madness, and once he has reminded us of
his bases for responding to them sympathetically, he
has work to do.

To deal with these formulations by analytic argument, he says, would be "supererogatory":

This is the intellectual mode that once went under the
name of cant. The disappearance of the word from the modern vocabulary is worth remarking. In characterizing the
position as I do it is not my purpose to minimize its cultural
significance, which, in fact, I take to be momentous.

It was . . . not quite cant that Norman O. Brown ut-
tered when . . . he spoke of the "blessing" and the "super-
natural powers" which he desired to attain and which . . .
come only with madness . . . Fully achieved cant is to be

seen in David Cooper . . . "Madness," he says . . . "is a way of seizing *in extremis* the racinating groundwork of the truth that underlies our more specific realization of what we are about. . . . Madness is a form of vision that destroys itself by its own choice of oblivion in the face of existing forms of social tactics and strategy. . . . [It] is a matter of voicing the realization that I am (or you are) Christ." . . . Laing [contends that] "transcendental experiences . . . break through in psychosis [and that] true sanity entails in one way or another the dissolution of the normal ego, that false self completely adjusted to our alienated social reality."

Cant neither merits analysis nor can be refuted by it. Instead, Trilling resorts to two majestically phrased questions that he asks us to consider as intimately and as profoundly as we can. They are questions that invoke the terrors of loneliness and the degree to which the very humanity of each of us as persons depends on social connectedness—on love, on shared work, on the mutual stimulation of friendly discourse and communication about common concerns, and even on the experience of finding our will locked in conflict with the will of another. First, "Who that has spoken, or tried to speak, with a psychotic friend will consent to betray the masked pain of his bewilderment and solitude by making it the paradigm of liberation from the imprisoning falsehoods of an alienated social reality?" And then, "Who that finds intelligible the sentences that describe madness (to use the word that cant prefers) in terms of transcendence and charisma will fail to penetrate to the great refusal of human connection that they express, the appalling belief that human existence is made authentic by the possession of a power, or the persuasion of its possession, which is not to be qualified or restricted by the coordinate existence of any fellow man?"

Trilling's sharpest and most trenchant criticism of our contemporary cultural experience rests on his obviously implied answer to these poignant and fundamental questions. We are endangered, he says, by the extent to which "many among us find it gratifying . . . that alienation is to be overcome only by the completeness of alienation, and that alienation completed is not a deprivation . . . but a potency." After analytically summarizing the most important reflections over four centuries on the clash between the personal sentiment of being and the exigent demands of social organization, he concludes, "no expression of disaffection from the social existence was ever so desperate as this eagerness to say that authenticity of personal being is achieved through an ultimate isolateness and through the power that this is presumed to bring." Not in his most uninhibited imaginings did the Diderot of *Rameau's Nephew* anticipate so self-defeatingly nihilistic an outcome to his criticisms of culture or so self-destructive an extension of his meliorative intent.

Yet for all the fervor that he atypically allows himself here, and despite his leveling the charge of cant against the advocates of madness, Trilling does not build his case *ad hominem*. Marcuse and Brown, Foucault and Laing and Cooper occupy him only because they serve so well as the spokesmen of a trend all too similar to the trends represented by Gifford Maxim and by Nancy and Arthur Croom. Buffeted by their own perceptive awareness of the ancient enemies of selfhood —poverty and deprivation, alienation and exclusion, oppression and its internalized equivalent of repression —decent people are sorely tempted to overreact, to politicize their compassion, and to attempt to write their goodwilled impulses into prevailing social attitudes, into social policy, and into a mandated form of social reality. When a sense of urgency, no matter how humane its intentions may be, engenders that "impassioned longing to believe," our best impulses lose the modulation and the regulation by an informed perception of complexity that an acceptance of the conditioned nature of human existence confers. Under these circumstances, ends come to justify means, and decent people who have no doubts think destructive thoughts, exercise destructive influences, and commit destructive acts. For Trilling, the most pernicious threats to human serenity, harmony, and creativity operate under this dissembling mantle of good intentions. To expose the weapons concealed beneath this garment was the unifying purpose of his career.

5

∞∞∞

Imagination
and Reality

The Matthew Arnold who "engaged my first interest,"
Lionel Trilling writes, "was . . . the melancholy poet,
the passive sufferer from the stresses and tendencies of
his culture. When the book [*Matthew Arnold*] was finished my concern was with the man who had pitted
himself against the culture, who had tried to understand
the culture for the purpose of shaping it—with the
critic."[1] What Trilling brought to his encounter with
Arnold and what, as a result of it, established Arnold
as his lifelong mentor go far toward accounting for one
of the major themes in his work. If Arnold's conception
of criticism provided the bases for Trilling's own ideas
of the proper task of the critic, and if Arnold's frequent
preoccupation with extraliterary issues and problems
legitimized Trilling's primary focus on moral and cultural matters, Arnold's most crucial legacy to Trilling
was an approach to the question of how society changes
and of how it *ought* to change.

Trilling came to his study of Arnold under at least
four powerful influences. First, he was a sensitive, intellectually disposed, and reflective child of his time.
Caught up in the radical idealism that followed the
First World War and swept painfully over the thresh-
old of the Great Depression, he deeply shared the
impression, confirmed by his exposure to Yeats and
Eliot, Proust, Mann, and Kafka, "that the culture of
humanism was at a point of crisis . . . That the society

which had sustained this culture was in dire straits . . ."[2]
Second, he had responded in a distinctive fashion to the
ideas of Marx and Freud. To Freud, of course, he maintained an increasingly sophisticated commitment. To
Marx, although Trilling had a brief experience in 1932
and 1933 as a Communist fellow traveler, he never fully
gave his allegiance. But his admiration for both rested
less on the specifics of doctrine than on the sense that
they gave him of the intimacy and the actuality of society, of culture, and of history as forces impinging on
personalities and as social processes, massive in their
dynamics but yet subject to some measure of human
direction and control.

Third, Trilling's novelistic ambitions cannot be
overestimated. Profoundly responsive from boyhood to
the genre in which he wanted to establish his own career, he derived "primarily from novelists" his conceptions and his convictions of "what is interesting and
problematical in life, of what reality consists in and
what makes for illusion, of what must be held to and
what let go."[3] Finding a fertile soil in his creative
aspirations, fiction early and permanently embedded itself in his consciousness as the criticism of life that
Arnold said it is, and works of the imagination furnished him with both the touchstones by which he
judged reality and the visions of possibility on which he
based his values. And finally, Trilling's disposition
toward ambivalence, his taste for subtlety, and his willingness to wrestle with complexity found warm and
productive nurturance in Arnold's similar qualities—
his insistence on seeing the object as in itself it really is,
including its contradictions, his concern for the intertwined Hellenistic and Hebraic tendencies in the intellectual and the moral life, his concurrent emphases on
politics and the great current issues of society and on
personal inwardness and the cultivation of the individual spirit.

Equipped in this manner, Trilling found in Arnold

the articulate assumptions and the general directions
that, despite his resolution to avoid becoming "an Arnold man" among English professors, significantly
guided him for the rest of his days. To hold, for example, as Arnold did, that literature is a criticism of life
is to affirm the power of thought in the governing of
humanity. It leads directly to Arnold's contention, so
fundamentally congenial to Trilling, that democracy is
characterized by its response to ideas and that it can
advance only by the discovery and maintenance of the
best of them. In the light of this notion, criticism becomes the instrument for the discovery and the evaluation of those ideas that matter most to the polity and to
the quality of life experienced by the persons whom it
comprises.

From this formulation, it follows that the "literature" that is itself a criticism of life and that provides
the stuff on which the critic works is not exclusively
literary. Of Arnold's principal critical essays between
1863 and 1865, "only four deal primarily with the literary life," Trilling notes a little triumphantly. "But
six," he continues, "deal, directly or indirectly, with
religion . . . one of the discoveries of Arnold's criticism
was that intellect was not enough, that it could not be
the guide to a multitude of matters for the multitude of
mankind . . . his criticism is the reconciliation of the
two traditions whose warfare had so disturbed his
youth—rationalism and faith." Written in 1938, this
characterization of Arnold becomes, in hindsight, something of a prescient anticipation of Trilling's own efforts. Arnold's criticism, he says, "is an attempt to bring
this synthesis to bear on all the aspects of modern life.
He steers a course both by compass and by stars; reason, but not the cold and formal reason that makes the
mind a machine; faith, but not the escape from earth-
binding facts." And then the sentence from Arnold that
expresses the animating principle in nearly all of Trilling's work: "The main element of the modern spirit's

life is neither the senses and understanding, nor the heart and imagination; it is the imaginative reason."[4]

The exercise of the imaginative reason entails two major principles—*disinterestedness*, and what Arnold, always with an upper-case letter, somewhat ambiguously referred to as *Joy*. Trilling, laboring conscientiously to understand them in Arnold, incorporated both of these conceptions not only into his intellectual apparatus but into his style of perception and his processes of judgment.

Arnold develops his argument for disinterestedness in his great essay on "The Function of Criticism at the Present Time." Disinterestedness rests on curiosity. Curiosity "obeys an instinct prompting it to try to know the best that is known and thought in the world, irrespectively of practice, politics, and everything of the kind; and to value knowledge and thought as they approach this best, without the intrusion of any other considerations whatever." In order "to produce fruit for the future," criticism finds in "flutterings of curiosity" its fundamental rule. That rule

may be summed up in one word,—*disinterestedness*. And how is criticism to show disinterestedness? By keeping aloof from what is called "the practical view of things"; by resolutely following the law of its own nature, which is to be a free play of the mind on all subjects which it touches. By steadily refusing to lend itself to any of those ulterior, political, practical considerations about ideas, which plenty of people will be sure to attach to them, which perhaps ought to be attached to them, which in this country at any rate are certain to be attached to them quite sufficiently, but which criticism has really nothing to do with. The business is . . . simply to know the best that is known and thought in the world, and by in its turn making this known, to create a current of true and fresh ideas. Its business is to do this with inflexible honesty, with due ability; but its business is to do no more, and to leave alone all questions of practical consequences and applications, questions which will never fail to have due prominence given to them.

As Trilling observes, Arnold insists on this total independence of criticism from the practical spirit for a particular reason. For him, the French Revolution had proved far less the fulfillment of the ideas of the great eighteenth-century philosophers of France than their large-scale betrayal. That betrayal, evidenced by the Reign of Terror and by the events that quickly brought Napoleon into authoritarian power, was the direct result of the impatient (and uncritical) desire of human beings to give "an immediate and practical application to all these fine ideas of the reason." Trilling does not make the parallel explicit, but it is difficult to imagine him—hardly twenty years after the Russian Revolution, with the Soviet purges and Stalin's pact with Hitler fresh in his consciousness, and with the agonies of the Great Depression still dominant in his experience—not responding strongly to this warning about the gulf that yawns between ideas and their too-prompt translation into political policy and social reality. Conceivably, that gulf could be narrowed, and the narrowing could save a great deal of human wretchedness, if the consequences of ideas could first be more extensively explored. One route of exploration lies through those thoughtful dreams called fictions, of which only men and women are capable; another route lies through disinterested criticism, as Arnold defined it.

In this light, Trilling's gloss carries a special intensity. "The spirit of criticism," he says, ". . . measures the actual and the practical by the ideal. It never relinquishes its vision of what *might be*." But on the other hand, it "never says that what *can be* is perfect merely because it is better than what *is*."[5] Above all, it strives to maintain that difficult but crucial discrimination between what is reasonable and beneficent in imagination but disruptive or corrupt in realization, and what may, in some way, serve beneficent practical ends but entail spiritual shortcomings.

In Arnold's case, Trilling takes pains to point out that

He welcomed the new democracy but he suspected it. He welcomed rationalism but feared its effects. He was far from being at one with established religion yet he feared the void which its disappearance would leave. He saw old institutions crumbling and was glad, but he was uneasy lest their fall bring down more than themselves. He wanted progress but he feared the "acridity" which would characterize the forward movement. Consequently, he found it necessary to formulate a point of view which, while it affirmed the modern spirit . . . would still allow him to defend the passing order.[6]

For Arnold, the social and intellectual ideas of the French Revolution deserved full-scale support, but he could supply that support only if the moral tone of the Revolution were supplanted by something more humane. Intelligence and energy were in themselves insufficient; they required melding with "moral balance" and "nobleness of soul and character," with love.[7] Trilling, who could have been a Marxist were it not for its ready corruption into Stalinism, who had looked through Freud's lens at the ways in which human hostility self-deceptively finds justification in the ideologies of decency, and who knew both from his direct experience and from remarkably wide reading about the imperfections of the human animal and the anxieties to which it is subject, understood. As centrally important as the intellect is, it does not encompass human wholeness, and it cannot provide the motive for morality. He set himself to comprehend what Arnold meant by "Joy."

What he learned was that Joy begins in the misty but critical region of personhood, where sincerity is rooted—in not only *knowing* oneself but in *being* oneself. "Resolve to be thyself: and know, that he/Who finds himself, loses his misery." Not only relief from misery, however, depends on being oneself; creativity and a functional moral sense operate only from a base

in personal integration, personal wholeness. The chief
threat to wholeness comes from a rationalistic society
that blunts the power to feel, that reinforces an evasion
of the emotional side of one's nature, and that prizes
practical and logical thought above the affects and the
imagination. At the same time, it is obvious that Arnold
was far from anti-intellectual in either his outlook or
his practice. Neither, just as obviously, was Trilling.
Trilling carefully points out that, for Arnold, as for
himself, "the antithesis to the head is not the heart but
the *whole being*," and he underscores the point by quoting Coleridge's comment that creative powers remain
unknown to "the sensual and the proud."[8]

Creative expression, then, cannot issue from "a
restless effort of the will"; it reflects "a precipitation of
the whole personality . . . a distillation of the complete
being." It is *not* a matter of simply releasing the emotions or of giving free play to the impulses. If the imagination and the intellect often war with each other
within the person, a creatively productive settlement
does not consist in the establishment of one over the
other. In that direction lie only the alternatives of a
sentimentality that borders on the maudlin or a chilly
and sterile didacticism. Only when thought and feeling
fuse, when the integration of the personality reaches
wholeness, does art result. There is no exaltation of the
artist as the prototype of happiness entailed by this
conception of creativity as a function of Joy, of the
exercise of the imaginative reason. Trilling quotes Coleridge again: Creative potency derives from "not mirth
or high spirits, or even happiness, but a consciousness
of entire and therefore well being, when the emotional
and intellectual faculties are in equipoise."[9] Joy serves
as both a condition and a concomitant of the ripening
and disciplined expression of the creative impulse; it is
neither a safeguard against the pains of life nor a
panacea for the vulnerabilities and the cruelties to
which human beings are subject.

A similar notion obtains in the moral sphere. For Arnold, "the real problem of conduct was not to know the rules," Trilling says: "these are easy to know and everybody knows them: the real problem was to put the rules into practice, an enormously difficult task." Morality is not a matter of reason alone but of the emotions as well. Arnold solved the problem to his own satisfaction by a reinterpretation of Pauline Christianity, in which the concept of "righteousness" plays a central role. In order to give "a fuller idea of righteousness, to reapply emotion to it, and thus by reapplying emotion, to disperse the feeling of being amiss and helpless, to give the sense of being right and effective," he defined religion as "not simply *morality*, but *morality touched by emotion.*" Trilling points out that the solution is a psychological one. It is not inappropriate because "religion's basis and method are psychological." But he also notes that Arnold's psychological approach deliberately cut away from Protestant Christianity virtually all of its usually associated metaphysics, its theology, its structure of beliefs about the nature of God and the destiny of the human world.

What remained was the model of Paul's "passionate attachment to Jesus by which he received strength for righteousness." Arnold justified the model of the love of Jesus as the foundation of morality by arguing simply that "everyone knows how being in love changes for the time a man's spiritual atmosphere and makes animation and buoyancy where before there was flatness and dullness." The idea of faith sheds its usual implication of commitment to dogma and becomes entirely a matter of relationship, of fidelity, which Arnold defined as a "holding fast to an unseen power of goodness." Through fidelity in the love of Jesus, one comes into possession of the method and the "secret" of this reconceived form of Pauline religion. The method is repentance, "the setting up a great unceasing inward movement of attention and verification" in matters of

conduct; the secret is that repentance, cultivated in the
context of fidelity, yields "joy and peace, missed on
every other line . . . reached on this."[10]

Skeptical, Jewish, and heir of an unreligious age,
Trilling cannot follow where Arnold would lead him.
But he recognizes, honors, and builds into himself Arnold's *sense*, his human agenda, his perceptively formulated goals. The sincerity based on *knowing* oneself and
the authenticity grounded in *being* oneself are fundamental values of both personhood and the inescapable
social life to which human beings are bound. Their psychological and cultural importance cannot be over-
stated. Each, however, can generate destructive ex-
cesses. Sincerity may develop into sheer egocentricity,
ranging from preening self-display to wallowing disrup-
tively and unproductively in one's own misery. Authenticity may eventuate in anarchy, a wanton disregard of
the feelings, the welfare, and the legitimate objectives
of others. As a corrective, they require the simultaneous constraint and support of a sense of unity, a
validation of one's own being by its participation in a
palpitant world greater than itself. That greater world is
both generally cosmic—there seems to be no better
word—and explicitly political. Only when the discipline
and the sustaining quality of unity are actively *sought*
does Joy result. Joy comes only to the person who
maintains himself as at once apart and *engagé*. Dogma,
neither the dogma of religion nor the dogma of social
theory, never suffices. "Whatever of sense and reason
Benthamism and Communism might bring," Trilling
writes, "they [do] not . . . bring the sense of Joy, of
wonder, of pleasure at being alive, of a world illuminated and bursting to tell a secret."[11]

Politically, Trilling found in Arnold the foundation of the liberal imagination. His experience, his education, his omnivorous reading had certainly prepared
him for this discovery. But Arnold furnished the conception, and it was in the context of Arnold's reflec-

tions and style that he made it his own. Once he had done so, he wrote little that did not either press for a fuller understanding and a fuller realization of Arnold's vision, or that did not call attention to defections and departures from it. Arnold had, he said,

the democratic insight that a human value exists in the degree that it is shared, that a truth may exist but be un-alive until it receives assent, that a good may have meaning but no reality until it is participated in. The very rewards which society bestows for virtue have their full reality only when bestowed by equals, and only the ungenerous mind finds satisfaction in receiving honor from inferiors. The artist has in a certain sense, failed, though through no fault of his own, when his intention is not understood by reason of the inferior capabilities of his fellows and his very artistic existence depends on the nature of his society. The en-lightened man must require a general development of his fellow-men as an effort of self-salvation.[12]

It was on this basis that "Arnold had formed his entire religious theory to supply the lacks of the French Revolution and he had to continue his fight against the Revolution's moral and psychological assumptions even while he fought for its social principles." The idea of faith, meaning fidelity in the love of Jesus, as Arnold developed it, "does not apply only to the individual man's relations with Christ. It implies the ideal of the State, the cooperative ideal. . . . It is with this concep-tion of unity in Christ that Arnold finds his way to solve the dilemma of community and assent in politics. For each man may discover the Socrates in his own breast by the religious act of . . . dissolving his lower nature in . . . finding accord with his fellows in Christ."[13] If the genuinely liberal imagination discriminates between the things that are Caesar's and the things that are God's, it also descries and takes seriously the connectedness be-tween matters of state and matters of spirit.

But Arnold's attempt to revise and revitalize the teachings of St. Paul also drew Trilling into a closer

relationship to Wordsworth, whose conception of the
sentiment of being came unfettered by Anglican, Protestant, or even Christian theological entailments.
Wordsworth's Christianity was, of course, incontest-
able, but it was not a necessary condition of the experience that he describes in Book Two of *The Prelude*:

> Contented, when with bliss ineffable
> I felt the sentiment of Being spread
> O'er all that moves and all that seemeth still;
> O'er all that, lost beyond the reach of thought
> And human knowledge, to the human eye
> Invisible, yet liveth in the heart;
>   ... Wonder not
> If high the transport, great the joy I felt,
> Communing in this sort through earth and heaven ...
> One song they sang, and it was audible,
> Most audible, then, when the fleshly ear,
> O'ercome by humblest prelude of that strain,
> Forgot her functions, and slept undisturbed.
>   ... I am content
> With my own modest pleasures ...
>   ... in these times of fear,
> The melancholy waste of hopes o'erthrown,
> ... 'mid indifference and apathy,
> And wicked exultation when good men
> On every side fall off, we know not how,
> To selfishness, disguised in gentle names
> Of peace and quiet and domestic love,
> Yet mingled not unwillingly with sneers
> Of visionary minds; ... in this time
> Of dereliction and dismay, I yet
> Despair not of our nature, but retain
> A more than Roman confidence, a faith
> That fails not ...
>   ... I find
> A never-failing principle of joy
> And purest passion.

Wordsworth's sentiment of being may well comprise a mystical, pantheistic element. But Trilling is
undoubtedly correct when he identifies it as consisting

essentially and fundamentally of four components: (a) an intense pleasure (b) in the validation of his own identity (c) through a sense of unity with the world (d) without a need to exercise the will.[14] He likens the sentiment of being to Hegel's definition of *Gemüt*, a personal state which has "no particular aims, such as riches, honors, and the like; in fact, it does not concern itself with any w rldly condition of wealth, prestige, etc., but with the entire condition of the soul—a general sense of enjoyment." Without the imposition of one's will on an object, a task, or another person, the sentiment of being evokes Joy simply through the intimate experience of existing selfhood confirmed by the perception of its unity with something larger than itself. Unique and actual, one's individual being presents itself as an integral part of the world, and that ontological fact gives rise to both delight and significance.

Understood in this fashion, the sentiment of being as the basis for Joy returns us, by two avenues, to that other component of the imaginative reason, disinterestedness. For Arnold, Trilling observes, himself sharing the principle involved, "the first premise of democracy . . . is that each individual has the capability—actual or potential—of interpreting the world for himself and of choosing his own course. Democracy is based on the intellect; it can progress only by the intellect, by the circulation of sound ideas so clear and distinct as to win general agreement."[15] If such is the case, then the ideas relevant to a democratic polity must take account of its members as persons with distinctive identities and with the potential for "expanding" their selfhood in rewarding ways.[16] Wordsworth's preoccupation with being carries, in other words, political implications.

Commenting on "The Old Cumberland Beggar," Trilling points out two of them. One Wordsworth makes explicitly: The old beggar cannot in good conscience be condemned to a workhouse because he serves a useful social function; his presence evokes an "habitual charity" and thus creates "a kind of communal institution, a communal bond."

> Where'er the aged Beggar takes his rounds,
> The mild necessity of use compels
> To acts of love . . .

But the implicit political proposition is still more important. The old beggar simply *is*; as a person who still finds pleasure in his own identity, he cannot justly be considered "a mere social unit." A good society, stimulating what Arnold called "the best selves" of its members, will include him willingly and gladly within the political unity.

> . . . man is dear to man; the poorest poor
> Long for some moments in a weary life
> When they can know and feel that they have been,
> Themselves, the fathers and the dealers-out
> Of some small blessings, have been kind to such
> As needed kindness, for this single cause,
> That we have all of us one human heart.

The liberal imagination, accepting the obligation of evaluating the real against the ideal, undertakes to explore the circumstances—personal, institutional, societal, and cultural—that may indeed make man dear to man and that will bring closer to realization the sense that we have all of us one human heart.

The other link between Joy and disinterestedness affects the critic himself, the practitioner of the imaginative reason. In order to learn "the best that is known and thought in the world, and by . . . making this known, to create a current of true and fresh ideas," the critic suspends in a significant degree and manner his own will. At the very least, it is incumbent on him to examine seriously and to curb his most basic and cherished preconceptions and prejudices and to make explicit any role that they may play in his critical effort. His obligation is not to take a firm position with respect to any particular issue until he has responsibly explored the implications and possibilities of alternative posi-

tions and the complex contexts in which important issues always are embedded. Most of all, he refuses to
align himself with contending forces in the arenas of
power. The critic's task is not to make his will prevail,
either alone or in concert with some party; it is to
"create a current of true and fresh ideas."

At the same time, the imaginative reason certainly
does not imply indifference. Its exercise leads typically
to passionate convictions and to the wish that the convictions should prevail. The fundamental distinction,
however, must be maintained: Although the realm of
ideas and the realm of politics and practice are intimately related, their confusion imperils both the soul
and the society. The realm of ideas encompasses
thoughts, ideals, sentiments, and feelings; the realm of
politics and practice operates under the mandate of will
and the might that will can summon. When a bill is to
be passed or defeated, a legislated act to be adminis-
tered in this way or that, a suit to be settled through the
adversarial processes of the courts, then ideas, principles, fundamental values, and sensibilities occupy
only a peripheral place and command little attention.
Mobilized force, focused on the immediacies of winning
or losing, does not define the atmosphere in which the
intellect most brilliantly blooms or in which the ideals
that the imagination can conceive most usefully acquire
form and articulateness.

Trilling learned from Arnold that "the grand error
of the French Revolution" was its "quitting of the intellectual sphere and rushing furiously into the political
sphere," with the result that it evoked "no such intellectual fruit as the movement of ideas in the Renas-
cence" and created a disfiguring and reactionary
"opposition to itself."[17] The effective "criticism of
life" that is the function of literature, and the "current
of true and fresh ideas" that it is the critic's job to
circulate, aim at creating a climate of "sweetness and
light" in public opinion; as that more enlightened

"movement of ideas" expands and takes hold, then, without "acridity," outmoded and inhumane institutions are dissolved and new social forms and political processes emerge to advance the humanization of man in society, which is the meaning of civilization.

Trilling's conception of the imagination and its proper uses derives directly from this Arnoldian base. Two observations seem especially important. The first and more obvious bears on his carefully maintained distinction between liberalism as "a large tendency" and liberalism as an effort to organize "the elements of life in a rational way." The other deals with that less explicit but pervasive and perhaps more fundamental component of his work, his concern for "character" as an aspect of selfhood, for a large-scaled but unsentimental sympathy in estimating the quality of life made possible by particular social and cultural circumstances, and for the nature of the individual's emotional experience—his access to Joy.

The first can be quickly disposed of. It is Arnold, fully integrated into Trilling as a man and a mind of the twentieth century, who stands firmly behind the statement,

when we approach liberalism in a critical spirit, we shall fail in critical completeness if we do not take into account the value and necessity of its organizational impulse. But at the same time we must understand that organization means delegation, and agencies, and bureaus, and technicians, and that the ideas that can survive delegation, that can be passed on to agencies and bureaus and technicians, incline to be ideas of a certain kind and of a certain simplicity: they give up something of their largeness and modulation and complexity in order to survive. The lively sense of contingency and possibility, and of those exceptions to the rule which may be the beginning of the end of the rule— this sense does not suit well with the impulse to organization . . . we have to expect that there will be a discrepancy between what I have called the primal imagination of liberalism and its present particular manifestations.[18]

Trilling could just as well have mentioned legislatures and adminstrative officers. He is discussing the fate of the liberal tendency when it quits the sphere of intellect and art and rushes into the arenas of political struggle. What transforms Arnold's insights and makes them contemporary is Trilling's sense of necessity and his perception of the conditioned nature of human effort. The politicizing of the liberal spirit is necessary for its actualization, but the entry of the liberal imagination into the realm of politics and practice lies under the law of costingness; liberal ideas and liberal values become conditioned by the reality of controversy and antagonism, compromise and contending forces. As in the inevitable warfare between self and culture, a tension that is at once delicate and grim must be maintained to elude disaster and to produce results that enlarge, in some measure and in some humane fashion, the zestful experience of human "variousness and possibility." The task of the artist and the task of the critic are to make that tension articulate and publicly available, to keep fresh the imagined outcomes of the liberal spirit at work in the world, and to make explicit the price that must be paid for its translation at any given moment into reality.

The second issue is more subtle, less immediately connected with Arnold, and complicated by the almost embarrassingly old-fashioned connotations of Joy. Yet Joy provides both the fortitude and the enthusiastic commitment necessary for the critical enterprise, the practice of the imaginative reason, if one engages in it responsibly, fully, and faithfully. What Trilling says of Arnold can be readily generalized: "Perhaps no man has ever formulated—though some have practised—so difficult an intellectual course . . . only the man of perfect equipoise and great spiritual strength may undertake it, the man utterly sure of the beneficent goal toward which he is striving."[19] And Trilling's comment is deeply informed by an awareness, acquired from

Freud, of the readiness by which surety about beneficent goals can serve self-deceptively as a mask for the
personal will. The critic of our time not only runs a
difficult intellectual course; he does so guarding himself
against the intrusions of self-deception to which he has
learned that he is susceptible. With reduced access to
"A presence that disturbs me with the joy / Of elevated
thoughts; a sense sublime / Of something far more
deeply interfused," and largely incapable of fidelity in
the love of Jesus, how does the critic of our troubled
and secular age find the sustaining and animating motive appropriate to the pursuit of the imaginative reason? What now are the grounds for discovering an intense pleasure in the affirmation of self through the
sense of something larger than oneself when the personal will is in suspension?

Although he never dealt with them in a head-on
fashion, Trilling obviously took such questions seriously. His concern for the self, which he gave a central
place by calling it the subject matter of literature, his
attentiveness to Wordsworth's sentiment of being,
which amounted to a lasting preoccupation, and his
unremitting focus on the embattled relationship between self and culture, which made psychoanalysis so
important to him, all testify significantly, if a bit indirectly, to the persistence of this theme. He appears to
have searched productively for his answers along two
routes.

First, Trilling was sharply aware of the intimate
interplay between ideas and emotions, especially in the
formation of those convictions that influence one's personal life and that enter into politics and public policy.
"Goethe says somewhere," Trilling writes, "that there
is no such thing as a liberal idea, that there are only
liberal sentiments." He continues,

This is true. Yet it is also true that certain sentiments con-
sort only with certain ideas and not with others. What is
more, sentiments become ideas by a natural and impercepti-

ble process. "Our continued influxes of feeling" said Wordsworth, "are modified and directed by our thoughts, which
are indeed the representatives of all our past feelings." The
converse is also true: just as sentiments become ideas, ideas
eventually establish themselves as sentiments.[20]

This insistent recognition that thought and sentiment interact continuously in vigorous and complex
ways carries at least three vital implications. First, the
imagination is "properly the joint possession of the
emotions and the intellect." Without the spur and nourishment of the emotions, the imagination grows torpid
and inactive; and without the imagination, the intellect
itself "withers and dies . . . the mind cannot work and
cannot properly conceive itself." Second, among the
affects that influence ideas, those that are unconscious
play determinative roles. The roles may be constructive
or ominous, insightful or self-deceiving, but they are
deeply at work. For this reason, Freud rather more
fully than most creators of literature provides us with
"the sense of the human mystery, of tragedy truly conceived in the great terms of free will, necessity, and
hope." And finally, what is "properly called an idea"
emerges when "two contradictory emotions are made to
confront each other and are required to have a relationship with each other." Ideas also spring from "the opposition of ideals and in the felt awareness of the impact of new circumstances upon old forms of feeling
and estimation, in the response to the conflict between
new exigencies and old pieties." The cogency of such
ideas depends on the "degree that the confronting emotions go deep, or in the degree that the old pieties are
firmly held and the new exigencies strongly apprehended."

Here is Arnold again, actively promoting the ideas
of the French Revolution but carefully defending the
passing order, finding in that deliberately sustained conflict a morally poised and zestful sense of self. In literary terms, the cogent imagination—in the best of

Hemingway and Faulkner, for example, among Americans—conveys "a sense that the amount and intensity of [its] activity are in a satisfying proportion to the recalcitrance of the material," which is precisely the fully apprehended conflicts that arise from the complex interlacing of sentiments and concepts, the clash between old pieties and new exigencies. Neither great works of literature nor great works of criticism pretend to say the last word about matters of such human depth and difficulty, but they are relentlessly active in their efforts to comprehend them. Comprehension, however, does not rest on the notion of ideas as "pellets of intellection . . . precise and completed, and defined by their coherence and their procedural recommendations." Rather, it bases itself in an awareness of "ideas as living things, inescapably connected with our wills and desires, as susceptible of growth and development by their very nature, as showing their life by their tendency to change, as being liable, by this very tendency, to deteriorate and become corrupt and to work harm."[21] In personal terms, this not entirely comfortable realization and a welcoming response to it, an eager willingness to cope with the oppositions and contradictions within one's deepest perceptions, and the use of the imagination in the unremitting but endless search for effective resolutions furnish the foundations for the sentiment of being, for the Joy that a sense of firm and active selfhood brings.

The other avenue of Trilling's effort here is suggested by a curious and characteristic meditation of his on Freud's notions of the relationship between the individual and his culture. A bit abruptly, he introduces the findings in 1954 of the Committee on Social Issues of the Group for the Advancement of Psychiatry. This body had considered the developmental effects of loyalty oaths, the requirement that people in positions of public importance swear a special allegiance to the United States and submit to governmental investigations of their ideas, their attitudes, and their previous personal associations.[22] In addition to reporting that a climate of surveillance and repression has a generally negative influence on public mental health, the psychiatrists found that if powerful interdicts by society interfere with the exploration of the world of objects (which includes persons and ideas), and if restrictions are placed on the impulse to adventure, then the growth of the ego is impaired. Similarly, the development of the superego suffers damage because "a mature superego can optimally develop only in a free and democratic society." Trilling fully assents: "If you enslave a man, he will develop the psychology of a slave. If you exclude a man from free access to the benefits of society, his human quality will be diminished." But he then asks, "What, to take a relevant example, was the cultural and political situation in which Freud's thought developed, and his ego and his superego too?" While Freud did not live under conditions of direct and actual oppression, the Vienna of his time was "anything but a free and democratic society . . . and Freud was not an enfranchised citizen of it until his middle years." His experience of Viennese society and politics may go far "to explain why some of his views are tragic or skeptical, and very far toward explaining why he conceived of the self as standing in opposition to the general culture. But the cultural circumstance in which he was reared did not, so far as I can make out, impair the functioning of his ego or superego."

The catalogue that Trilling enumerates in answer to the question of why it did not merits reproducing. There was, for instance, his family. If the family certainly serves as a conduit for the transmission of cultural values, it also provides a bulwark against cultural impingements; like individuals, families are distinctive, and one of their realms of distinctiveness has to do with the manner in which they modulate, screen, and soften particular cultural influences while enthusiastically en-

hancing and enforcing others. There was also Freud's
ethnic situation. "He was a Jew; and enough of the
Jewish sub-culture reached him to make a countervail-
ing force against the general culture." Nor can the
worth here of Freud's education be minimized. Who
can say "what part in his self-respect, in his ability to
move to a point beyond the reach of the surrounding
dominant culture, was played by the old classical education, with its image of *the other culture,* the ideal
culture, that wonderful imagined culture of the ancient
world . . . ? The schoolboy who kept his diary in Greek,
as Freud did, was not submitting his ego or his superego to the debilitating influences of a restrictive society." In addition, Freud's love of England, generated
early, furnished still another defense in the form of a
contrasting model of social organization and individual
expression. He became deeply involved with science
and with the requirement of intellectual freedom that
science levies, and, in his imagination, Freud reflected
on what his own culture, given its very real strengths,
could have been and could be. And then there was his
sense of himself as a biological fact, unduplicated and
unduplicable, his "naive belief that there is a human
given in all persons."

What Trilling is saying is straightforward and important. The validation of selfhood through a sense of
unity with something larger than itself, which brings
such intense pleasure that it qualifies as Joy, can derive
from many sources. Wordsworth's extolling of an upper-
case Nature is entirely appropriate but not at all restrictive. The sentiment of being emerges from the supports
of the family and of enduring and reciprocated love
generally. It is facilitated by commitments to large-
scale enterprises like science. Most of all, it gains
strength from identifications, which are partially acts of
the imagination—identification with an ethnic tradition, identification with an idealized culture of antiquity,
identification with an adopted culture like Freud's Eng-

land, and, although Trilling does not mention it explicitly in this context, identification with the worlds revealed in great fiction. Running through all these processes is the power of the imagination to create ideals out of conflicting emotions, out of oppositions between received pieties and new exigencies. Those ideals, those visions of possibility, approximate what Arnold called "a power not ourselves" which, when suitably wedded to disinterestedness, makes if not for "righteousness," then for the quest for righteousness, meaning a full engagement with the complexities and difficulties in clarifying cogent ideas and in exploring the potentials and the perils of translating them into dynamisms of social and cultural change. This quest is the quest of criticism, the quest of the imaginative reason in the twentieth century.

Out of this quest comes Trilling's conception of politics and of the relation of imaginative literature to politics:

. . . our fate, for better or worse, is political. It is therefore not a happy fate, even if it has an heroic sound, but there is no escape from it, and the only possibility of enduring it is to force into our definition of politics every human activity and every subtlety of every human activity. There are manifest dangers in doing this, but greater dangers in not doing it. Unless we insist that politics is imagination and mind, we will learn that imagination and mind are politics, and of a kind that we will not like.[23]

Within this political context, the question of power inevitably arises, and one aspect of this question bears on the power of writers and of the literature that they create. For Trilling, the appropriate power of the imagination takes its form and energy from the conditions of a democratic culture.

From the democratic point of view, we must say that . . . nothing should be done *for* the people. The writer who defines his audience by its limitations is indulging in the unforgivable arrogance. The writer must define his audience by its abilities, by its perfections, so far as he is gifted to conceive them. . . . The writer serves his daemon and his subject. And the democracy that does not know that the daemon and the subject must be served is not, in any ideal sense of the word, a democracy at all.[24]

In other words, the power of ideas and ideals, the rightful realm of literature as a criticism of life, must be protected first from underestimation and then from "the temptations of grossness and crudeness" which appear whenever the question of power is raised. If, as Trilling insists, the activity of politics is to be "united with the imagination under the aspect of mind," then poets, novelists, and critics fall under the obligation of maintaining their focus on the judgment of social reality by a vision of the humane ideal that can be generated through the mating of reason and the sentiment of being, of thought and a full awareness of the demanding, self-related, extrarational elements that are integral to human experience.

Pervading this notion of politics is a disciplined faith to which Trilling remained steadfast, although the momentous events of his lifetime often severely shook him in it. That faith holds that the success of liberal democracy, if its success is attainable at all, depends on three vital processes. Each is closely intertwined with the others.

The first of these processes entails an ever sharper discrimination by increasingly large numbers of people between the realm of ideas and ideals and the realm of practical politics. Obviously, this discrimination includes greater and greater clarity in the perception of the interplay between the two domains. If the world of ideas and ideals furnishes the function of evaluation and critical judgment essential to a democratic polity, then the world of practical politics supplies the approximations in actual society to those human goals and aspirations that begin in dreams—or, if not in dreams, in exigent experience that has been deeply reflected upon. Such a relationship has no end; it simply identifies the ongoing interaction between imagination and reality that makes viable the "large tendency" that is liberalism. In the light of this state of affairs, citizenship imposes the requirement of a respectful comprehension of these two quite different but actively interrelated elements in political life. One is the role of art and criticism, keeping themselves free from the immediate demands and the hurly-burly of practical politics. The other is the inevitably approximate nature of achievements in legislation and public policy, won through the inescapable climate of conflict and compromise that permeates institutional deliberative bodies and bureaucratic agencies.

Fastening on this basic discrimination and the respectful understanding bound up with it, Trilling judged such overly engaged works as the proletarian novels of the 1930s—the writing of, for example, Upton Sinclair and Albert Maltz—as a form of what Arnold had called philistinism. They were essentially propagandistic efforts that inappropriately and self-defeatingly subordinated the realm of ideas and ideals to the realm of practical politics. Consequently, while they articulated a "code of excited humanitarianism," they did little to facilitate the movement of imaginative reason that enriches the culture and that brings a somewhat greater degree of wisdom to political decisions. Such a literature finally amounts to little more than a kind of "flattery by which the progressive middle-class reader is cockered up with a sense of his own virtue and made to feel that he lives in a world of perfect certainties in which critical thought or self-critical feeling are the only dangers."[25] If we come close once more to the notion of rendering unto Caesar the things that are Caesar's, so that we can render unto God the things that are God's, we also hear echoes of the Socratic observation that the unexamined life is not worth living. Trilling remains entirely consistent in his stress on crucial distinctions and in his insistence on grappling with modern life's complexities.

Second, this insightful appreciation of art and criticism in our overarching political fate implies a slowing down in the implementation through legislation and executive action of those programmatic concepts that reason, *without* its imaginative component, tends to produce in the realm of practical politics as responses to the press and urgency of societal realities. Two considerations operate to lend centrality to this plank in Trilling's platform of faith. One grows obviously and directly from Arnold's conviction, hardly subject to serious challenge, that the French Revolution destroyed —by its violence, by its rapid deterioration into authoritarianism, and by its arousal of implacable resistances against itself—the creative ideas and ideals of a more generously distributed decency that originally gave it its impetus. That destruction of the humane spirit of the revolution occurred because of a premature rush from the domain of ideas into the domain of practical politics. The result was not the approximations, those acceptable if imperfect translations into reality of the visions shaped by the imaginative reason, that citizens may properly expect; it was cruelty, corruption, and the frustration of hopes. As it was with the French Revolution, so it is typically when thoughts and principles are too hurriedly transformed into law and social programs and into self-interested agencies of implementation. For a polity to realize democratic purposes, the pace of implementation must be reduced and the tests of disinterestedness applied more fully to explore possibilities and implications.

The other consideration here stems from an observation of Freud's to which Trilling repeatedly gave his attention. Genuinely concerned with social reform, Freud saw political relief as limited not by defects in governmental systems or political procedures, but by inherent factors. As he put it in *Civilization and Its Discontents,*

In rightly finding fault . . . with our present state of civilization for so inadequately providing us with what we require to make us happy in life, and for the amount of suffering of a probably avoidable nature it lays us open to—in doing our utmost to lay bare the roots of its deficiencies by our unsparing criticisms, we are undoubtedly exercising our just rights and not showing ourselves enemies of culture. We may expect that in the course of time changes will be carried out in our civilization so that it becomes more satisfying to our needs and no longer open to the reproaches we have made against it. But perhaps we shall also accustom ourselves to the idea that there are certain difficulties inherent in the very nature of culture which will not yield to any efforts at reform. Over and above the obligations of putting restrictions upon our instincts, which we see to be inevitable, we are imminently threatened with the dangers of a state one may call *"la misère psychologique"* of groups. This danger is most menacing where the social forces of cohesion consist predominantly of identifications of the individuals in the group with one another, whilst leading personalities fail to acquire the significance that should fall to them in the process of group-formation.[26]

Two themes, both of great significance for Trilling, are stated here. Both comment trenchantly on the tragic quality in the human condition. The first focuses on the civil war within the personality of the socialized individual, the eternal conflict, sometimes violently and agonizingly disruptive, between what Trilling calls "the hidden and the visible" elements in human nature.[27] The parties to that civil war are our innate motivational and emotional equipment on the one side, and on the other, the executive and self-regulatory capabilities and habits, themselves not always in a comfortable alliance, that we acquire from our experience as members of a culture. And yet, because none of us can realize in any sense or in any degree our potentials as human beings without that socializing discipline, without the nay-say-

ing that the culture—that all cultures—subject us to,
we have no alternative to the internal battles that incorporate into our individual identities the opposition
between self and society that Trilling, a committed student of Freud, so fully and poignantly documents.[28]
This struggle with the inevitable "restrictions upon our
instincts" limits reform through political processes and
must condition our expectancies. Such contentment as
we may achieve rests on our learning to enjoy approximations to our dreams and our ideals, on our neither
asking too much of politics nor permitting politics to
override the satisfactions afforded by mind and imagination.

The second theme in Freud's statement has to do
with the problem of democracy and leadership. The
issue is an old one. Arnold did not solve it; neither have
political scientists before or since *Culture and Anarchy*
was published. Not surprisingly, Trilling did no better.
Recalling in 1971 his concerns in the 1930s, he reports
his perception of a "kind of self-deception" in the
prevailing intellectual-political climate—"an impulse
toward moral aggrandizement through the taking of extreme and apocalyptic positions which, while they
seemed political, actually expressed a desire to transcend the political condition—which, as I saw things,
and still do, meant an eventual acquiescence in
tyranny." We have previously noted[29] this side of Trilling's meditations on politics, his well-grounded fear of
substituting a kind of "final solution" for the endless
clash of individual wills in the open political marketplace. But, he continues, this "impulse toward moral
aggrandizement" could mean the covert but imperious
desire to exercise raw power:

I account as one of the most significant moments of my
intellectual life an encounter that I had in my late twenties
with a Russian emigre, an aging man of impressive mien,
a Menshevik who had spent years in the Czar's prisons and
in Siberia, who had fled his native land after the defeat of

the revolutionary programs of his party by the Bolsheviks. In the course of conversation he said that what motivated intellectuals was the desire for *power*. He did not mean merely that they wished to make their ideas prevail, believing them to be good for mankind—he meant that behind the ideals there lay the desire for power in itself. He meant that the intellectual, however disinterested he claimed to be, was not *innocent* . . . Power blinds us to the object; to the work of art, to the complexity.[30]

When Freud speaks of *la misère psychologique* of groups, including states and societies, he refers to the condition under which individuals, identifying with each other rather than with a unifying leader, grow hungry for power. Their tendency is to extend an appropriate effort to prevent, to escape, or to overthrow *authoritarian* controls to an inappropriate refusal to acknowledge *authority*. Anarchy then threatens through the rise of a revolutionary spirit that acquires potency but that embodies a dangerous self-deception. Characteristically, rebellion against authority (*not* a totalitarian regime or authoritarian rule, but authority) claims its legitimacy and license from some ideology of decency. Marxism is a clear modern example. That ideological justification is the "visible" element. The dominant dynamics of rebellion, however, lie in the "hidden" components of human motivation. They consist in precisely that imperious yearning to impose one's will on others that Trilling's Menshevik mentioned. They include the energies of frustration undirected by the humane imagination, accumulated resentments unmodulated by rational considerations, the aggressions that are inherent in human nature, and raw wishes for immediate self-gratification. Because they are so seldom under the direction of conditioned and ripened ideas and so frequently motored by these hidden components of our humanity, revolutions typically leave histories of either brutal and bloody failure or, as in the case of the French and Russian revolutions, a quick corruption and destructive betrayal of their presumably animating ideals. The first of these themes, the limited nature of politics and the appropriate relationship between politics and the life of the mind and the imagination, commanded a central place in Trilling's thought when he published *The Liberal Imagination* in 1950. The second theme, the tendency, by virtue of *la misère psychologique*, of the revolutionary impulse to betray and pervert itself, proved paramount when he wrote *Sincerity and Authenticity* in 1972. The continuity and integrity of his outlook remained quite of a piece; his emphases differed because of the different conditions of American life and American culture.

Finally, the third article of Trilling's faith turned on the cultivation of the sentiment of being. For him, self-knowledge is fundamental, and self-knowledge implies a sense of the self as distinctive, existent, *real*. Alienation and opposition define that sense of self. The groundwork of our recognizable and recognized identity takes form from our realization of our separateness from others and from society and from our perduring conflict with the demands of our culture. The "very principle of society," Trilling writes, "is the individual's abnegation of personal autonomy in order to win the forebearance and esteem of others." Consequently, "society, though necessary for survival, corrupts the life it fosters."[31] Imperfectly and with difficulty, personhood emerges from the endless struggle by the individual to conduct simultaneously two contradictory ventures. One entails maintaining a relationship with society that maximizes survival; the other involves the virtually deliberate development of anomie, an active and often hostile divorcing of the self from culture. Once again we confront the issue with which Trilling was unremittingly preoccupied. As human beings, we are social animals who need the love, the approval, and the support of our kind, but as human beings, we are also individuals who need to feel ourselves in some measure autonomous, unique, and self-contained—whole in ourselves.

In his conception of the sentiment of being, Trilling reminds us that it is a synonym for "that 'strength' which, Schiller tells us, 'man brought with him from the state of savagery' and which he finds it so difficult to preserve in a highly developed culture. The sentiment of being is the sentiment of being strong." But being strong is *not* synonymous with being powerful. It is not concerned "with energy directed outward upon the world in aggression and dominance, but, rather, with such energy as contrives that the centre shall hold, that the circumference of the self keep unbroken, that the person be an integer, impenetrable, perdurable, and autonomous in being if not in action."[32] To avoid the confusion of strength with power—the power that "blinds us to the object," that prevents our seeing the object as in itself it really is—two conditions, as we have seen, are necessary. One is the person's identification with something larger than himself; the other is the capacity on crucial occasions to suspend the individual will.

Trilling insists on the importance of these requirements in the cultivation of the sentiment of being, even when he sympathetically acknowledges the "violence" that may be demanded in the face of particular cultural circumstances to make possible the cultivation of selfhood. In speaking of the position taken in the nineteenth century by writers like Schiller, Wilde, and Nietzsche, and of the later works of Gide, Mann, and Kafka, he observes,

Sometimes we are a little puzzled to understand why this art was greeted upon its first appearance with so violent a resistance, forgetting how much violence there was in its creative will, how ruthless an act was required to assert autonomy in a culture schooled in duty and in obedience to peremptory and absolute law, and how extreme an exercise of personal will was needed to overcome the sentiment of non-being.[33]

Among his illustrations of non-being are Melville's Bartleby and Flaubert's Frederic Moreau. In *Bartleby the Scrivener*, the protagonist finds the social world so deficient in authenticity that he "prefers not to" exert any effort at survival but literally to die in his preferred isolation. In *The Sentimental Education*, Moreau experiences only duplicity and hollowness in every human venture—love, friendship, art, politics. The world is perceived as providing only preconceived roles to play; there is no room for an authentic self, for the delight and strength that the sentiment of being furnishes. To overcome such cultural impingements and limitations on personhood, a degree of violence is justified, but Trilling conceives of that justified violence as occurring primarily in the imagination, in the envisioning of possibilities and the routes by which they may be attained, by "dealing with the universe in the peculiarly human spirit of play. In that spirit the universe might be taken apart and put together in a new way."[34]

This tripartite faith—in firmly maintaining the distinction between the realm of ideas and ideals and the realm of practical politics, in the slowing down of the processes of implementing political concepts, and in the cultivation of the sentiment of being—specifies the implicit undergirding of almost all of Trilling's work. Because Trilling, like Arnold, held systems in a kind of hostile mistrust, he never systematically articulated these principles. Strategically, his permitting them to operate without explicit statement gave him his flexibility, his ability to deal with the always shifting character of social and aesthetic circumstance and with the always changing configurations of the culture. Twice, however, in his treatments of Keats and of Joyce, and both treatments, interestingly, dealt with those authors' presentations of themselves through their letters—he came close to making manifest this loosely held but functional credo of how the imagination is best related to reality.

Keats's primary (although far from his sole) appeal for Trilling resides in his gracefully embodying an ideal of character. That ideal "implies a direct relationship to the world of external reality, which by activity, it seeks to understand, or to master, or to come to honorable terms with; and it implies fortitude, and responsibility for both one's duties and one's fate, and intention, and an insistence upon one's personal value and honor." Consistent with that characterological ideal, Keats was acutely attuned to what Freud called the reality principle. "Was it ever by anyone more starkly asserted," Trilling asks, "than in the phrase he used to Fanny Brawne: 'I would mention that there are impossibilities in this world' "? And yet Keats's capacity for uninhibited pleasure—in his fundamental appetites, in his creative processes, in what he called "the continual drinking of Knowledge"—richly balanced his intimate familiarity with despair, with conflict, and with the world's intractability. The balance that he achieved reflects what Trilling calls his "dialectical view of any large question,"[35] a disposition to respond fearlessly and unhurriedly when confronted by contradictions and oppositions, either within himself, in his environment, or in his relationship to society and the universe.

Out of this dialectical view, Keats formulated his notion of Negative Capability, which he described as "when a man is capable of being in uncertainties, mysteries, doubts, without any irritable reaching after fact and reason." In clarification of the famous conception, Trilling carefully points out that Negative Capability is not appropriate to problems like those of science. But it *is* appropriate to large and significant human problems, including "nothing less than the problem of evil." Developing his argument, he quotes Keats

further: "The excellence of every art is its *intensity*
(italics added), capable of making all disagreeables
evaporate, from their being in close relation with
Beauty and Truth . . . with a great poet the sense of
Beauty overcomes every other consideration, or rather
obliterates all consideration."[36] Understanding the objections and misunderstandings to which this formulation is subject, Trilling explains that Beauty was neither
a term of aesthetic judgment for Keats nor a concept
through which he could evade issues. Keats knew full
well the extent to which human experience includes ugliness, heartache, and pain; he comprehended evil as
integral to reality. For this reason, as Trilling points
out, he believed that "to see life truly; that is, as it must
be seen if we are to endure to live it," one must see it
tragically. The "matter of tragedy is ugly or painful
truth seen as beauty," and the tragic poet, confronting
"the terrible truth of . . . evil . . . sees it so intensely
that it becomes an element of the beauty which is created by his act of perception." The beauty achieved
through intensity (and the courage that this kind of
perceptual intensity requires) links, Trilling says, two
kinds of truth: "through the mediation of beauty, truth
of fact becomes truth of affirmation, truth of life." Although his reading of Keats describes the response to
evil that tragedy, in the literary sense, both reflects and
encourages, Trilling's focus characteristically centers on
more than literary concerns. What we must understand
about Keats, he insists, is "that he sought strenuously
to discover the reason why we should live, and that he
called those things good, or beautiful, or true, which
induced us to live or which conduced to our health."[37]
Keats's mode of perceiving life is certainly that of the
great poet, the poet of Shakespeare's caliber, but what
gives it force and high importance is that it is profoundly moral.

That moral vision, characterized by the intensity
that engenders beauty, depends on at least two factors.

First, "doctrinal utterances about the nature of life, about life's goodness or badness or perfectibility" must be avoided. Resting in available ideologies blocks the intensity that full moral perception requires. Protection against this temptation derives from Negative Capability, the ability to remain in uncertainty and doubt without grasping at the straws of conventional wisdom or of ready-to-hand systems. What psychologists call "tolerance of ambiguity" is a condition and facilitator of those moral insights that conduce to our health. But the second factor is even more significant. "Negative Capability, the faculty of not having to make up one's mind about everything, depends upon the sense of one's personal identity and is the sign of personal identity. Only the self that is certain of its existence, of its identity, can do without the armor of systematic certainties." The essential truth with which Keats is concerned, Trilling says, speaking as much for himself as for the poet, is "that truth which is to be discovered between love and death, between the sense of personal identity and the certainty of pain and extinction."[38] That truth, attained by an intense exercise of the imagination, accords entirely with the reality principle. Politically, Keats was an active partisan of socially liberal, meliorative ideas and programs. But "he had no hope whatever that life could be ordered in such a way that its condition might be anything but tragic."

Twinned, however, with that clear-eyed ability to face the fact of evil was Keats's self-knowledge and his affirmation of "the creativity of the self that opposes circumstance, the self that is imagination and desire, that . . . assigns names and values to things, and that can realize what it envisions." Unlike most of us, who "suppose that what is grim and cruel is more real than what is pleasant," Keats, although never deceiving himself that "the power of the imagination is sovereign," found the experience of selfhood—the sentiment of being and the intense pleasure that it makes possible—

just as real as the evil that destroys it. He "brought his two knowledges face to face, the knowledge of the world of circumstance, of death and cancer, and the knowledge of the world of self, of spirit and creation, and the delight in them. Each seems a whole knowledge considered alone; each is but a half-knowledge when taken with the other; both together constitute a truth."[39]

The positive, affirmative nature of that truth, made accessible through Negative Capability, means much to Trilling—as well it might. Keats concludes that human life, at even its most remotely imaginable best, can only prove tragic. Nature's very components, it seems to him, are hostile to humanity, and human nature itself is hardly conducive to happiness. Having made as extreme a case as he can for the inevitability of misery, frustration, and wretchedness as inherent to the fate of humankind, he "breaks out," Trilling admiringly comments, "with a sudden contempt for those who call the world a vale of tears." Trilling quotes Keats's words as an impassioned and lyrical articulation of his own thoughts:

What a little circumscribed straightened notion! Call the world if you please "The vale of Soul-making!"—I say *Soul making*—Soul as distinguished from Intelligence— There may be intelligences or sparks of the divinity in millions—but they are not Souls until they acquire identities, till each one is personally itself. . . . Do you not see how necessary a World of Pains and troubles is to school an Intelligence and make it a Soul? A place where the heart must feel and suffer in a thousand ways! . . . the Heart . . . is the Minds Bible, it is the Minds experience, it is the teat from which the Mind or intelligence sucks its identity.[40]

Trilling gives his unstinting admiration to "the idea . . . of souls creating themselves in their confrontation of circumstance" and to "the implicit and explicit commitment to the self even in the moment of its extinction." Keats's vision of human wholeness, his zestful acceptance of struggle, his rejection of political or

psychological resolutions of life's problems simply because they are available and conventionally approved,
his refusal to be rushed—to be forced into reaching
irritably after fact and reason when in doubt, when
uncertain, when anxious—all inspire a degree of ex-
hortation not typical of Trilling. We "cannot now attain" Keats's "spiritual and moral health" merely by
"wishing for it. But we cannot attain it without wishing
for it and clearly *imagining* it" (italics added). And he
gives the last word properly to Keats himself. "The
imagination may be compared to Adam's dream—he
awoke and found it truth."[41]

Trilling puts us in his debt by demonstrating in a
writer as different from Keats as James Joyce the same
positive affirmation, achieved through an intensity that
is at once vigorous and almost infinitely patient in the
confronting of circumstance. Joyce, too, was a soul-
maker. In 1935, he ended a letter to his son, "Here I
conclude. My eyes are tired. For over half a century
they have gazed into nullity, where they have found a
lovely nothing."[42] Joyce, Trilling says, "can be understood to say that human existence is nullity right
enough, yet if it is looked into with a vision such as his,
the nothing that can be perceived really *is* lovely,
though the maintenance of the vision is fatiguing work."
Once again, the rigorous use of the imagination reveals that "Beauty is truth, truth beauty." In Joyce's
case, the cost of the energy necessary to attain this
insight proved high. There was much that was unattrac-
tive in Joyce's personality; and in his later years, "the
personal life seems to have been burned out, calcined."
But there remained a strange serenity, a rare courage,
and an eye that, however weary, continued to see the
world *sub specie aeternitatis*, even when there are no
longer "any indications of an interplay between the self
and the life around it." In the making of his own soul,
Trilling observes, Joyce achieves a view in which "a
thousand years are as but a day, or the other way

around, and the fall of the sparrow does not go unno-
ticed. The round of birth, copulation, and death receives his sanction . . . in the awful silence of the infinite spaces, and his inscrutable but on the whole
affectionate irony is directed upon all that men contrive
in their cities for their survival, with a somewhat wryer
glance toward what they contrive for their delight."

But, if Joyce alienated himself from the usual involvement with life and society to a degree that Trilling
finds "chilling," he also celebrates "human existence
even in the pain, defeat, and humiliation that make up
so large a part of its substance." He "consciously intended Molly Bloom's ultimate 'Yes' as a doctrinal
statement, a judgment in life's favor," and he fashioned
"a rich poetry out of the humble and sordid, the sad
repeated round of the commonplace, laying a significant emphasis on the little, nameless, unremembered
acts of kindness and of love." He could speak in what
Trilling calls a "thrilling archaic phrase" of "the fair
courts of life" even as he responded only with apathy to
society's developments and culture's elaborations.

Obviously, a fierce ambivalence is at work here.
Trilling regards as unparalleled and perhaps unmatch-
able the "focus [of] this much power of love and hate
into so sustained a rage of effectual intention as Joyce
was capable of, so ferocious an ambition, so nearly
absolute a commitment of himself to himself." Toward
his Ireland, Joyce's "hatred was as relentless as the love
was unfailing." He looked upon *Dubliners* as an effort
to construct a conscience for his "wretched race," and
he referred to himself on occasion as a "socialist artist"; but he contemptuously avoided political activity
and associations. Overtly interested in subverting existing society, he was preoccupied with his own social
status, with being a "gentleman," and looked upon his
family's crest as his most treasured possession. Sexu-
ally, his passions had a powerfully polymorphous-
perverse quality, but he cherished an authentic part of

his personality as "austere, almost priestly propriety."

Under the steel sway of his imagination, that ambivalence provided what Trilling characterizes as "the controlling tendency of Joyce's genius—to move through the fullest realization of the human, the all-too-human, to that which transcends and denies the human." In Trilling's eyes, Joyce does not contradict the principle that the fulfilled self is marked by the nature of the alienation that it achieves. He simply creates an existence for himself on the far side of all the carefully sampled, experienced, and evaluated fulfillments that human life has to offer. Unhurried, steadily confronting circumstance, after a long period in uncertainties, mysteries, doubts—with never any irritable reaching after fact and reason—Joyce arrived at his summing up. As Trilling puts it,

The fair courts of life still beckoned invitation and seemed to await his entrance. He was to conclude that their walls and gates enclosed nothing. His genius is defined by his having concluded this rather than taking it for granted, as many of the generations that came after him have found it possible to do.[43]

What is important here for Trilling is not just Joyce's "discovery" that "the world is a cheat, its social arrangements a sham, its rewards a sell." The point is that, in the light of that discovery, the fair courts of life continue to beckon, and the "nothing" within them is "lovely." Entirely aware of the vital affirmation of the "Here Comes Everybody" theme in *Finnegans Wake* and the buoyancy and genuine gaiety in the "funferall" that Joyce puts in progress in his great last work, Trilling praises Joyce for his Keatsian intensity and Negative Capability that lie at the base of the moral courage necessary for looking long and deep into nullity and finally finding it beautiful. By keeping the realm of ideas and ideals distinct from the realm of practicality, Joyce taught us perhaps more than anyone else that although "as getters and spenders we take (the world) to be actual and there," a reality with which some accommodation must be reached, "as persons of moral sensibility, we *know* that the values of the world do not deserve our interest," that it is "at most . . . an absurdity."[44] By refusing to participate in the urgencies of Ireland's politics, Joyce contributed to the development of the Irish national conscience and to the value of its culture. And above all, by making the prodigious empathic effort necessary, Joyce identified himself with the human "nothing" that he perceived as so "lovely." In doing so, his personal will suspended despite the energies of his creative will, he affirmed humanity through making manifest his own sentiment of being.

When Trilling emerged from his long initial encounter with Matthew Arnold, his concern had shifted from the melancholy poet to the man who "had tried to understand the culture for the purpose of shaping it." What Trilling acquired from Arnold and truly possessed as his own was the sense that humanly positive changes in culture occur most frequently from the consequences of energetic and persistent efforts of the imagination. As a thoroughly modern man, profoundly educated and almost painfully perceptive, Trilling could not share Arnold's goal of "human perfection." But in fashioning Arnold's insights and method into intellectual processes distinctively his own, Trilling believed that the cultural changes that "induce us to live or conduce to our health," that improve in some measure the quality of life as we experience it in this vale of soul-making, depend on the manner in which the imagination, interacting with rational disinterestedness, can transform reality as we perceive it, and therefore alter in humane ways our relationship to it. Throughout his career, he held to this faith without sentimentality and, like Freud, Keats, and Joyce, without winking at the tragic nature of human destiny.

6

~~~~~~

The Honest Place "Between"

Reacting to Lionel Trilling's insistent examination of all aspects of an issue, to his characteristic acknowledgment of the merits of quite contrary cases, Richard Sennett once accused him, "You have no position; you are always in between." Trilling's reply poignantly illustrates his fundamental critical stance. "Between," he said, "is the only honest place to be."[1]

Trilling fashioned "between," the honest place within which he conducted his quiet but intensely dramatic dialectic, from two basic materials. One was his deep and enduring sense of human existence as a continuous struggle, of culture itself as "not a free creation but a continuous bargaining with life."[2] The other was his conviction that the quality of personal experience results less from the outcomes of that struggle than from the comprehensiveness, the subtlety, and the energies of mind and imagination with which it is managed. These persuasions gave the distinctive color to his work as critic and as writer of fiction.

Because he invested the utmost seriousness in Matthew Arnold's conception of literature as a criticism of life, and because his consistent focus was on the destiny of the individual self in its often painful relationship to civilization, Trilling's consistent effort revolved around two poles: One was the honest, open exploration of the "variousness and possibilities" with which the inevitable and conflict-filled encounter be-

tween person and culture can be conceived. The other
was an examination of the criteria by which the forms
of variousness and possibility may appropriately be
judged. Although a man of finely honed tastes with a
disposition toward elegance, his aesthetic concerns always remained secondary. His fundamental interests
were moral and therefore psychological and sociopolitical. Like the Arnold that he so richly understood and
admired, he disliked and mistrusted systematic theories
of literature as overly rarified and as essentially irrelevant to the complexly related and central problems of
how personal integrity may be achieved and how corporate life can be humanely arranged. More than that,
he regarded these issues as inevitably recurrent. They
cannot be resolved; they reject systemization. They can
only be dealt with—*struggled* with—in the mind and
imagination and then in the political marketplace,
where individual wills contend with one another under
social rules.

Trilling early claimed the honest place "between"
and rarely left the position that he established there. It
was apparent in *Matthew Arnold*, his first book, in his
advocacy of the Arnold who sought so unremittingly
for ways to support the social principles of the French
Revolution, but who simultaneously extolled the benefits and virtues of the passing order and attempted to
ground the political notions of liberty, equality, and
fraternity in a firmer and nobler psychological and
moral base. It found expression four years later, in
1943, in Trilling's admiration of E. M. Forster's moral
realism, of what he perceived in Forster as "not the
knowledge of good and evil, but the knowledge of good-
and-evil." In his treatment of Vernon Parrington, one
of Trilling's few explicit acts of intellectual demolition,
his assault on *Main Currents in American Thought*
arose not from revulsion at Parrington's favorable comparison of James Branch Cabell with Herman Melville
or from dissent against Parrington's disapproving judg-

ment of Hawthorne. Trilling concentrated his artillery on what he disdained as Parrington's "limited sense of what constitutes a difficulty," and he found weak and offensive Parrington's belief in "a thing called *reality*; it is one and immutable, it is wholly external, it is irreducible. Men's minds may waver, but reality is always reliable, always the same, always easily to be known. And the artist's relation to reality . . . [is] a simple one." Out of these fundamental shortcomings, Trilling charges, grows Parrington's tendency to meet "evidence of imagination and creativeness with a settled hostility the expression of which suggests that he regards them as the natural enemies of democracy." The foundations have been laid for Trilling's ultimate verdict:

Parrington's characteristic weakness as a historian is suggested by his title, for the culture of a nation is not truly figured in the image of the current. A culture is not a flow, nor even a confluence; the form of its existence is struggle . . . it is nothing if not a dialectic. And in any culture there are likely to be certain artists who contain a large part of the dialectic within themselves, their meaning and power lying in their contradictions; they contain within themselves . . . the very essence of the culture, and the sign of this is that they do not submit to serve the ends of any one ideological group or tendency. . . . Parrington . . . expresses the chronic American belief that there exists an opposition between reality and mind and that one must enlist oneself in the party of reality.[3]

Two of the major entailments of occupying that honest place "between" strongly manifest themselves here. One is the emphasis on the dialectical struggle inherent in human experience; the other is the possibility of transforming reality—meaning always, for Trilling, social reality, the reality of culture—by the power of the imagination.

The heart of that struggle beats with the active and unremitting warfare between the individual self and the civilization that simultaneously gives it its life and its

central character and yet restricts, cabins, and imprisons it. In Trilling's eyes, as in Freud's, selfhood requires
and depends on alienation. To be a person demands not
only an active declaration of difference from the dominant tendencies of culture but a stubborn and combative resistance to culture's rules, to culture's nay-saying.
As it is in life, so it is in serious literature:

In its essence literature is concerned with the self; and the
particular concern of the literature of the last two centuries
has been with the self in its standing quarrel with culture.
We cannot mention the name of any great writer of the
modern period whose work has not in some way, and usually
in a passionate and explicit way, insisted on this quarrel,
who has not expressed the bitterness of his discontent with
civilization, who has not said that the self made greater
legitimate demands than any culture could hope to satisfy.
This intense conviction of the existence of the self apart
from culture is, as culture well knows, its noblest and most
generous achievement.[4]

In the phrase of William James that Trilling so often
found useful, the life of the individual consistently
"*feels* like a fight." What gives art, especially literature,
its importance is the way that it articulately reflects and
illuminates the subtleties, the complexities, and the intensities of that inescapable battle for selfhood that persons must wage with the civilization that is at once the
powerful opponent and the basic groundwork of their
being.

But if Trilling consistently sided with the self in its
unceasing strife with civilization, he remained clear-
eyed about culture's furnishing the foundations of personal being. Beside his conviction that the self makes
greater legitimate demands than any civilization can
satisfy, he maintained, beyond that of any other modern critic, a focused awareness on the cultural *nature* of
human beings; the notion of a feral humanity was for
him a flat contradiction in terms. With Freud, he knew
that the alleged freedom of primitive life was a roman-

tic illusion, and he found no opposition between finding
extensive fault with contemporary sociocultural forms
and, with Arnold, committing himself to the humanization of man-in-society. That commitment, Trilling believed, defines the quest that lies at the core of an en-
lightened politics. Without society, without culture,
Homo sapiens can claim neither humanity nor selfhood.

In consequence, Trilling could respond with a tenderness that never became sentimental to social institutions like the family. Perceptive about the way in which
Dickens, for example, "specializes in the depiction of
inadequate parents and no one knew better than he how
truly the Victorian family could be . . . a hell," he is
impressed by how, "if we now look back over the great
literary enterprises of our time, we cannot but be struck
by how deeply preoccupied these are with the family
idea." Given all the stress on alienation, the force and
persuasiveness of its images derive "from the sense of
the violation of . . . childhood peace and familial
security." And after noting that "Lawrence, Proust,
Joyce, Faulkner give to the family a place in their vision of life which is no less fundamental than that of
Dickens," Trilling observes that Dickens is one of the
strongest articulators of "the great modern theme of
'little boy lost,' of the child's elemental emotions and
familial trust being violated by the ideas and institutions of modern life."[5] The trust, the experience of
love, the security that a good childhood may provide
lay down the foundations for character, for one's sentiment of being, and for the interpersonal sensitivity
upon which both a proud selfhood and a viable society
depend.

This point of view and these values underlie Trilling's reaction to the first Kinsey Report, *Sexual Behavior in the Human Male*. That reaction, incidentally,
illustrates how the honest place "between" was not at
all a home for indifference or neutrality; it frequently

proved the breeding ground and the platform for strongly held convictions. In the case of Kinsey, Trilling quotes a key sentence from the discussion of premature ejaculation: "It would be difficult to find another situation in which an individual who was quick and intense in his responses was labeled anything but superior, and that in most instances is exactly what the rapidly ejaculating male probably is, however inconvenient and unfortunate his qualities may be from the standpoint of the wife in the relationship." The response reveals much about Trilling's style, his eye for details, his concern for relationships and for the decencies and decorum that make corporate life fruitful as well as inevitable. Most of all, it encapsulates his conception of humanity. "But by such reasoning," he writes, in answer to Kinsey,

the human male who is quick and intense in his leap to the lifeboat is natural and superior, however inconvenient his speed and intensity may be to the wife he leaves standing on the deck, as is also the man who makes a snap judgment, who bites his dentist's finger, who kicks the child who annoys him, who bolts his—or another's—food, who is incontinent of his feces. Surely the problem of the natural in the human was solved four centuries ago by Rabelais, and in the simplest naturalistic terms; and it is sad to have the issue all confused again by the naiveté of men of science. Rabelais' solution lay in the simple perception of the *natural* ability and tendency of man to grow in the direction of organization and control. The young Gargantua in his natural infancy had all the quick and intense responses just enumerated; had his teachers confused the traits of his natural infancy with those of his natural manhood, he would not have been the more natural but the less; he would have been a monster.[6]

Growth in personal organizations, in self-regulation, and in respect for others may seem old-fashioned virtues. Similarly, the idea of a natural adulthood that differs markedly from the self-indulgences appropriate to a natural childhood may hold little appeal for an age that worships youth if not infancy and that puts a premium on self-expression through acting uninhibitedly on impulse. For Trilling, they were basic features of an authentically human life. His insightful affection for children, demonstrated in his treatment of Susan Caldwell in *The Middle of the Journey* and of the daughter in "The Other Margaret," reflects this view of human development no less than does his admiration of Keats, of Jane Austen, and of Arnold as models of adult maturity.

That same moral vision of the basic features of a human life embraces Trilling's concern for order, for civil peace. Order in society, however, must be organic; the parts of a polity must enjoy an intimate connection with each other, created by processes of historical development. His long hostility to Stalinism in all its forms attests to Trilling's unshakable rejection of what he regarded as the pseudo order achieved through authoritarian rule. Order conducive to civilization can only be achieved; it cannot be imposed. Yet the achievement, like all achievements as he conceived them, is precarious. Social order always entails an expense of the self, a bending of the individual to conform to the contours of the community, a surrendering of some portion of personal autonomy to corporate authority.

The proper response of the individual to such pressures is opposition; the authentic self is an opposing self. Yet selfhood depends on relationships, on a sense of belonging to a group and to history, on the status of being a protected citizen in some kind of organized association of human beings. Once again we encounter the motif of struggle, the embattled state that relates self to culture, even when the conditions of social order are genuinely achieved and not tyrannically imposed. The complexities and ramifications of this motif of struggle give literature its high importance. On the one hand, "the idea that preoccupies . . . literature

and is central to it . . . [is] the idea of the self."[7] On
the other hand, "what constitutes the matter of literature is the discordant and destructive reality that threatens the peace which makes literature possible"[8]—that
is, that makes possible the contemplation and development of selfhood under the aegis of the imaginative
reason.

Literature and life for Trilling are clearly not distant cousins or related only through the intellectual
tracing of common lineages, like the anthropological
demonstration of a primitive kinship system. They are
inseparable. This insistence on the *cogency* of literature
informed his work as a critic and accounts for his skeptical view of art as a self-justifying venture. Art "does
not always tell the truth or the best kind of truth and
does not always point out the right way . . . it can even
generate falsehood and habituate us to it."[9] Literature
has consequences, and those consequences can be dangerous. The dangers are greatest when literature flirts
with the cultish, when it becomes organized, however
loosely, into an "adversary culture" that threatens individual autonomy by virtue of its taking on those organizational characteristics that always entail costs to
selfhood. Fashionable art, whether it reflects the qualities and aims of the dominant or the adversary culture,
does not do and cannot be the work of artists who
contain within themselves the dialectic of their place
and time, who derive their meaning and power from
their internal contradictions, and who do not "submit
to serve the ends of any one ideological group or tendency." It was on this basis that Trilling in the 1930s
could find little merit in writers like James T. Farrell
and George Sklar, whose doctrinal positions he found
congenial. On the same basis, in the sixties and seven-
ties, he reacted negatively to Beckett, Burroughs, and
Sartre, whose ideas struck him as both wrongheaded
and perilous. In both instances, he characteristically
condemned the lack of that dialectic quality that

emerges from experience examined by the imaginative reason.

Trilling acquired the idea of the imaginative reason from Arnold and transformed it into a concept all his own. It combines three elements: a rather severe and broadly informed rationality, a deliberate and habitual envisioning of alternatives (again the characteristic emphasis on "variousness and possibility"), and an insistence on *feeling*, on the integral relationship of emotion and will to ideas. This last factor has seldom been understood as essential to Trilling's approach and method. Passion is part of the atmosphere of the honest place "between." But it is passion controlled, made to motor thought but not to dominate it.

The sources of the deliberate control of emotion bear on Trilling's substance as well as on his critical style. To begin with, there is his notion of courtesy as a component of morality. Good manners are more than mere forms. They are at once the interpersonal mucilage that holds society, always subject to the centrifugal force of individual selves and individual wills, together and the means by which we minimize our tendency to hurt each other. Trilling had no compunction about combat or about giving or receiving wounds as entailments of battle. But for him, the distinction was crucial between principled and justified hostilities as against indulging the aggressive impulse, acting vindictively, or salving one's own ego by damaging another person.

Second, he deeply believed that "objectivity" of judgment depends on "a programmatic prejudice in favor of the work or author being studied"; "sympathy and even admiration"[10] serve as routes to insight and as the bases for critical appraisals of genuine value. Aversion and dislike rarely promote acuity in either perception or evaluation.

When Trilling occasionally broke this self-imposed discipline—as in his treatments of Parrington and Dreiser,[11] of Gheorghiu's *The Twenty-Fifth Hour*,[12] of C. P. Snow and F. R. Leavis for their roles in the so-called two-cultures controversy,[13] and of R. D. Laing and comparable psychoanalytic revisionists[14]— he did so only because his sympathy and admiration and commitment to explicit principles, which he saw as seriously contravened by those whom he defined as his opponents, required it. Positive passion, the passion of dedication and enthusiasm, enjoyed free rein as the energizer of creative and critical powers; negative passion, the passion of hostility and hatred, Trilling kept closely curbed.

Finally, there is just a hint of the omnipresent Wordsworth. Like poetry, criticism flowers most brightly and most enduringly when powerful emotions are recollected in tranquillity—that is, when the critic, although quite in tune with his own strongest feelings, places them in perspective and fully comprehends their meanings rather than accepting them at their manifest values. The critic as an opposing self works under the obligation of self-knowledge and of the self-restraints demanded by his mission of cultural change.

Cultural change, of course, is precisely the function of the imaginative reason and was just as precisely what Trilling sought and hoped for. The ways in which he bridled his passion in his exercise of the imaginative reason provide clues to the directions that for him specified desirable modifications in our common life. Trilling saw both creativity and a democratic civil experience as necessarily entailing "aggression" in the sense of persistence in the face of frequent frustration, a full-scale investment of the will, consciously directed and determinedly sustained energies—the doctrine, once again, of *ad astra per aspera*. He worked consistently to distinguish this kind of human aggressiveness from hostility, bigotry, and authoritarianism, the aggressions of person against person, the aggressions of the imperial self and of the imperial nation.

Trilling perceived alienation as an essential condition of selfhood, and he understood the manner in which opposition and difference become definitive of one's sense of personal being. But he also felt and articulated the functions of group membership, of personal relationships, and of identification with others in the forging of personhood. Together with the promotion of individuality—his preoccupation with human variousness and possibility—Trilling pressed for the recognition of human commonalities, of the unheroic but genuine worth of what Eliot called "the common routine"[15] and even of the dutiful, dull, thoughtless "morality of inertia"[16] embodied in Willa Cather's *Ethan Frome*. He understood William James's characterization of habit as "the enormous fly-wheel of society, its most precious conservative agent,"[17] and Alfred North Whitehead's similar observation that "Civilization advances by extending the number of important operations which we can perform without thinking about them."[18]

For Trilling, caring so deeply about the stability and peacefulness of society and about the quality of civilization led directly to his concerns with the requirements of civility and with the dynamics of character formation. The interaction between a society's standards of decency and the processes of character development deeply influences two major components of selfhood. One is the contours of the individual's sentiment of being, the shape and central tendency of one's identity. The other is the quality and tone of the judgments that each person makes about himself. The peculiar mix of contentment and despair, of esteem and doubt, of pride and self-loathing with which we evaluate ourselves derives primarily from the interplay between the moral norms of one's culture and the form and furnishings of one's own character. Similarly, when the rules of civility command respect and the attributes of character elicit honor, then our social experience enjoys a reduction in the abrasiveness, the untrust-

worthiness, and the crass getting-and-spending elements
that otherwise permeate our corporate life. Both good
manners and morality, in this sense, matter as much
by virtue of their political implications as through their
being the outward manifestations of inward graces.

Because he held the point of view as inherent to
the topography of the honest place "between," Trilling,
when he identified himself as a liberal, did not—any
more than Arnold did—mean that he supported the
received ideology of practical liberal politics. Nor did
he endorse by reflex action the catchwords and slogans
of progressive opinion at any particular moment. At
times, when he publicly aligned himself on some special
issue, he assumed the characteristic liberal stance. For
example, along with a large number of his Columbia
colleagues, he signed a strong statement, which appeared in *The New York Times* (October 16, 1952),
in support of the presidential candidacy of Governor
Adlai Stevenson in his first campaign against General
Dwight D. Eisenhower, then serving as Columbia's
president. Late in 1953, in the heyday of Senator Joseph McCarthy's witch-hunts and investigations of
"subversives," Trilling was vigorous and active in his
defense of intellectual and academic freedom.

During that difficult period on college and university campuses, he led the Columbia faculty in register-
ing its opposition to a proposed inquiry into Communist sympathies and influences among university
professors. Chairing a drafting committee that comprised Polycarp Kusch, a Nobel laureate in physics,
David B. Truman, a distinguished political scientist,
and Harold E. Lowe, the director of admissions, Trilling argued that such attempts to impose criteria of
political acceptability on education and on artists and
scholars are beside the point and work harm. They are
unnecessary because only a handful of faculty members
have had even remote associations with Communism;
they work harm by creating a climate of "apprehension

and distrust that jeopardize(s) the cause of free inquiry and the right to dissent, which is the foundation of civil liberties in a free society." Trilling and his committee held that, although membership in Communist organizations suggests "submission to an intellectual control which is entirely at variance with the principles of academic competence," issues of academic capability must be resolved within the academic community and not by governmental intervention; "professional competence and personal integrity" are and must remain the only proper tests of fitness for university teaching, and only academic scholars and educators hold the qualifications to apply these tests in an appropriate fashion.

But these and other acts were undertaken simply as a responsible citizen, voicing his will in contention with others in the arena of practical politics. As a writer and critic, Trilling's point of view toward sociopolitical change emphasized quite different efforts. The Arnoldian trend in those efforts found a voice in his discussion of John Dos Passos as early as 1938.[19] One of the considerable virtues that Trilling identifies in U.S.A., John Dos Passos's great trilogy of the 1930s, is its subordination of politics to morality; the criterion of political action for those who participate in it and live under its consequences is the quality of moral experience that it promotes. If "Dos Passos is a social historian . . . he is that in order to be a more complete moralist. It is of the greatest significance that for him the barometer of social breakdown is not suffering through economic deprivation but always moral degradation through moral choice." Trilling consistently used the same barometer, regarding it as peculiarly sensitive to modern moral and political weather.

In a time that combines intense self-consciousness with high and anxious uncertainty about social directions and a breakdown in the persuasiveness of traditional codes of conduct, moral choice turns on the probable consequences of action for the personality. When the ends and outcomes of one's decisions appear dim, inconclusive, or unpredictable, the central question becomes one of how choice will affect the character of the chooser. The issue is less one of what he should *do* than one of what he will *become* as a result of his choosing, of how his choice will influence the quality of his selfhood, of his sentiment of being. This moral criterion, which Trilling salutes Dos Passos for applying in *U.S.A.* with insight and a compassionate but wide-ranging rigor, derives from John Dewey, who put the case in this fashion:

What shall the (moral) agent *be*? What sort of a character shall he assume? . . . The distinctively moral situation is . . . one in which elements of value and control are bound up with the processes of deliberation and desire; and are bound up in a peculiar way: *viz.*, they decide what kind of a character shall control further desires and deliberations. When ends are genuinely incompatible, no common denominator can be found except by deciding what sort of character is most highly prized and shall be given supremacy.[20]

But if this view derives from Dewey, it also illustrates the process of soul-making that Trilling so deeply admired in Keats and in Joyce's creation of "loveliness" out of the "nullity" that he regarded as human life. And it is very much of a piece with Arnold's emphasis on "culture"—by which he means reading, observing, and reflecting—as a means to transcend the "ordinary self" by achieving one's "best self" and therefore to infuse the realm of practical politics and social change with some of the beauty and intelligence ("sweetness and light") that depend on the disinterestedness and Joy that mark the realm of ideas and ideals.

In other words, the moral growth and transformation of persons lay at the root of Trilling's notion of social change in a democratic polity. Personal moral

growth and transformation depend in significant measure on a rich flow of fruitful ideas clothed in the emotions that are integral to the human estate. The central
task of the intellectual, the artist, and the critic is to
maintain that stream of ideas touched with feeling.
Without discounting the importance of economics,
Trilling understood the limitations and the contradictions in economic solutions to problems arising from
cultural and psychological sources. He was aware, for
example, of the mounting tension between capitalism
and democracy, despite the popular view that they
complement each other. Capitalism depends on risk-
taking initiative, and democracy provides the freedom
for that kind of boldness to succeed. But the same sort
of freedom also defines the condition under which heart-
rending, destructive, and socially disruptive failures
occur with a punishing frequency. Political redress for
economic inequities and governmental protection
against at least the most grinding forms of failure become humanly necessary.

As a result, conflicts arise, and impediments to the
processes of both capitalism and democracy begin to
operate. Politicians in a democratic state preserve public confidence in both themselves and society's institutions through responsiveness to their constituencies.
Yet their responsiveness may strain the system with a
load of obligations and rising expectations that it cannot safely carry. In an effort to extend equality and to
broaden the base of economic security, high taxes and
restrictive regulations may sap capitalism of its vitality
and deprive citizens of their self-reliance, their independence, and their privacy. Industrious and clever
strivers lose their economic rewards; those who have
encountered failure in their experience must wear its
label on their personhood. Neither economic performance nor democratic satisfactions are enhanced.

Perceiving these complexities, Trilling invested no
faith in economic wizardry. Rather, he looked to politi-

cal leadership responding to a people affected by the imaginative reason. His goals included a redefinition of the responsibilities of the state, of both profit and non-profit private enterprise, and the individual. That re-definition entailed the restoration and preservation of trust in government, of strength in private effort, and of dignity in persons. Overwhelmingly, the achievement of these objectives and purposes rested, in Trilling's eyes, on raising the level of moral awareness and elevating the plane of moral meaning throughout the nation. For him, that moral function was the chief (though never the sole) justification for the efforts of intellectuals and artists, especially of novelists. Those efforts supply, however imperfectly—and the prime task of the critic is to assess their effectiveness—the models and the stimuli out of which individuals at least partially fashion their own moral selves, what Arnold called their "best selves" in contrast to their "ordinary selves." When those moral selves set their distinctive wills in political con-tention, subject to the procedural regulations of democ-racy, the quality of legislation and of executive leader-ship and executive responsiveness tends to transcend the otherwise dominant considerations of party solidar-ity, discipline, and expedience. The tone and substance of the dialectic, of the inherent and unremitting human struggle, become a bit more elevated. Sympathies grow more comprehensive; expressed interests are less in-tensely parochial and therefore less divisive, and the im-mediate outcomes are more tempered by realism. "In the long run," Trilling asks, "is not the political choice fundamentally a choice of personal quality?"[21]

The question stands, of course, as entirely rhetori-cal. Trilling's affirmative answer constitutes one of the blocks out of which the honest place "between" is con-structed. From that vantage point flow some of his representative judgments. He liked Ignazio Silone's *Bread and Wine*, for example, because of its depiction of how membership in a revolutionary party, whatever

its values may be, clearly fails to solve in itself the
personal, moral, and even the political problems that
beset modern men and women. In the "heartbreak" of
Bernard Shaw's *Heartbreak House*, he found "the beginning of new courage, and I can think of no more
useful *political* job for the literary man today than, by
the representation of despair, to cauterize the exposed
soft tissue of too-easy hope."[22] He rejects the Utopian
element in Herbert Marcuse's politics, as he rejects
Utopian political thought generally, on the grounds that
it promotes "a character-structure and a culture . . . as
deficient in grace as in authenticity."[23] And he energetically reverses the verdict on Dos Passos's trilogy,
rendered by T. K. Whipple and Malcom Cowley, as
expressing a political despair that is "negative to the
point of being politically harmful." Despair that aban-
dons illusion, Trilling argues, "is very different from
despair which generates tender new cynicism." *U.S.A.*'s
achievement lies in its presentation of the intimately
personal as well as the political consequences of moral
choice: "If it is made on the wrong (the safe) side, the
loss of human quality, so that instead of a man we have
a Success and instead of two lovers a Statue and a Bust
in the public square."[24]

These illustrative judgments reflect a personality
engagé but far from orthodoxly partisan, a mind and a
character discriminating between the sphere of ideas
and ideals and the sphere of practical politics but
understanding the connections between them, an intellect passionately concerned with the quality of quotidian life for the *persons* caught up in the endless
conflict between selfhood and civilization. They also
reflect a rejection of the chic and the currently approved
in assessments of literature and contemporary life, in
favor of a commitment to the complexity and the
necessity for some effective balance among the contending drives, interests, and perilous contingencies of
the contemporary world. This commitment, so integral

to the honest place "between," has enraged not a few. Roger Sale, by no means an ungenerous critic, represents those who have responded to Trilling's disinterested-ness with explosive frustration.

Sale, a proponent of "our own voice, our ignorant voice, our American voice," characterizes Trilling as "a voice that one could not expect to adapt itself easily to the sixties," and charges—the word is used advisedly—that he "wanted to be Matthew Arnold." Sale con-cludes, in a final dismissal of Trilling, that "we had best be done with models, that we can keep the past alive not by imitating or emulating it but by reading its words aloud and by answering them in whatever authentic voice we have, wildly, loudly, or in hushed tones."[25] Saul Bellow, whom Sale much admires, disagrees. "What one sees on Broadway while bound for the bus," muses the wise old title character of *Mr. Sammler's Planet*:

All human types reproduced, the barbarian, redskin, or Fiji, the dandy, the buffalo hunter, the desperado, the queer, the sexual fantasist, the squaw, bluestocking, princess, poet, painter, prospector, troubadour, guerrilla, Che Guevara, the new Thomas à Becket. Not imitated are the businessman, the soldier, the priest, and the square. . . . They sought originality. They obviously were derivative. And of what—of Paiutes, of Fidel Castro? No, of Hollywood extras. Act-ing mythic. Casting themselves into chaos, hoping to ad-here to higher consciousness, to be washed up on the shores of truth. Better, thought Sammler, to accept the in-evitability of imitation and then to imitate good things. The ancients had this right. Greatness without models? Inconceivable. One could not be the thing itself—Reality. One must be satisfied with the symbols. Make it the object of imitation to reach and release the high qualities. Make peace therefore with intermediacy and representation. But choose higher representations. Otherwise the individual must be the failure he now sees and knows himself to be.

And there is Bellow's comment on the sixties, the *Zeitgeist* of which, according to Sale, lay beyond Trilling's powers of "adaptation." Asked to address a seminar at Columbia University, Mr. Sammler has had his lecture broken up under the vulgar leadership of a presumed student "in Levi's, thick-bearded but possibly young, a figure of compact distortion." Out of the amphitheater, Sammler

was not so much personally offended by the event as struck by the will to offend. What a passion to be *real*. But *real* was also brutal. And the acceptance of excrement as a standard? How extraordinary! Youth? Together with the idea of sexual potency? All this confused sex-excrement-militancy, explosiveness, abusiveness, tooth-showing. Barbary ape howling. Or like the spider monkeys in the trees, as Sammler once had read, defecating into their hands, and shrieking, pelting the explorers below.[26]

Although there is nothing simian in Roger Sale's informed and intelligent appraisals, when he speaks so ardently of "our own voice, our ignorant voice, our American voice . . . whatever authentic voice we have," he illustrates precisely the defects of authenticity that Trilling took pains to document. Three points seem worth making. First, in contrast to the rule of sincerity, which requires that public statements be congruent to private thoughts and feelings, the rule of authenticity demands self-disclosure, especially the disclosure of one's affects and feelings. Exercised judiciously, authenticity carries the twinned values of being oneself and of enhancing the self through a courteous and courageous outspokenness. Without the element of judiciousness, it degenerates quickly into an obliteration of the boundary between the private and the public realms; the result destroys relationships and sunders the community. The principle of sincerity remains intact, for example, if, in order to avoid hurting another person needlessly, one withholds from him a damaging feeling or judgment. When authenticity becomes warped and overblown, such a consideration loses all significance, and the notion of interpersonal or social decency undergoes a degree of erosion. The virtue of respect and the potential for learning from someone else, from a tradition, or from an imperfect but functioning society are undermined.

Second, authenticity unconstrained makes self-disclosure into a kind of fundamental measure of credibility and truth. Only when I am telling you what I feel do I have a sense of meaningfully expressing myself, and the precondition of this kind of expression is a central concentration on my own raw affects. Psychologists have long known this state of affairs as narcissism. Although he chooses not to use the term, Trilling has sharply exposed this narcissistic tendency in authenticity, especially in his analysis of Sartre.[27] Narcissism denies the degree to which the self grows organically out of the culture in which it is embedded, and it makes subjectivity an end in itself, entailing a focus on the nature of private feeling to the neglect of what is objectively felt. Under these conditions of self-absorption, expression tends to lose its force, turning, at best, eccentric and crotchety rather than original, and the process of self-disclosure itself becomes amorphous and recedes from any real communicative enterprise among persons.

Finally, the notion of authenticity, as it acquired meaning and force during the decade of the 1960s, represents what Trilling calls "something like a mutation in human nature." Emerging as a response to the hypocrisies and dark violence of the war in Vietnam, its intensity grimly follows Sainte-Beuve's observation that "nothing resembles a hollow so much as a hill." Confronted by horror, the devotee of authenticity copes with it by merging with it, by becoming a part of it. Trilling's brilliantly chosen example is Conrad's Kurtz in *Heart of Darkness*. Kurtz does not, like most Belgians and other whites in the Congo, look away from the savagery that exists there, essentially denying it. But neither does he face it, attempt to understand it, and make an effort to master it. Instead, he incorporates it and exploits it, and his famous judgment, "The horror, the horror," amounts to an evaluation of himself as well as of the culture that he has joined. Authenticity at the extreme, as in Kurtz, undoes the nay-saying that civilization imposes on the self; the result is the primitivation of the personality, the feralizing of the self, rather than the humanization of man-in-society.

These considerations anxiously preoccupied Trilling during the latter part of the 1960s and run like the threads of the Fates through the pages of *Sincerity and Authenticity*. The same considerations lie at the base of Bellow-Sammler's reflections on the brutality of being "real" and on the importance of good models and their imitation. The humanization of man-in-society requires traditions and the inheritance of moral distinctions between what is humane and what is destructive of humanity. The importance and desirability of changes in those traditions and moral legacies cannot be doubted, and change, it must be remembered, was Trilling's foremost goal. But change, if it is to support and enhance the fragile potentials of humanity, cannot occur too abruptly or without an adequate moral base, and certainly not through the process of joining horror in its essence if not in its particular forms.

Trilling's unflagging opposition to Stalinism had its roots in precisely this concern. The justification for the Russian Revolution was to end the horrors of the Czarist regime and to replace that brutal totalitarianism with a more just and egalitarian culture. In actuality, internal dissensions within the Communist Party led to Stalin's purges, which grimly outdid the repressive acts of the Czars, to social control through terror in a fashion that made the aftermath of the French Revolution seem pale, and to a despotism that at least matched that of the Romanoffs in its reality if it differed in its appearance. Like Conrad's Kurtz, the Communists—or at least their leadership—had fused with the horror,

becoming one with it, instead of combatting it or containing it. This perception of the central core of Stalinism underlay Trilling's response to the upsets and disruptions of the 1960s. Interviewed in the spring of
1968, when Columbia was beset by a student uprising
of a kind then epidemic in American universities, Trilling characterized the issues posed by the student dis-
senters as "gratuitous," "factitious," "symbolic."[28]

The resulting misunderstandings have proved
startling. William Chace illustrates the point when he
claims that Trilling's "attitudes were akin to those of
William Butler Yeats when he said of the First World
War that 'We should not attribute a very high degree of
reality to the Great War.' "[29] Few comments could
stand farther from accuracy. Trilling meant precisely
what he said: The *issues* presented during the Columbia
crisis were symbolic and adventitious, and the gratuitous quality of the *issues* flowed from what worried
Trilling most deeply and impressed him as the heart of
the student revolt—its Stalinist style. As he saw things,
the issues served as a rhetorical mask behind which
destructive impulses, the wish for power for sheer power's sake, and the narcissistic indulgence and exhibition
of the ego were given unbridled play. The horror of the
American involvement in Indochina and of American
race relations had not been faced, understood, and attacked; the horror had been joined and participated in
after the manner of the Communists emulating the bru-
talities of the Czars. License the beast within one's own
bosom by pointing to the beasts in other hearts. When
Roger Sale talks, then, of Trilling's inability to "adapt
. . . easily to the sixties," he simply fails to comprehend
Trilling's steadfast position. Trilling had no wish to
"adapt" to the spirit of that time. He deplored it, opposed it, and suffered real anxieties about its probable
consequences.

One illustration should suffice. Trilling quotes a
comment by Archibald Cox, the author of the *Report*

*of the Fact-Finding Commission to Investigate the Dis-
turbances at Columbia University in April and May
1968:* "The present generation of young people in our
universities are the best informed, the most intelligent,
and the most idealistic this country has ever known."
With this somewhat bewildering assertion on the record, Trilling points out that through television and
radio, mass journalism, and other cultural agencies,
"there is unceasingly borne in upon us the consciousness that we live in circumstances of an unprecedented
sort." These circumstances entail unprecedented difficulties, but, according to the messages of the communi-
cations media, we are entitled to believe "not only that
we can properly identify the difficulties . . . but also that
we can cope with them . . . and that . . . our consciousness of difficulties to be coped with gives us moral distinction." In the light of this situation, what Cox celebrates "as knowledge and intelligence . . . is merely a
congeries of 'advanced' public attitudes." Superficiality
and fashion have been misinterpreted as information
and idealism. But Cox's deference to students seems
less significant than another implication of his statement in the report—its acceptance of "another of the
master traits of our contemporary culture; its willingness—its eagerness—to forgo the particularization of
conduct. Recognizing the great store now placed on
selfhood and the energies of the self, Professor Cox met
and matched the culture in its principled indifference to
the intellectual and moral forms in which the self
chooses to be presented."[30]

Trilling perceived the primary choice exercised
during the Columbia disturbances as a Stalinist one.
The strong presence at Columbia of the Weathermen, a
terrorist group formed out of the original Students for a
Democratic Society, makes it at least unlikely that he
was entirely wrong, and crude posters reading,
"Wanted: Dead or Alive—Lionel Trilling," appear
hardly irrelevant to his judgment. Sale and Chace are

certainly entitled to different readings of that turbulent
period, but their remarks about Trilling seem badly
mistaken on two important counts. They fail to note the
courageous consistency with which Trilling maintained
a lifelong stance against *all* forms of authoritarianism,
against merging with the horror, and they charge him
with not adapting or with being intellectually distant
from events in which he was actually heavily implicated, about which he was profoundly and articulately
concerned, and toward which he took a definite and
clear position.

That position characteristically found its locus,
however, in the honest place "between." Although *Sincerity and Authenticity* carries a tincture of nostalgia
for the "moral lyricism" of the old culture of sincerity,
it welcomes and affirms the strenuousness, the exigence,
and the combative siding with self against culture that
inhere in the style of authenticity. What else would one
expect from a thoughtful man who sees struggle as the
root metaphor of human life, whose work has always
reflected "the idea that society, though necessary for
survival, corrupts the life it fosters," for whom the
Latin tag of *ad astra per aspera* has consistently held
such rich meaning? But, like the Arnold who wholeheartedly supported the ideas of the French Revolution
but simultaneously sought to defend what was humane
in the passing order, Trilling at once hails authenticity
and warns of its vulnerability to serious pathology.

Human beings remain culture-made animals; to
deny culture, to make the goal of the self's autonomy
into an absolute unrelated to society, to accord moral
authority to the "authenticity" of disorder, violence,
and unreason, are to destroy the peace on which creativity depends and to put beyond the pale the wholeness on which personhood rests. The state becomes
ungovernable and therefore dangerous to individuals
and to individuality; the idea of community loses all
significance, and history suggests that a repressive back-

lash, led by a Napoleon, a Stalin, a Hitler, will not be far behind.

Meanwhile, "The falsities of an alienated social reality are rejected in favour of an upward psychopathic mobility to the point of divinity, each one of us a Christ—but with none of the inconveniences of undertaking to intercede, of being a sacrifice, of reasoning with rabbis, or making sermons, of having disciples, of going to weddings and to funerals, of beginning something and at a certain point remarking that it is finished."[31] The notion that "alienation is to be overcome only by the completeness of alienation, and that alienation completed is not a deprivation or deficiency but a potency" is a mindless one. It may reflect a desperation that warrants wholesale trembling for the precariousness of civilization, but it also reflects an ominous and sad failure to understand that no man is an island, that the life of each person remains forever conditioned and qualified but also enriched by the interdependent lives of others. Narcissism is not autonomy, and susceptibility to blatant narcissism is the inherent defect of authenticity. The pathology is not inevitable, but it must be guarded against.

In Trilling's simultaneous welcoming of authenticity and his warning of its narcissistic pathology, as in other instances where his dual-mindedness has been characteristic, two components of the honest place "between" reveal themselves. One consists in Trilling's sense of the tragic quality in human experience. The other reflects his adaptation of Keats's principle of negative capability, the capacity to sustain doubt and uncertainties and to forgo easy or doctrinaire resolutions. Both undergird the wide sweep of his work, providing it with the quality of combined solidity and ambivalence that has puzzled many in relation to the variety and range of the works, the writers, and the issues that Trilling addressed.

Roger Sale again represents the failure of compre-

hension that often greeted efforts that somehow commanded admiration at the same time that their lack of
system, or declared theory, proved baffling. Symptomat-
ically, Sale writes that "the whole idea of being plumply
judicious about subjects of concern is one which has
seen better days," and he couples this derogating comment with the quite accurate observation that Trilling
"is a thinker, he is generous, but he is no theoretician."
Trilling was quite clear about his stubborn but reasoned
and explicitly deliberate resistance to theory, to system,
and, if one charitably ignores that snide adverb
"plumply," one can ask a serious and too frequently
ignored question. Not only what is wrong with being
judicious about subjects of concern, but what better—
what more humane—approach is there to subjects of
concern? Trilling's judiciousness grounded itself in his
angle of regard, and that angle of regard comprised his
tragic view of human life and the utility that he found,
following Keats, in the requirements of negative capability.

The notion of tragedy lends itself to at least two
quite different conceptions, not at all antithetical to
each other. One takes its definition from the great tragic
literature of the Greeks, Shakespeare and the Eliza-
bethans, Racine and Corneille, Melville and Hardy and
Dostoevski. It entails a figure of heroic proportions engaged in an action of extraordinary painfulness and difficulty that pits the self against some implacable force—
its own fatal flaws, the unyielding power of circumstance, or the dictates of destiny whether fate rests on
the decrees of the gods or on the interplay of character
and the conditions of the world. In this essentially classic sense, tragedy has a monumental quality; it invades
and disturbs our minds and hearts with the impact of
myth and through the transfiguring conceptions that
myths embody.

But another idea of tragedy, far less grand and
mythic but more pervasive, immediate, and intimate,

enjoys its own validity. As Paul Elmer More phrased it, all men and women live under "the law of costing-ness,"[32] the rule that one pays for what one gets, and one gets what one pays for. The universal temptation to evade the expense of what one has received or to obtain more than one has paid for defines the bedrock of moral experience. That temptation complicates the process of our living as human beings, and it endows virtually all our exercises of choice with tragic poten-tials.

To select one object or course means the foregoing of another. That foregoing of other options has conse-quences that we cannot fully predict; it may demand a price that we ultimately find exorbitant, and we not infrequently encounter situations where we cannot meet the cost of what we most want—one of the conditions that arouses and lends force to that universal tempta-tion to deny, to escape, or somehow to override the ineluctable law of costingness.

Thoreau had something of this pattern in mind when he movingly observed that "most men lead lives of quiet desperation." And Whitehead's somber com-ment on the implications of modern science goes to the heart of the same matter: "The essence of . . . tragedy is not unhappiness. It resides in the solemnity of the remorseless working of things. This inevitableness of destiny can only be illustrated in terms of human life by incidents which in fact involve unhappiness. For it is only by them that the futility of escape can be made evident."[33] Destiny cannot be discounted; although we may be captains of our fate, our captaincy remains subject to the remorseless working of things and to the law of costingness.

When Trilling refers to the "conditioned" nature of human existence, as he does insistently, he reflects the tragic vision in this second sense. From "Impedi-ments," the short story published when he was twenty, through "Whitaker Chambers' Journey," the introduc-

tion to the reissue of *The Middle of the Journey* in the
last year of his life, and the posthumous "Why We
Read Jane Austen,"[34] this conception of tragedy functions as a powerful undercurrent to his perceptions and
his sensibility. It explains why, in spite of his frequent
invocation of the idea of tragedy, Trilling so seldom
dealt directly with any of the great literary expressions
that spring to mind when that idea is given voice. Only
in his commentaries on *Oedipus Rex* and *Lear* in his
anthology, *The Experience of Literature*, does he address himself in any comprehensive fashion to works of
this sort. His main interests lay elsewhere—with the
problems of life faced not by the extraordinary heroes
of Sophocles and Shakespeare but by relatively common
folk with no more than a reasonable sensitivity to the
nature of their efforts to cope with reality.

This concern and his special conception of the
tragic as a widespread and crucial aspect of personal
experience stand in flat contradiction of the charge of
"mandarin exclusiveness"[35] sometimes brought against
him. Deeply conscious of the tragic threads that run
through most lives, Trilling cared, and his caring
emerged from and was intertwined with his sharp
awareness of the futility that frequently besets human
endeavor, of the pain that attends the struggle for a
moral identity, and of the hard-won and often deficient
quality of self-respect when its bases are directly and
honestly examined. He knew a good deal about the
secret grades that people give themselves when they confront themselves in those hours that at once are darkest
and present the most undeniable forms of self-knowledge. Those who avoid that kind of confrontation,
those who mask their wills even from themselves, refusing to acknowledge the tragic—the conditioned—
nature of the human estate excited his impatience and
probably his fear. His distinctive sense of tragedy accounts in many ways for his opposition not only to

Stalinism but to the Stalinist personality in all its variations.

Trilling's most direct statement of his view of tragedy takes a fictional form. "Of This Time, Of That Place,"[36] remarkably successful in its evocation of academic life, enmeshes its protagonist, Dr. Joseph Howe—a poet, who, like many poets, earns his livelihood by conscientiously teaching literature—with two students. Ferdinand Tertan exudes a genuine brilliance and, as Howe writes in his endorsement of Tertan for membership in the college literary society, "is marked by his intense devotion to letters and by his exceptional love of all things of the mind." He also proves to be diagnosably and, presumably, incurably psychotic. Theodore Blackburn, on the other hand, walks as an undergraduate the road of professional sycophancy. Energetically self-serving, he holds the vice-presidency of the student council, manages the debating team, serves as secretary of the literary society, and has never received a grade lower than B−. But he can write an examination in which he characterizes the world of Coleridge's "The Ancient Mariner" as a "warm and honey-sweet land of charming dreams" where "we can relax and enjoy ourselves."

The story's context involves a stunning gallery of representative students and a series of people and scenes that capture the essence of college life. De Witt appears, exhibiting a "beautiful and clear, if still arrogant, mind." Johnson displays a "stolid mediocrity." Stettenhoven, a football player who could have served as a model for Phidias, responds to discussions of Ibsen's *Ghosts* with an irritated boredom that clearly arises from his bafflement. Casebeer combines flawless coherence with marginal understanding and unfailing dullness. The college dean is a thoughtful man, largehearted and incisive, who still embodies that quality of distance from the front lines of instruction and scholarship that marks most academic administrators. Familiar as they are, none of these figures degenerates into stereotype; each is individual, convincing, and obedient to the distinctive laws of his own character. Similarly, the details of classroom and campus life have a firmness and a credibility that pay homage to Trilling's eye and to his ability to create precisely the right image, to describe exactly the relevant action, which evoke assent from anyone who has spent time in an academic environment. And the dialogue, though colored by the vanished courtesies of 1945, continues to ring true for all its lack of four-letter words.

Within this framework, Dr. Howe develops a "various and warm" relationship with Tertan, the shambling, passionately intellectual freshman who opens his theme on the conventional topic of "Who I am and why I came to Dwight College" in an arresting fashion: "Existence without alloy," he writes, "is the question presented . . . Tertan I am, but what is Tertan? Of this time, of that place, of some parentage, what does it matter?" As the academic year wears on, Howe discovers Tertan's power to "hit, deviously and eventually, the literary point of almost everything," but he also recognizes that that power is vitiated by the young man's wild verbosity that consistently obscures insight with meaninglessness. "Their conferences had been frequent and long but had done nothing to reduce to order the splendid confusion of the boy's ideas. Yet, impossible though its expression was, Tertan's incandescent mind could always strike for a moment into some dark corner of thought." Forced to the realization, Howe acknowledges finally that Tertan is probably insane—technically, certifiably mad.

That acknowledgment requires Howe to think of his student as a "case" to be put before the dean. Yet he hesitates. Tertan has been very much a person—interesting, touching, authentically literary, and intellectual in a way that most undergraduates are not—and

Howe has felt a real affection for this strange youngster. That affection lifts a barrier against "official" solutions, against the necessity of obtaining a psychiatric final answer to the question, "What is Tertan?" Howe "alone could keep it still a question. Some sure instinct told him that he must not surrender the question to a clean official desk in a clear official light to be dealt with, settled and closed." In spite of that "sure instinct," he suddenly hears himself asking a secretary, "Is the Dean busy at the moment? I'd like to see him."

Later, when he reviewed the events . . . [of] that year, it was over this moment . . . that he paused longest. It was frequently to be with fear and never without a certainty of its meaning in his own knowledge of himself that he would recall this simple, routine request and the feeling of shame and freedom it gave him as he sent everything down the official chute. In the end, of course, no matter what he did to "protect" Tertan, he would have had to make the same request and lay the matter on the Dean's clean desk. But it would always be a landmark of his life that, at the very moment when he was rejecting the official way, he had been, without will or intention, so gladly drawn to it.

The situation becomes still more complicated by a letter that Tertan has sent to the dean: ". . . certain are chosen out of the human race to be the consoler of some other. Of these, for example, is Joseph Baker Howe. . . . Of intellects not the first yet of true intellect and lambent instructions . . . what is judged by him is of the heart and not the head. . . . To him more than another I give my gratitude. . . ." Howe acknowledges the statement for what it is. "This was love. There was no escape from it. Try as Howe might to remember that Tertan was mad and all his emotions invalidated, he could not destroy the effect upon him of his student's stern, affectionate regard."

The conclusion cannot be avoided. Howe had diminished himself in dismissing Tertan from the status of complex and unique personhood to that of a "case," a generalized and simply factual instance of psychosis. "He had betrayed not only a power of mind but a power of love." The betrayal cannot be undone by invoking the necessity, the inevitability of Tertan's psychiatric referral through the dean. Such an effort leads only to the remorseless working of things, which defines the central point. The remorseless working of things *entails* the betrayal of a power of mind and a power of love. In doing what is necessary and even what is just— for as Tertan's madness worsened, his presence at Dwight College would have become corporately intolerable—we violate the personhood of others, including others who command our interest, our loyalty, and our affection.

But if this powerful implication of Trilling's quiet little microcosm represents the essence of his conception of tragedy, he presses home an intensifying observation. On a midterm examination, Howe fails Blackburn, the other student with whom he is entangled, for his discussion of the "honey-sweet world where all is rich and strange" as the atmosphere of "The Ancient Mariner." In their conference, although Blackburn is furious and exhibits little understanding of his teacher's explanations of the F, Howe suggests that the student "really prepare" and take another examination in two weeks. "We'll forget this one and count the other." On this second try, Blackburn does no better. Howe gives him a C—, "carefully and consciously committing a cowardice." Telling himself that the overly generous grade results from wanting no more to do with a youngster whom he dislikes, he cannot still the awareness that he fears Blackburn. Blackburn spurns the grade, and this time he threatens to complain to the dean about Howe's arbitrary imposition of his own opinions and about Howe's having recommended Tertan to the college literary society—"a student who is crazy, who threw the meeting into an uproar." Howe takes the bluebook, strikes out the C—

and writes an F. "Now you may take the paper to the Dean," he says. "Tell him that after reconsidering it, I lowered the grade." Blackburn comes apart, changes his approach from bullying threats to abject pleading, and goes down on his knees in supplication. Howe, thinking "The boy is mad," rises abruptly and orders him out of the office.

On the college's commencement day, Howe and Blackburn have two more encounters. Blackburn, a graduating senior, expresses satisfaction at having finally met Howe's standards. Howe blazes, "You didn't pass my course. I passed you out of my course. I passed you without even reading your paper. I wanted to be sure the college would be rid of you. And, when all the grades were in and I did read your paper, I saw I was right not to have read it first." In the teacher's recollections, "The paper had been fantastic. The paper had been, if he wished to see it so, mad." At this point, the dean comes upon them and takes their arms, "linking Howe and Blackburn," and comments warmly that Blackburn already has a job, "the first man of his class to be placed." The story ends as Howe "hurried off to join the processional."

Howe has behaved toward Blackburn as virtually any self-respecting college professor would, and, although the relationship has hardly tested his mettle in any stringent sense, he has shown both fairness and a degree of courage. Yet his passing Blackburn out of his course to insure the college's being quit of him has contributed to the boy's receiving his baccalaureate degree and therefore to his obtaining a job, "the first man of his class to be placed." The contrast to the consequences for Tertan are a bit overwhelming. Tertan's academic career and probably far more than that are coming to an unhappy termination, whereas Blackburn, equally mad but in quite a different way, seems embarked on a life of success. If there are some forms of madness that society abhors and will not tolerate, there are others that it rewards. Howe, although doing the defensible "right thing" in both instances, has allied himself with society, connecting himself through officialdom and ceremony—the dean's arms linking him to Blackburn and his hurrying to join the academic processional on graduation day—to the remorseless working of things. His selfhood has been twice defeated, twice diminished—by his betrayal of Tertan and, ironically, by his calling of Blackburn's bluff—and on both occasions by his necessarily folding himself into the contours of ineluctable cultural demands.

Robert Boyers, a sympathetic and sensitive critic, denies the tragic element in "Of This Time, Of That Place," although he admires its fictional success.[37] His error derives from two sources. One is the common tendency to conceive of tragedy only in the first, classical, and almost exclusively literary sense and to judge it in terms of literary conventions like harmony, reconciliation, catharsis, and transfiguration. The other is the failure to realize that Trilling's deepest concerns were only secondarily literary. His focus was on "moral questions . . . the questions raised by the experience of quotidian life and by the experience of culture and history." He was consistently "a little skeptical of literature, impatient with it, or at least with the claims of literature to be an autonomous, self-justifying activity."[38] To read him, either as a critic or as a writer of fiction, without an understanding of that quietly passionate connection that Trilling always made between literature and life is to miss what is essential in him. At one with Freud's, Trilling's tragic vision encompassed Everyman, noting with an unsentimental empathy the diminutions of self that each of us suffers in his encounters with the law of costingness and the remorseless working of things, especially that expense to the self demanded by its inescapable engagements with the remorseless working of technically civilized society.

Speaking of his career as an undergraduate and of

his frustrated but lifelong yearning to be a novelist, Trilling once remarked, "I did not count myself among those who were intelligent . . . intelligence . . . did not seem a quality that a novelist needed to have, only a quick eye for behavior and motive and a feeling heart."[39] Intelligence he accumulated in abundance; it became the trait by which he was best known. But the feeling heart remained central in virtually all of his work, expressed most richly in his perception of the tragic destiny of the Toms, Dicks, and Harriets of this world. Those who overlook this dimension of both his criticism and his fiction overlook one of the defining characteristics of his mind and his character.

A comparable component of Trilling's human angle of regard—of that honest place "between," from which he examined experience—derived from Keats's conception of Negative Capability. In his well known letter to his brothers, Keats referred to Negative Capability as "when a man is capable of being in uncertainties, mysteries, doubts, without any irritable reaching after fact and reason." For Trilling, that idea amounted, in some measure, to a rationale for his often remarked ambivalence, an ingrained element of his cognitive style if not of his temperament. More importantly, it specified an aspect of the *struggle* that he perceived as inherent to the human quest, an entailment of the dialectic appropriate to any large issue that presents itself to the imaginative reason.[40] The power to sustain over time an intense and open-minded consideration of contradictory and conflicting ideas and values becomes the condition of sound judgment and significant artistry. Trilling's praise of Dos Passos's *U.S.A.* contrasts with his disappointment in the later work, beginning with *Number One*, less because of Dos Passos's rapid slide toward the political right than because of his loss of dialectical tension, of Negative Capability. He no longer embodied within himself the contradictions of America, forcing their deeper understanding through his novelistic gifts; he had submitted "to serve the ends of . . . one ideological group or tendency," and, in doing so, he foreswore the coping with complexity, the dealing with reality's contrarieties, that mark writers of genuine distinction and critics of the first rank.

But Negative Capability cuts still more deeply. "Man is neither angel nor brute," observes Pascal,[41] adding, "and the unfortunate thing is that he who would act the angel acts the brute." And in another of the *Pensées*, he reflects,

It is dangerous to make man see too clearly his equality with the brutes without showing him his greatness. It is also dangerous to make him see his greatness too clearly, apart from his vileness. It is still more dangerous to leave him in ignorance of both. But it is very advantageous to show him both. Man must not think that he is on a level either with the brutes or with the angels, nor must he be ignorant of both sides of his nature; but he must know both.

From these two meditations, a third follows: "Man does not know in what rank to place himself. He has plainly gone astray, and fallen from his true place without being able to find it again. He seeks anxiously and unsuccessfully everywhere in impenetrable darkness."

Pascal represents one of the subterranean foundation stones of Trilling's thought. There are five references to him in *Matthew Arnold*; his perceptions figure prominently in *The Middle of the Journey*, and the pivotal role assigned in *Sincerity and Authenticity* to *Rameau's Nephew* is precisely a function of the way in which "Diderot's dialogue continues and further particularizes Pascal's sense of the human contradiction of man as the opposite of himself." The passage cited from Pascal as the text for Trilling's discussion of Diderot's novel is the famous one: "What a chimera then is man! What a novelty! What a monster, what a chaos, what a contradiction, what a prodigy! Judge of all things, imbecile worm of the earth; depository of truth, a sink of uncertainty and error; the pride and refuse of the universe!" With none of Pascal's religious faith, Trilling responded with profound seriousness to his intense sense of humanity's contradictory nature and to the insoluble ambiguity of the notion of human beings as *neither* beasts *nor* angels.

That ambiguity lies at the base of the appeal that Negative Capability held for Trilling; it accounts for the parallels between his affirmations of life and his dark warnings of its inherent hazards. Unable—and *unwilling*—to resolve the issue of humankind as the pride and refuse of the universe by resorting to religion, he found in the *Pensées* much of the groundwork of his twinned convictions: that struggle defines the proper and telling metaphor for personal existence and for cultural experience, and that the style with which the struggle is managed specifies the substance of character. An ideal entailment of that style is the perception of human contradictions without demanding that they be reconciled. Moral insight depends on the intensity of the perception, not on solutions that can only prove expedient or spurious.

Conceived in this fashion, the high value of Negative Capability is the high value that Trilling finds in Hawthorne despite (or perhaps because of) his being "not gratifying."[42] Like Kafka's, Hawthorne's main concern revolves around "man's dark odyssey in an alien world," and, like Kafka's, Hawthorne's "fiction does not make a very determined reference to the concrete substantialities of life." Society as Hawthorne conceives it is "thinly composed," thereby facilitating his "representation of the world as . . . susceptible to penetration and suffusion by agencies not material and mundane." Because of that thin composition of culture, "the autonomy of the spirit is the more easily imagined." But "if it is indeed true that Hawthorne's world is thinly composed . . . whatever its composition lacks in thickness is supplied by an iron hardness . . .

for Hawthorne the world is always and ineluctably *there* and in a very stubborn and uncompromising way." The intractability of life-in-society holds sway through all of Hawthorne's works, even though he consistently displays "the moral life as existing beyond the merely pragmatic . . . as a mystery, as being hidden, dark, and dangerous, and as having some part of its existence in a world which is not that of our ordinary knowledge. This other world . . . interpenetrates the world of material circumstance, and . . . provides . . . [it] with its most intense significances." At his best, Hawthorne has an instructive and "quick response to the non-rational," a "lively awareness of the primitive and chthonic, of the dark roots of life," but these qualities never "deflect the naturalistic and humanistic tendency of his mind . . . however successfully he may project illusion, he must point beyond it to the irrefrangible solidity."

Yet over this hard and funereal conception of the self in its relation to culture, Hawthorne's imagination literally *plays*: "He takes," Trilling says, "somber moral principles and makes them into toys." But through the playfulness, elements of ambivalence and ambiguity operate. Unlike the ambivalence and ambiguity that also characterize Kafka, whom Hawthorne so much resembles, these attributes lead not to Kafka's "mute, riddling power." Rather, in Trilling's judgment, they provide an avenue by which he approaches Montaigne's *Que sais-je?*—"the ironic childlike question, the question which conscious or calculated modesty asks, out of which all the questions come. It is *questions* which Hawthorne leaves us with" (italics added).

For Trilling, a crucial test of mature personhood is the ability to live with questions—critical and profound questions—without an irritable, or an anxious, grasping for fact or reason to achieve a reassuring but bogus answer. Humanity remains neither beast nor angel, and the determination of what humankind *is* becomes the object of the often frightening quest of the self in its alien world. As was the case in the great quests of antiquity—the quest for the Grail, for example—what matters in this one is less the location of its object than the style, the seriousness, the courage, the intelligence, and the grace of its pursuit.

Boyers, in his genial, receptive, and informed fashion, sees Trilling's commitment to Negative Capability as a jusifying rationale for a "wisdom of avoidance," for a disposition to stand above the battles of both politics and intimate and immediate interpersonal relationships.[43] In his perception, he approximates the judgment of Joseph Frank.[44] Frank charges Trilling with a preference for "stability and stasis" that underestimates and derogates the individual will. In one sense, Frank says, Trilling's position amounts to little more than an effort to reincarnate Irving Babbitt's notion of the "inner check" (the *frein vital* in contrast to the *élan vital*). In another, it entails a substitution of "contemplation for an active grappling with social reality" and an effort to cloak "social passivity and quietism" with an undeserved and quite false dignity. Trilling, Frank argues, is simply a rhetorically elegant reactionary.

Boyers errs, once again, because of his overstrict attention to literary matters. We have had repeated occasion to note that the honest place "between" was no neutral eremite's retreat. It was consistently the locus of frequently passionate convictions, but convictions emerging from an insistent concern for complexity, for difficulty, and for avoiding the relatively easy but regularly misleading solutions that ideology provides. For Trilling, ideology was perhaps the prototypical form of an irritable grasping for fact or reason as a way of escaping from serious and complicated questions. And the issues confronted from the honest place "between" were only secondarily literary. Those issues were, however, conceived and dealt with under the aegis of the

Arnoldian distinction between the sphere of ideas and ideals and the sphere of practical politics. That distinction makes Frank's evaluation of Trilling into something of a curiosity.

When an intellectual (and Frank's bona fides here lie beyond dispute) disparages "contemplation" in favor of "an active grappling with social reality," one wonders what is afoot. Such a contention comes close to denying that the imaginative reason has anything to do with the achievement of political wisdom and that mind has any relevance to the problems that "social reality" presents. Similarly, when Frank talks about Trilling's depreciation of the will and, in the same breath, his attempt to reinstate Babbitt's "inner check," he makes two flat mistakes. First, Trilling summarizes and recapitulates the case he made over his entire career when he writes, "The issue, which I believe must occupy the consciousness of our culture for a long time to come, is whether life is the better or the worse for putting a high valuation on the will. It is my position that it is the better."[45] Nothing could be plainer. Further, Babbitt's *frein vital* requires precisely an act of volition and finds its base in that spiritual strenuousness that the New Humanists most prized.[46] If more linkages exist between Babbitt and Trilling than the latter may have been aware of, they do not and cannot consist of either a disparagement of the will or a taste for quietism.

Finally, the notion of Trilling as a reactionary holds meaning to almost exactly the same extent that the notion of Arnold as a reactionary would hold meaning. If the critical attempt to conserve what is humane and functional from a passing order amounts to reaction, if the investment of a degree of skepticism in virtually any radical politics amounts to reaction, if a measure of mistrust in absolutist commitments of almost any sort and especially in ideological fanaticisms amounts to reaction, then Trilling, like Arnold, is a reactionary. Meanwhile, such an inference must cope with Trilling's awareness that much of the evil of the world is accomplished by decent people who have no doubts, and one has room to wonder if such a consciousness, such an insistent effort to deal with complexity, dwells even in the neighborhood of either reaction or "social passivity." In any event, Trilling's reflections on Morris's *News from Nowhere*,[47] where he once yet again asserts the doctrine of *ad astra per aspera*, stands as a straightforward answer to Frank's rather astonishing evaluation.

Trilling's treatment of Henry James's *The Princess Casamassima*[48] also provides an answer to Frank in the capaciousness, depth, and subtlety of the attitudes that it both displays and advocates and in the warmth and novelty of the understanding that it exhibits. Trilling begins with one of James's self-characterizations to which he was peculiarly resonant: "I have the imagination of disaster," James wrote in a letter of 1896, "and see life as ferocious and sinister." Set in a context of anarchist terrorism, *The Princess Casamassima* certainly fulfills in two respects expectations of ferocity and danger: in the detailed evocation of an anarchist organization in which assassination is coldly conceived as an ethical instrument of politics, and in the fate of Hyacinth Robinson, the novel's protagonist. Hyacinth elects to commit suicide when he finds that he can neither betray the anarchist cause with which he has aligned himself nor execute the order that he has received from the organization to murder the duke. Trilling trenchantly summarizes the reasons for this decision: "Sometimes society offers an opposition of motives in which the antagonists are in such a balance of authority and appeal that a man who so wholly perceives them as to embody them in his very being cannot choose between them and is therefore destroyed. This is known as tragedy."

Hyacinth's tragedy, however, is that of a very

human hero who dies not innocently but under a burden of guilt. Hyacinth recognizes, Trilling points out, "what very few people wish to admit, that civilization has a price, and a high one . . . all civilizations . . . renounce something for something else." In general, the civilized ideal of widespread security works against the equally civilized ideal of high and distinctive achievement and of nobility of artistic expression. The first reflects the emphasis and spirit of radical democracy; the second embodies the aristocratic aspiration of individual distinction. Hyacinth, caught up in the egalitarian desire to increase and broaden the experience of both justice and security by destroying the dominance of the ruling class, also has become aware that "the monuments of art and learning and taste have been reared upon coercive power." As Hazlitt once noted, Trilling reminds us, "poetry has an affinity with political power in its autocratic and aristocratic form and . . . is not a friend of the democratic virtues." Committed to anarchy as a political principle, Hyacinth is also "of the company of Rabelais, Shakespeare, Scott, Dickens, Balzac, and Lawrence, men who saw the lordliness and establishment of the aristocrat and the gentleman as the proper condition for the spirit of man, and who, most of them, demanded it for themselves."

Hyacinth's conflict, then, entails a double guilt. He has discovered something of what typically lies behind abstract radical ideals: envy, the impulse to revenge, the desire for personal dominance, narcissism. But he has also discovered that a "passion for life at its richest and noblest" entails consenting to the coercive power of the established order. Hyacinth's tragedy is a genuine and moving one, because "he dares to do more than civilization does: embodying two ideals at once, he takes upon himself, in full consciousness, the guilt of each. . . . By his death," Trilling says, "he instructs us in the nature of civilized life and by his consciousness he transcends it."

Here is the kind of moral realism that Trilling first identified and discussed in E. M. Forster, a clear-eyed knowledge not of good and evil but of good-and-evil. But he adds a dimension here, in an essay first published in 1948, that, although he seldom refers to it explicitly, he carries with him as moral equipment for the remaining twenty-seven years of his life. Calling it "the imagination of love," Trilling either discovers it or creates it from James's handling of the characters in *The Princess Casamassima*. If we think, he says, of

a father of many children who truly loves them all, we may suppose that he will see very vividly their differences from one another, for he has no wish to impose upon them a similarity which would be himself; and he will be quite willing to see their faults, for his affection leaves him free to love them, not because they are faultless but because they are they; yet while he sees their faults he will be able, from long connection and because there is no reason to avoid the truth, to perceive the many reasons for their actions. The discriminations and modifications of such a man would be enormous, yet the moral realism they would constitute would not arise from an analytical intelligence as we usually conceive it but from love.

Trilling concretizes his perception through a series of vignettes from James's book. Rosy Muniment is crippled, sharp-tongued, courageous, quaint, and unkind. James "forces us to admire her courage, pride, and intellect and seems to forbid us to take account of her cruelty because she directs it against able-bodied or aristocratic people." Only at the end of the novel do we discover that Hyacinth doesn't like Rosy "and that we don't have to." That insight provides "an emotional relief and a moral enlightenment." But, although James explicitly permits us to dislike Rosy, he himself "does not avail himself of the same privilege. In the family of the novel Rosy's status has not changed."

Millicent Henning has a "strength, affectionateness, and warm sensuality" that James depicts with un-

bridled admiration. At the same time, he clarifies un-
sparingly "not only . . . her desire to pull down what is
above her but also . . . her desire to imitate and conform to it and to despise what she herself is." In Paul
Muniment, genuine idealism couples with a secret desire for personal power. Radiating charisma and a gift
for leadership, he illustrates at once the authenticity
of humane dreams and some characteristic modern
ironies. To a moral realist, those ironies include "the
liberal exhausting the scrupulosity which made him
deprecate all power and becoming extravagantly toler-
ant of what he had once denounced, and the idealist
who takes license from his ideals for the unrestrained
exercise of power." Yet Paul is consistently an attractive and admirable if highly complex and not entirely
trustworthy man.

As for the Princess herself, she is the Christina
Light of James's earlier *Roderick Hudson.* As one of
the other characters, Madame Grandoni, says of her,
"she sold herself for a title and a fortune. She regards
her doing so as such a terrible piece of frivolity that she
can never for the rest of her days be serious enough to
make up for it." Trilling's comment is that "Seriousness
has become her ruling passion, and . . . it is her fatal
sin, for seriousness is not exempt from the tendency
of ruling passions to lead to error. And yet it has an
aspect of heroism, this hunt of hers for reality, for a
strong and final basis of life." In the Princess, Trilling
finds "the very embodiment of the modern will which
masks itself in virtue, making itself appear harmless,
the will that hates itself and finds its manifestations
guilty and is able to exist only if it operates in the name
of virtue, that despises the variety and modulations of
the human story and longs for an absolute humanity,
which is but another way of saying a nothingness."
But the Princess continues to command our compassion.

Trilling's assessment of *The Princess Casamas-*

sima is that it is "an incomparable representation of the spiritual circumstances of civilization." That assessment, however, enjoys less importance than Trilling's insight into moral realism as the basis for James's undeniable achievement:

. . . the novelist can tell the truth about Paul and the Princess only if, while he represents them in their ambiguity and error, he also allows them to exist in their pride and beauty: the moral realism that shows the ambiguity and error cannot refrain from showing the pride and beauty. Its power to tell the truth arises from its power of love. James had the imagination of disaster and that is why he is immediately relevant to us; but together with the imagination of disaster he had what the imagination of disaster often destroys and in our time is daily destroying, the imagination of love.

If his literary perceptions were notably acute, Trilling's focus in his treatment of James's novel centered, as always, on the moral ideas of which the literary work gives rise, and on the connections between those moral ideas and the quality of our corporate—our political—life.

A distinctive sense of tragedy as an inherent component of daily experience, a feeling for the intellectual and moral power of negative capability as a means of coping with complexity, and a concept of moral realism humanized by the imagination of love, then, are the tools with which Trilling worked on the authors, the works, and above all, the issues that struck him as important in the ongoing struggle between the self and its at once nurturing and imprisoning culture. They also define the primary avenues by which he enters our moral consciousness. Gracefully and accurately, William Chace has caught his essence: "Rather than historian, philosopher, or theorist, Lionel Trilling was a sensibility who patiently cultivated thinking in order to subsume it to the rhythms of his search for wisdom."[49]

It is hard to conceive of a more humane model of self-aware and socially responsible personhood.

Chace's accuracy slips a little when he characterizes Trilling's career as revolving around two major themes, "the power of death and the corruption of doctrinaire politics."[50] The statement, while true enough, lacks trenchancy. Four brief comments may sharpen the point of Chace's perception.

First, at the root of anything that may be called the tragic sense of life lies the distinctive human awareness of mortality, of finitude, of death. Like all who share that tragic sense, Trilling invested a suitable seriousness in the fact of death and in our awareness that, whatever our state of being at any given moment, we cannot live forever. His main concern, however, focused on the moral and political implications of the various attitudinal forms that that awareness may assume. In *The Middle of the Journey*, for example, he examined the tendency of American liberals to regard death as a taboo topic because of its "reactionary" denial of progressive trends and of human perfectibility through the restructuring of society. Trilling found this tendency disturbing because it entails a winking at an ultimate reality, a wishful rejection of the final "conditioned" state to which all human beings are subject, a major failure to see the object as in itself it really is. But his disturbance grew far more richly out of the conception of life that these faults involve than out of any special concentration on the ineluctable fact of death.

Second, although Trilling was indeed preoccupied with "the corruption of doctrinaire politics," his stern and committed opposition to Stalinism extended beyond political corruption and doctrinaire positions. Ideologies, panaceas, Utopias, all impressed him as inappropriately and dangerously easy solutions to society's profoundly complex problems and as violations of the advantage and virtues of negative capability. In his Arnoldian way, he fought them unremittingly. More immediately, he stood always embattled against all forms of authoritarianism, whether of the polity or of the personality. If anything, the authoritarian style, the incorporation into the self of a disposition to subordinate the wills of others to one's own and to curtail arbitrarily and through might alone the freedom of others, struck him as more damaging and frightening than authoritarian governments.

Third, as central as politics—conceived typically in the domain of ideas and ideals rather than in the realm of current practicalities—was for Trilling, he looked upon politics as a component of culture. The larger sweep of the culture, of which politics was only a part, and the quality of life that that cultural movement promoted, commanded his first interest. That interest occupied itself most diligently with society's moral climate, the network of ideas and sentiments that influence our relationships with one another, that determine our feelings about social responsibility and the ways in which we can properly come to terms with the corporate dimension of our lives, and that shape our imaginations of how we can and should conduct our interactions on both intimate and societal levels. In a sense, his concerns with death and Stalinism found their fullest meaning only within this always shifting moral matrix of civilization as it impinges on individual consciousness.

Finally, Trilling's curiosity, patient but passionate, fastened most avidly on questions of personal development, of the contours of the sentiment of being, of the nature and dynamics of character. Issues of individual identity and integrity appeared in his eyes as axiomatically fundamental. Experience as a self and of the self is the quintessence of the human condition.

His finding in literature a criticism of life so broadly and so deeply conceived constitutes Trilling's tribute to the literary enterprise and forms the basis of his vigorous seriousness as both a critic and a writer of fiction. In the latter role, he produced two short stories, "The Other Margaret" and "Of This Time, Of That Place," that merit the status of minor masterpieces, beautifully crafted, fully persuasive in their characterizations, and complexly significant and essentially timeless in their themes. "Notes on a Departure" stands not far behind in richness of conception and quality of execution. *The Middle of the Journey,* so disappointingly received when it first was issued and so ironically successful after its author's death, patently serves a dialectical purpose and has a logical sequence and structure perhaps more suitable to argument than to art. Nevertheless, when this point has been made, the novel still achieves a high economy of episode, builds the tensions relevant to its subject matter and its characters with a convincing inevitability, and explores with a brilliant cogency the interplay of private passions and public ideologies in contemporary experience. Nowhere else in American fiction since the end of World War II has the relationship of personality to politics found so subtly perceptive a student.

As a critic, Trilling continues, in a fashion finely tuned to the crises, turbulences, and stridencies of the twentieth century, the great humanistic tradition that takes its course from Dr. Johnson through Hazlitt and Arnold. As an heir—one is tempted to say *the* heir—of that tradition, Trilling is the child of both the Enlightenment with its realistic empiricism and its emphasis on decorum, and Romanticism, with its idealistic expansiveness and its insistence on individuality.

His range and professional seriousness invite comparison with Edmund Wilson, the magisterial dean of modern literary critics. Wilson certainly covered more critical ground, demonstrated a weightier and more catholic learning, and was sharper, more forthright, and more challengingly quirky in his opinions. Both Wilson and Trilling regarded life, including political life, as more important than art, but both found in literature a window on the world that enlarged and lent perspective to their perceptions of life. Both mistrusted systematic literary theories as breakers of the connection between literary art and the common human experience, and neither depended to any significant degree for his critical judgments on either the apparatus or the fruits of formal literary scholarship, although both were somewhat distantly respectful of the scholarly profession.

Trilling, working consistently at the problem of the relationship of the self to the character of culture, probed more deeply than Wilson did into the actualities of living, and he was more successful in using literary materials for the exploration of the moral problems that the struggle between the individual, striving for autonomy, and civilization, insisting on homogeneity and order, complexly poses. In achieving that success, he fulfilled, in a greater measure than Wilson, one of the requirements of the humanistic tradition. He demonstrated both the positive importance and the hazards of literature as a moral force in society.

Most of all, Trilling built the honest place "between." Never a home for evasive neutrality, it was a kind of debaters' hall where, in conscious and articulate forms, the conflicting, contradictory trends in a contemporary culture could contend with each other, each assured of a carefully attended hearing and a just and accurate interpreter. The careful attention and the just and accurate interpretation took precedence over any service to a particular point of view or party. As a result, Trilling's formulations from the honest place "between" had a richness of both texture and implication that only fully apprehended complexity can confer, and his ideas enjoyed a moral cogency that can only be attained through enduring the often painful tension that is entailed by incorporating within oneself the clashing contradictories of one's civilization. By sustaining that

tension within himself for precisely half a century, Trilling, as both a discerning mind and an exemplary character, taught us much about ourselves and the civilization that is both our groundwork and our albatross.
Fortunately for all of us, his works embody both the
mind and the character, and they remain.

Notes

1. LIONEL TRILLING: THE OPPOSING SELF

Detailed biographical information about Lionel Trilling is scarce. This chapter is heavily indebted to Diana Trilling, both for generous conversations about her husband and for her extremely useful "Lionel Trilling, A Jew at Columbia" in *Commentary*, 1979 (March), Vol. 67 (No. 3), pp. 40–46. This essay has been reprinted as an appendix (pp. 411–429) to *Speaking of Literature and Society*, the final volume in the Uniform Edition of the Works of Lionel Trilling. Mrs. Trilling carries no responsibility, of course, for the inferences, interpretations, and speculations here; but her helpfulness, her kindness, and the centrality of her contribution should be thoroughly understood. In addition, the material in this section derives from personal acquaintance between 1950 and 1965, from correspondence from 1965 until Trilling's death ten years later, and from a number of conversations (rather than formal interviews) with Trilling's colleagues and students.

1. *E. M. Forster*, p. 37.
2. *The Liberal Imagination*, pp. 206–207, xv.
3. *A Gathering of Fugitives*, p. 90.
4. *Sincerity and Authenticity*, p. 120.
5. *The Liberal Imagination*, pp. 3–22.
6. *Beyond Culture*, pp. 145–178.
7. *Sincerity and Authenticity*, pp. 167–172.
8. *A Gathering of Fugitives*, p. 114.
9. *A Gathering of Fugitives*, p. 87.
10. *The Last Decade*, p. 158.
11. *A Gathering of Fugitives*, p. 55.
12. *A Gathering of Fugitives*, p. 65.
13. *The Opposing Self*, pp. 118–150.

14. *Of This Time, Of That Place, and Other Stories,* pp. 3–10.

15. Lionel Trilling, "Introduction" to Robert Warshow, *The Immediate Experience* (Garden City, N.Y.: Doubleday, 1962), p. 15.

16. "Introduction," pp. 14–15.

17. Since the Second World War, the circumstances of Jews in the United States have improved dramatically, and, despite the memories of Hitler and the Holocaust, it is difficult for the postwar generations to understand the extent and the effects of American anti-Semitism in the 1920s and 1930s. Nevertheless, anti-Semitism still has its measure of virulence, and, while it represents a distinctive form of prejudice, it is closely related to other forms of racism, including the massive variety that takes blacks as its object. The literature, of course, is huge. One of the best vehicles for developing a sense of the Jewish immigrant community in New York City in the early decades of the twentieth century is Henry Roth's novel, *Call It Sleep,* first published in 1934 and reissued thirty years later in a paperback edition by Avon Books. A great deal of information is available in the comprehensive volume edited by Louis Finkelstein, *The Jews* (New York: Harper, 1960). On the dynamics of prejudice, see the still richly seminal book by Leonard Doob, *et al., Frustration and Aggression* (New Haven: Yale University Press, 1939); Gordon Allport, *The Nature of Prejudice* (Cambridge, Mass.: Addison-Wesley Press, 1954); and Kenneth Gould, *They Got the Blame: The Story of Scapegoats in History* (New York: Association Press, 1942). More recent work concentrates much more on black-white relations than on anti-Semitism and its consequences, but it remains highly relevant psychologically. Excellent sources are Charles V. Willie, Bernard M. Kramer, and Bertram S. Brown, eds., *Racism and Mental Health* (Pittsburgh: University of Pittsburgh Press, 1973); Louis L. Knowles and Kenneth Prewitt, eds., *Institutional Racism in America* (Englewood Cliffs, N.J.: Prentice-Hall, 1969); Joel Kovel, *White Racism: A Psychohistory* (New York: Vintage Books, 1971)·

and Pierre L. van den Berge, *Race and Racism* (New York: Wiley, 1967).

18. *The Last Decade*, pp. 11–12.

19. *A Gathering of Fugitives*, pp. 58–59.

20. The best and most available brief account of the General Honors program and its rationale is John Erskine's *My Life as a Teacher* (Philadelphia: Lippincott, 1948), pp. 165–175 *et passim*. See also his *The Moral Obligation to Be Intelligent* (New York: Bobbs-Merrill, 1921), especially the title essay, pp. 3–32. Quotations here are taken from *My Life as a Teacher*.

21. *The Last Decade*, p. 231.

22. *The Last Decade*, p. 234.

23. *A Gathering of Fugitives*, pp. 135–136.

24. For Trilling on education, see "Preface" in *Beyond Culture*, pp. ix–xviii, and the essays "On the Teaching of Modern Literature," pp. 3–30, and "The Two Environments: Reflections on the Study of English," pp. 209–234. In *The Last Decade*, "Mind in the Modern World," his Jefferson Humanities Lecture, pp. 100–128, "The Uncertain Future of the Humanistic Educational Ideal," pp. 160–176, and "Why We Read Jane Austen," pp. 204–225, all exemplify his concern with teaching, learning, and the importance of educational institutions. Throughout his writings, Trilling sprinkles observations and reflections on education, the significance of some of his interactions with students, and the ways in which education does or should provide a liberating, developmental experience for persons both young and old.

25. *The Liberal Imagination*, pp. 34–37.

26. *The Last Decade*, pp. 236–237.

27. The peculiar and complex role of Communism in the United States between the Russian Revolution and the Second World War, especially its appeal to intellectuals and its importance in shaping the Ameriican *Zeitgeist*, was an extensive one. See Christopher Lasch, *The American Liberals and the Russian Revolution* (New York: McGraw-Hill, 1972); Theodore Draper, *The Roots of American Communism* (New York: Viking Press, 1957) and his *American Communism and Soviet Russia* (New York: Macmillan,

1960); Daniel Aaron, *Writers on the Left* (New York: Harcourt, Brace and World, 1961); and—perhaps best of all for its special subject—David Caute, *The Fellow Travellers* (New York: Macmillan, 1972).

28. *The Last Decade*, pp. 14–16.

29. *Of This Time, Of That Place, and Other Stories*, pp. 38–57.

30. This statement of Trilling's is most accessible in Theodore L. Gross, ed., *The Literature of American Jews* (New York: Free Press, 1973), pp. 358–360. It is reprinted from the *Contemporary Jewish Record* for February, 1944.

31. Alfred Kazin, *New York Jew* (New York: Knopf, 1978). Quotations here are taken from the Vintage Books edition of 1979, pp. 64–70. See also pp. 292–298 and p. 391.

32. *The Last Decade*, p. 238.

33. *The Last Decade*, p. 164.

34. *The Last Decade*, pp. 238–239.

35. *The Last Decade*, p. 227.

36. Bernard Kalb, "The Author," *Saturday Review*, 12 February, 1955, p. 11.

37. Lionel Trilling, "Introduction" to the reissue in 1975 by Avon Books of *The Middle of the Journey*. The essay is reprinted in *The Last Decade* under the title of Whittaker Chambers' Journey," pp. 185–203.

38. "Introduction," *The Immediate Experience*, pp. 14–15.

39. Warshow, pp. 42–48. The review appeared originally in *Commentary* for December, 1947.

40. Richard Cordell, "Clash of Ideas," *Saturday Review*, 11 October, 1947, p. 25.

41. *The Last Decade*, p. 227.

42. Lionel Trilling, *Mind in the Modern World* (New York: Viking Press, 1972). The Jefferson Memorial Lecture is reprinted under the same title, "Mind in the Modern World," in *The Last Decade*, pp. 100–128.

43. Irving Howe, *Celebrations and Attacks* (New York: Horizon Press, 1979), p. 214. Howe's discussion of

Trilling's *Sincerity and Authenticity* first appeared in *Commentary*, February, 1973.

44. R. H. Super, *The Time-Spirit of Matthew Arnold* (Ann Arbor: University of Michigan Press, 1970), pp. 90–91.

2.   CIVILIZATION AND ITS DISCONTENTS

1. Sigmund Freud, *Civilization and Its Discontents*. (London: Hogarth Press, 1930). In translations by either Joan Riviere or James Strachey, paperback editions are widely available.

2. Much of this introductory statement draws heavily on two papers: E. J. Shoben, Jr., "The Tragic Nature of Human Destiny," *American Journal of Orthopsychiatry*, 1979 (October), Vol. 49 (No. 4), pp. 564–570; and E. J. Shoben, Jr., "Tragedy as Moral Concept and as Moral Problem," a keynote address to the Eighth Annual Conference on Piagetian Theory and the Helping Professions in Los Angeles, February, 1978.

3. Walter Cannon, *The Wisdom of the Body* (New York: Norton, 1932). See also Carroll E. Izard, *Human Emotions* (New York: Plenum Press, 1977), and Howard S. Liddell, *Emotional Hazards in Animals and Man* (Springfield, Ill.: Charles C. Thomas, 1956).

4. A large literature documents this point. Among the best and most readable references are C. Judson Herrick, *The Evolution of Human Nature* (Austin: University of Texas Press, 1956); Albert Szent-Gyorgyi, *The Crazy Ape* (New York: Philosophical Library, 1970); and Bernard Campbell, *Human Evolution* (Chicago: Aldine Press, 1974).

5. *The Opposing Self*, xiii.

6. Jean Kinney, *An American Journey: The Short Life of Willy Wolfe* (New York: Simon and Shuster, 1979).

7. *Beyond Culture*, p. 13.

8. *Sincerity and Authenticity*, p. 156.

9. Trilling's insistent attention to moral issues and his
    emphasis on judgment, restraint, and a framework
    of articulate values in the conduct of life suggest
    linkages between his ideas and those of the New
    Humanists—Irving Babbitt, Paul Elmer More, Stuart
    Pratt Sherman, and Norman Foerster. Similarities,
    such as the congruence of Trilling's stress on self-
    control as a personal virtue to Babbitt's concept of
    the *frein vital* (as opposed to the romantic or Berg-
    sonian *élan vital*) or "inner check," do appear and
    seem significant. Trilling's only direct references to
    Babbitt and More, however, occur in *Matthew
    Arnold*. For the most part, they simply acknowledge
    Arnold's considerable influence on the New Human-
    ists. In one instance, with noticeable asperity, he
    "disposes," not with one weapon but with two, of
    one of Babbitt's condemnations of the romantic
    melancholy that colors Arnold's poetry. He first doc-
    uments Arnold's awareness that melancholy is
    "always bad" and his persistent and deliberate
    cultivation of *Tüchtigkeit*, a kind of cheerful inner
    peace. He then refers to a bit of scholarship, pub-
    lished some dozen years after Babbitt's attack,
    demonstrating that the lines from "The Scholar
    Gypsy" that Babbitt had submitted as damning
    evidence referred not at all to Arnold himself but
    to Goethe. (See *Matthew Arnold*, p. 140.) Never-
    theless, if the New Humanists did not directly im-
    press themselves on Trilling or become a part of his
    conscious intellectual and moral equipment, they
    and he derive from common traditions—witness their
    mutual admiration of Arnold as critic if not as poet—
    and Trilling's affinity for their ideas may have been
    greater than he himself thought. That likely affinity
    is often remarked by those who charge Trilling with
    "conservatism." Joseph Frank exemplifies this dis-
    position in *The Widening Gyre* (New Brunswick,
    N.J.: Rutgers University Press, 1963), pp. 253–254,
    257.

10. *The Last Decade*, p. 238.

11. *The Experience of Literature*, pp. 900–901.

12. Although his inclusion in this list may jar, Philip

Roth's popularity should obscure neither his crafts-manship nor his subtlety. He certainly must rank among the best of our contemporary stylists. More importantly, his bumptiousness of manner and his taste for the outrageous mask a curious and serious concern for precisely the power to feel that is under discussion here. Even in *Portnoy's Complaint*, wit serves as a kind of substitute for the power to feel, and the undercurrent of this theme accounts for much of the touching quality of the novel. In *My Life as a Man*, the inhibition of feeling through the deterio-ration of a relationship, and the generalizing of that inhibition to all relationships and to the power to feel itself, are what the book is essentially "about." *The Professor of Desire* is essentially an explicit study in the mutability and evanescence of feeling, and *The Ghost Writer* involves the substitution of fantasy for feeling in a manner that is reminiscent, despite a quite different matter, of *Portnoy's* ex-amination of wit as a shadowy alternative to genuine feeling. What makes many of Roth's characters interesting for us is their clear retention of the "fierce necessity" as against their loss of "the power" to feel.

13. *Beyond Culture*, pp. 113, 115.
14. *Matthew Arnold*, p. 124.
15. *Matthew Arnold*, p. 136.
16. Trilling refers frequently to Jane Austen, and on at least three occasions he devoted rich essays to her work. His consideration of *Mansfield Park* is in *The Opposing Self*, pp. 206–230. He deals with "Emma and the Legend of Jane Austen," in *Beyond Culture*, pp. 31–56; and *The Last Decade* includes his post-humous and unfinished treatment of "Why We Read Jane Austen," pp. 204–225. From the last piece, it is clear that his appreciation of her stemmed in large part from the trenchancy with which she portrayed society at the very beginning of the modern period and from the prescience of her psychological insights into the ways that changes in that society were to im-pose additional burdens on selfhood.
17. *Beyond Culture*, pp. 8, 13.

18. Basically, the psychological concept of "modeling" refers simply to our learning new forms of behavior by observing their performance in other people. At more complex levels, it has to do with deliberate emulation, the acceptance of another person, in limited or comprehensive ways, as a kind of master. In its most developed form, modeling entails one's guiding one's own behavior in problematic situations by asking, in effect, the question, "What would my model do, how would he respond, were he in my shoes at this moment?" A counterpart of this process involves the use of the model's probable behavior— including his attitudes, his feelings, and his values— as a touchstone for judging one's own conduct and in directing one's own will. The idea has clear connections with that of indentification, the incorporation into the essential structure of the self of attributes of another. Sentiments of liking and admiration tend to be associated with the choice of a model, but fear and helplessness can sometimes also promote the selection of models. The latter phenomenon was first clearly recognized and studied in the curiously positive responses of some inmates of Nazi concentration camps to their guards; it plays a major role in the reactions of some hostages to contemporary terrorists. See T. W. Adorno, *et al.*, *The Authoritarian Personality* (New York: Harper, 1950); and Albert Bandura, *Aggression: A Social Learning Analysis* (Englewood Cliffs, N.J.: Prentice-Hall, 1973). More familiarly, modeling functions importantly in both the socialization of children and the processes of psychotherapy. In the present case of Wordsworth and the leech-gatherer, the analogue to the latter is a striking one. The best general reference is probably Albert Bandura's *Social Learning Theory* (Englewood Cliffs, N.J.: Prentice-Hall, 1977).

19. David Riesman, *The Lonely Crowd* (New Haven: Yale University Press, 1950). See also Riesman's *Individualism Reconsidered* (Glencoe, Ill.: The Free Press, 1954). Trilling, enthusiastically and at some length, reviews both books in *A Gathering of Fugitives*, pp. 85–100.

20. *Beyond Culture*, pp. 16–17. For detailed and current documentations of the charges that Trilling abstractly summarizes, see Kurt Glaser and Stefan Posony, *Victims of Politics* (New York: Columbia University Press, 1979).

21. *The Liberal Imagination*, pp. 98–99. In the same passage, Trilling speaks of "the tendency of our educated liberal class to reject the tough, complex psychology of Freud for the easy rationalistic optimism of Horney and Fromm." He may have erred in regarding Horney and Fromm as peas from the same pod, but he was certainly correct in his contrasting of Freud and Fromm. It is impossible to imagine Freud, with his painstakingly and often unwillingly developed tragic reading of the human condition, bypassing character for technique and artfulness in so sentimental a fashion as Fromm does in his *The Art of Loving* (London: George Allen and Unwin, 1957).

22. *Beyond Culture*, p. 167.

23. *Beyond Culture*, p. 169.

24. *Beyond Culture*, p. 52.

25. *Beyond Culture*, pp. 53–54.

26. Alienation as a concept came into general use through Marx's use of the term in *Das Kapital* to describe the remoteness of the worker from the end products of his labor and the resulting dissatisfaction and emptiness associated with assembly-line jobs and other highly specialized operations in industry. It has since been variously defined and is closely linked to the sociological notion of anomie. See Robert K. Merton, *Social Theory and Social Structure*. (Glencoe, Ill.: The Free Press, 1957). Trilling's frequent use of the term tends to be a trifle hazy, and it is touched with cloudiness in the present context (*Sincerity and Authenticity*, pp. 122–125). He concisely distinguishes the early Marx's meaning of alienation from Hegel's; but we cannot be sure of the precision with which he is identifying similarities among the ideas of Marx, Arnold, Wilde, and Ruskin. In his *Economic and Philosophical Manuscripts*, written when he was only twenty-six but not published until as late as 1932, Marx was somewhat clearer than Trilling suggests

about the meaning of that remarkable but rather gnomic statement, "Let us assume *man* to be *man*, and his relation to the world a human one." See Karl Marx, *Early Writings* (New York: McGraw-Hill, 1964).

27. *Sincerity and Authenticity*, p. 106.

28. The idea of the "noble savage" has great mythic appeal. As Trilling uses it in his consideration of *Heart of Darkness*, it refers to a frequent component of the romantic faith—the belief that human beings are intrinsically good, that their "natural" dignity and integrity are ruined only by the imposition of the conventions and requirements of civilized society, and that primitives embody a capacity for nobility of conduct that has been stripped away from Euro-Americans by the dehumanizing constrictions of "advanced" culture. The instinctual life enjoys high honor in this view, and childhood takes on the aura of a primitive innocence out of which a strange and wonderful wisdom can emerge. The idea cuts, however, in two other directions. One deals with the notion of the internal wild man, the primitive within ourselves; it poses the question of the degree to which life will be enhanced or damaged by the degree to which we control or unleash the primitive tendencies that are an inherent part of human nature. The other has to do with the operation of primitive as against civilized forces in society. The great portrayal of this conception is *The Tempest*, where Shakespeare pits Prospero against Caliban in a dramatic tension that remains unresolved at the play's ending. Cervantes also develops this theme, at about the same time as Shakespeare, in his character of Cardenio. This young nobleman, under crisis, disintegrates into a wild man, but, with the help of Don Quixote, reconstitutes his civilized humanity on a broader and more generous basis. Shakespeare, a little like the Greek tragedians, conceives of humankind as caught forever in an unresolvable conflict between demonic forces and the gods; Cervantes, while hardly optimistic, has the redemptive view that the person can find both God and himself on his life's quest. One can only regret that

Trilling never dealt directly with this pervasive theme of humanity's conception of itself and of its cultures. The standard work on this interesting topic remains Hoxie Neale Fairchild's *The Noble Savage* (New York: Columbia University Press, 1928. Also useful and stimulating are the essays collected under the editorship of Edward Dudley and Maximillian E. Novak, *The Wild Man Within* (Pittsburgh: University of Pittsburgh Press, 1972).

29. *Sincerity and Authenticity*, p. 108.
30. *Beyond Culture*, p. xvi.
31. *Beyond Culture*, p. 23.
32. *Matthew Arnold*, pp. 150, 153.

3. Freedom vs. Necessity

1. *The Liberal Imagination*, p. xi.
2. *The Liberal Imagination*, p. xii.
3. *The Experience of Literature*, pp. 131–132.
4. *The Experience of Literature*, pp. 960–964.
5. *A Gathering of Fugitives*, pp. 79–84.
6. *The Liberal Imagination*, p. xii.
7. *Of This Time, of That Place, and Other Stories*, pp. 11–37.
8. *The Last Decade*, pp. 238–239.
9. *The Opposing Self*, p. 137.
10. Although Trilling's love for poetry was obvious, he seems oddly to have been uncomfortable with it in his role as critic. Surprisingly little of his work focused on poets. Even Matthew Arnold, one of his chief mentors, whose verse he dealt with extensively and competently in *Matthew Arnold*, is treated in Trilling's introductory essay "Matthew Arnold, Poet," in *Major British Writers* (New York: Harcourt Brace & World, 1954) as primarily a man of ideas whose poetry represents essentially an early expression of the concepts later developed in his literary criticism, his social thought, and his writings on religion. His extensive admiration for Keats is founded far more in Keats's personal character and in the insightfulness of his letters than in his poetry. In his commentaries on

poems in *The Experience of Literature*, Trilling appears sympathetically workmanlike and professional rather than deeply involved. The contrast with his commentaries on fiction in the same anthology is striking, although the difference must be understood as one of tone and not of intellectual penetration.

With one exception, the only poet to whom he devotes an entire essay is Robert Graves, and his romping, joyous "A Ramble on Graves" (*A Gathering of Fugitives*, pp. 20–30) takes its color from Graves's Englishness of style and diction, which appealed to Trilling's acknowledged Anglophilia, and from Graves's uninhibited "passion for pleasure, for love, for sexuality, for masculinity, for femininity, for activity, for rest . . . a passion for integrity of the self—and a passion for civilization."

The one exception is Wordsworth. In *The Liberal Imagination* there is an affectionate, strongly positive reading of "The Immortality Ode." In *The Opposing Self* "Wordsworth and the Rabbis" is an engaging and subtle *jeu d'esprit* concerned with the sentiment of being, and in *Sincerity and Authenticity* Wordsworth is cited much more frequently than any other poet except Shakespeare and is used more systematically than any other including Shakespeare. What appears to give Wordsworth so much centrality for Trilling is the variousness and subtlety with which the poet explores the ways in which the personal will finds "its own affirmation by its rejection of the aims which the world sets before it and by turning its energies upon itself in self-realization" (*The Opposing Self*, p. 150). The quotations used here are from Book Two, lines 401–405, and Book Six, lines 603–613, of *The Prelude*.

11. *Sincerity and Authenticity*, p. 92.
12. William James, *Principles of Psychology* (New York: Henry Holt, 1890), vol. II, pp. 297–298.
13. *E. M. Forster*, pp. 12–14.
14. *The Last Decade*, pp. 148–159.
15. Asa Briggs, "Introduction," *William Morris: Selected Writings and Designs* (Baltimore: Penguin Books, 1963).

16. Paul Elmer More, *The Catholic Faith* (Princeton, N.J.: Princeton University Press, 1931).

17. *The Liberal Imagination*, pp. 243–254.

18. *The Liberal Imagination*, pp. 118–128.

19. In order to perpetuate itself and to preserve its core identity through the processes of change, every society, regardless of how simple and primitive or how complex and industrialized, must deal with the problem of transforming its children into citizens. While a human baby is by no means a tabula rasa, the character that it acquires and the kind of adult that it becomes are largely the result of the social influences that play over it. Without exception, all cultures vigorously attempt to mold the plastic material of the infant into those forms—and only those forms—of personality that are believed to be contributory to the survival and to the welfare of the group. Many of the functions of such core institutions as the family and the school derive their legitimacy from participating in this process of influencing, of deliberately shaping, the young in socially acceptable directions.

Known to psychologists and other social scientists as *socialization*, the training of children in the manners, the morals, the valued skills, and the likes and dislikes of society is a key to cultural stability. For the most part, it goes on more through informal channels and through the weight of tradition and convention than through explicit and articulately directed efforts. In the United States (and pretty much throughout the Western world), however, public concern for the last forty years with child-rearing practices and options attests to the degree to which socialization has become an increasingly conscious and rather anxiety-laden matter. Its complexity is, of course, very great, and it is the essence of that lifelong conflict between the individual and his culture that Freud discussed with tragic sensitivity in *Civilization and Its Discontents*.

To sample the voluminous and fascinating technical literature on socialization, see, for example, John Whiting and Irvin Child, *Child Training and Personality* (New Haven: Yale University Press, 1953);

Erik Erikson, *Childhood and Society* (New York: Norton, 1950); and Louis Breger, *From Instinct to Identity* (Englewood Cliffs, N.J.: Prentice-Hall, 1974). All children's literature in some fundamental sense has implications for socialization, as, for that matter, have all children's television programs. In the case of *The Jungle Book*, Kipling's alluringly presented conception of the Pack and the Law represents in a feral world the conditions that young wolves (and by logical extension all young, including children) must meet in order to enjoy the benefits of truly "belonging" to their society, the all-powerful Pack.

20. This statement was published in 1950, when perceptions of social class membership, ideas of a world state or of a United Nations Organization that would genuinely constitute a "parliament of man," and conceptions of a Good Society, perhaps like that of "the great experiment" being conducted in the Soviet Union, all enjoyed a more positive and more hopeful ambience than they do now. The point, however, remains unchanged. In "the culture of narcissism," where privatistic goals predominate, self-aggrandizement and self-gratification take clear precedence over any sort of commitment to the nation, and sentiments of patriotism typically seem hollow, false, or jingoistic. See Christopher Lasch, *The Culture of Narcissism* (New York: Norton, 1978).

21. *A Gathering of Fugitives*, p. 82.

22. *A Gathering of Fugitives*, p. 98.

23. *The Last Decade*, p. 140.

24. Strenuous opposition to the American involvement in Indochina had ample legitimacy without this romanticizing of the North Vietnamese government and without the deification, remarkable figure that he was, of Ho Chi Minh. Indeed, the dressing of North Vietnam's regime in the clothing of righteousness may have, in some significant degree, diverted attention from the real issue—the moral errors and the serious mistakes in international politics that marked from the first the actions of the United States in Southeast Asia. The literature here remains of high importance, despite the understandable desire to forget that sullied

decade between 1963 and 1973. See especially Paul Mus, *Vietnam: Sociologie d'une Guerre* (Paris: Editions du Seuil, 1952); Jean Lacouture, *Ho Chi Minh* (New York: Random House, 1968); Frances Fitzgerald, *Fire in the Lake* (Boston: Little, Brown and Co., 1972); and Alexander Kendrick, *The Wound Within* (Boston: Little, Brown & Co., 1974).

25. William L. O'Neill, *Coming Apart: An Informal History of America in the 1960s* (Chicago: Quadrangle Books, 1971), pp. 263–265 *et passim*; and Milton Viorst, *Fire in the Streets* (New York: Simon and Shuster, 1979). See also the anthology edited by Edward Quinn and Paul J. Dolan, *The Sense of the 60s* (New York: The Free Press, 1968); and the second volume of William Manchester's *The Glory and the Dream* (Boston: Little, Brown & Co., 1974).

26. *The Last Decade*, p. 175.

27. Joseph Frank, *The Widening Gyre* (New Brunswick, N.J.: Rutgers University Press, 1963), p. 268.

4. Decent People Who Have No Doubts

1. *Beyond Culture*, p. 13.
2. *The Liberal Imagination*, pp. 218–219.
3. *The Liberal Imagination*, p. 220.
4. *The Liberal Imagination*, p. 221.
5. *The Liberal Imagination*, pp. 221–222.
6. Richard Sennett, "Lionel Trilling," *The New Yorker*, 5 November, 1979, p. 204.
7. *The Last Decade*, p. 198.
8. See ch. 1, pp. 36–45.
9. *The Last Decade*, pp. 185–203.
10. *The Last Decade*, p. 200.
11. *The Last Decade*, p. 200.
12. *The Liberal Imagination*, p. 221.
13. T. S. Eliot, ed., *Pascal's Pensées* (New York: E. P. Dutton, 1958), pp. 49–50 (*Pensée* 182).
14. *Of This Time, Of That Place and Other Stories*, p. 78.
15. *The Liberal Imagination*, pp. xiv–xv.
16. There are some interesting parallels between Trilling's ideas on this score and the notions of Robert Penn Warren. See "Pure and Impure Poetry" in Warren's

Selected Essays (New York: Vintage Books, 1966), pp. 3–31.

17. The effort by Herbert Marcuse, an authority on Hegel, to "radicalize" Freud has a special importance by virtue of both its sophistication and its intent. Marcuse knows psychoanalysis intimately; his purpose in attempting to revise it is to specify the psychodynamic conditions of human development that will produce a society marked by peace, freedom, and pleasure. His argument, although far too complex to summarize without doing violence to it, concentrates on the lessened need for a harsh superego by virtue of technological and economic changes. As these environmental conditions continue to alter, what he calls "surplus repression" and the "performance principle" will lose their force within the personality; competition among persons will markedly decline, and neither the inhibitions nor the frustrations associated with sexuality will interfere with intrapsychic serenity or interpersonal relatedness.

Marcuse's vision entails an uncompromising attack on Freud's famous criteria of individual mental health, the ability to work and the capacity for love. For work to prove satisfying, the worker must contend with difficulty and challenge and must respond to at least the threat of failure with persistence and discipline. For love to occur on what Freud regarded as the fully genital level, earlier modes of gratification—for example, the "polymorphous perverse" patterns of childhood—must be renounced. What Marcuse seeks is a culture in which human beings can develop without acquiring strong achievement needs and without guilt.

In the course of sketching the lineaments of such a society, he abrogates civil liberties in favor of his conception of civil rights; he bypasses the inherent conflict between egalitarian values and the values of excellence that undergird the technological advances on which the lessened influence of the superego depends; and, although his touchstones of appropriateness are less than precise, he legitimizes violence when it reflects resistance to a repressive established order.

Trilling's objections to such a view are clearly predictable. Perhaps the best entries into Marcuse's thought
are *Eros and Civilization* (Boston: Beacon Press,
1969) and his essay on "Repressive Tolerance" in *A
Critique of Pure Tolerance,* written with Robert Paul
Wolff and Barrington Moore, Jr. (Boston: Beacon
Press, 1965).

5. IMAGINATION AND REALITY

1. *The Last Decade,* p. 239.
2. *The Last Decade,* p. 235.
3. *The Last Decade,* pp. 227–228.
4. *Matthew Arnold,* pp. 192–194. The sentence from
    Arnold occurs in "Pagan and Medieval Religious
    Sentiment" in *Essays in Criticism,* First Series.
5. *Matthew Arnold,* p. 205.
6. *Matthew Arnold,* p. 206.
7. *Matthew Arnold,* p. 208. Arnold's concern with
    "acridity" and its dangers is expressed in his essay on
    Heinrich Heine, in *Essays in Criticism,* First Series.
8. *Matthew Arnold,* pp. 24–25. Coleridge's observation
    occurs in "Dejection: An Ode." The conception of
    creativity formulated here is entirely consonant with
    the formulations of modern psychology. See Frank
    Barron, *Creativity and Psychological Health* (New
    York: Van Nostrand, 1963); Arthur Koestler, *The
    Act of Creation* (New York: Macmillan, 1964); Sil-
    vano Arieti, *Creativity: The Magic Synthesis* (Berke-
    ley, Calif.: University of California Press, 1952). Of
    special interest is Brewster Ghislin's *The Creative
    Process* (Berkeley, Calif.: University of California
    Press, 1952), a collection of accounts of their own
    creative processes by people as various as Albert Ein-
    stein, Carl Jung, D. H. Lawrence, Vincent Van Gogh,
    Amy Lowell, Wolfgang Amadeus Mozart, Jean Coc-
    teau, and many others.
9. *Matthew Arnold,* p. 26.
10. *Mathew Arnold,* pp. 339, 349, 336. Arnold's rationale
    for the love of Jesus as morally transformative comes
    from his *St. Paul and Protestantism* (1870).

11. *Matthew Arnold,* p. 352.

12. *Matthew Arnold,* pp. 269–270.

13. *Matthew Arnold,* pp. 370, 351.

14. *The Opposing Self,* pp. 141–145. Trilling also speaks here of Wordsworth's "conception of the world as being semantic." This phrase is one of the extremely rare instances in which he uses language that, if it is not completely meaningless, seems quite without communicative effectiveness.

15. *Matthew Arnold,* pp. 161–162.

16. For Trilling's summary and commentary on Arnold's notion that "Civilization is the humanization of man in society" and his concept of "expansion" as a means of achieving this end, see *Matthew Arnold,* pp. 381–388. The primary source in Arnold is the preface and the essays on "Democracy," "Equality," and "George Sand" in *Mixed Essays,* originally issued in London in 1879.

17. See Arnold's "The Function of Criticism at the Present Time" in *Essays in Criticism,* First Series, first published in London in 1865, and *Matthew Arnold,* pp. 204–208 and pp. 216–218.

18. *The Liberal Imagination,* pp. xiv–xv.

19. *Matthew Arnold,* p. 205.

20. *The Liberal Imagination,* p. xi. This passage is redolent of William James's "The Sentiment of Rationality," first published in *The Will to Believe and Other Essays* (New York: Holt, 1912). It also echoes much in John Dewey's *How We Think* (New York: D. C. Heath, 1910). Trilling was familiar with both works, admired them, and acknowledged them as part of his formative intellectual background.

21. *The Liberal Imagination,* pp. 298–303.

22. *Beyond Culture,* pp. 108–113. See the report of the Committee on Social Issues, *Considerations Regarding the Loyalty Oath as a Manifestation of Current Social Tension and Anxiety* (Topeka, Kans.: Group for the Advancement of Psychiatry, 1954).

23. *The Liberal Imagination,* p. 100.

24. *The Liberal Imagination,* pp. 101–102.

25. "The Situation in American Writing," *Partisan Review,* 1939 (Fall), Vol. 6 (No. 5), p. 109.

26. Sigmund Freud, *Civilization and Its Discontents*, Joan Riviere trans. (London: Hogarth Press, 1930), pp. 92–93. The closing portion of this passage, for all of Irving Babbitt's dislike of psychoanalysis, has striking affinities to themes developed in his *Democracy and Leadership* (Boston: Houghton Mifflin, 1924).

27. *The Liberal Imagination*, p. 36.

28. See Chapter 2.

29. See Chapter 3, especially pp. 112–117.

30. *The Last Decade*, pp. 240–241.

31. *Sincerity and Authenticity*, p. 60.

32. *Sincerity and Authenticity*, p. 99.

33. *Sincerity and Authenticity*, pp. 131–132.

34. *Sincerity and Authenticity*, p. 31.

35. *The Opposing Self*, pp. 24, 31.

36. *The Opposing Self*, pp. 34–35.

37. *The Opposing Self*, pp. 36–37.

38. *The Opposing Self*, p. 37.

39. *The Opposing Self*, pp. 40–42.

40. *The Opposing Self*, p. 44. Keats's statement occurs in the long letter, begun on February 14, 1819, and completed on the following May 3, to his brother George and his sister-in-law, Georgiana Wylie Keats. See Trilling's edition of *The Selected Letters of John Keats* (New York: Farrar, Straus and Young, 1951), pp. 203–217, especially pp. 215–216.

41. *The Opposing Self*, pp. 45, 48–49.

42. *The Last Decade*, p. 25. Joyce always wrote to his children in Italian. The original reads as follows: "*Adesso termino. Ho gli occhi stanchi. Da più di mezzo seculo scrutano nel nulla dove hanno trovato un bellisimo niente.*" See the third volume, edited by Richard Ellmann, of *The Letters of James Joyce* (New York: Viking Press, 1966).

43. *The Last Decade*, p. 56.

44. *The Last Decade*, p. 30.

6. The Honest Place "Between"

1. Richard Sennett, "On Lionel Trilling." *The New Yorker*, November 5, 1979, p. 209.

2. *A Gathering of Fugitives*, p. 65.
3. *The Liberal Imagination*, pp. 1–10.
4. *Beyond Culture*, p. 118.
5. *A Gathering of Fugitives*, pp. 43–44.
6. *The Liberal Imagination*, pp. 236–237.
7. *The Opposing Self*, p. ix.
8. *A Gathering of Fugitives*, p. 55.
9. *Beyond Culture*, p. xvii.
10. *The Last Decade*, pp. 226–227.
11. *The Liberal Imagination*, pp. 3–21.
12. *A Gathering of Fugitives*, pp. 79–84.
13. *Beyond Culture*, pp. 145–178.
14. *Sincerity and Authenticity*, pp. 167–172.
15. *The Opposing Self*, pp. 145–148.
16. *A Gathering of Fugitives*, pp. 31–40.
17. William James, *Principles of Psychology* (New York: Henry Holt, 1890), vol. I, p. 121.
18. Alfred North Whitehead, *An Introduction to Mathematics* (New York: Oxford University Press, 1948), p. 42.
19. Lionel Trilling, "The America of John Dos Passos," in Andrew Hook, ed., *Dos Passos: A Collection of Critical Essays* (Englewood Cliffs, N.J.: Prentice-Hall, 1974), pp. 93–100. First published in *Partisan Review*, 1938 (April), Vol. 4 (No. 5), pp. 26–32.
20. John Dewey and J. H. Tufts, *Ethics* (New York: Henry Holt, 1908), p. 210.
21. "The America of John Dos Passos," p. 100.
22. "The America of John Dos Passos," p. 96.
23. *Sincerity and Authenticity*, p. 167.
24. "The America of John Dos Passos," pp. 97, 100. The assessments of Dos Passos by Cowley and Whipple are available in Hook's *Dos Passos: A Collection of Critical Essays*, pp. 76–86 and 87–92.
25. Roger Sale, *On Not Being Good Enough* (New York: Oxford University Press, 1979), pp. 148–157.
26. Saul Bellow, *Mr. Sammler's Planet* (New York: Penguin Books, 1979), pp. 135–137, 42–43. (Originally published by Viking Press in 1970).
27. *Sincerity and Authenticity*, pp. 100–105, 144–149.
28. Stephen Donadio, "Columbia: Seven Interviews,"

Partisan Review, 1968 (Summer), Vol. 35 (No. 3), pp. 386–387.

29. William Chace, *Lionel Trilling: Criticism and Politics* (Stanford, Calif.: Stanford University Press, 1980), p. 150.

30. *The Last Decade*, pp. 173–174.

31. *Sincerity and Authenticity*, pp. 171–172.

32. Paul Elmer More, *The Catholic Faith* (Princeton, N.J.: Princeton University Press, 1931).

33. Alfred North Whitehead, *Science and the Modern World* (New York: Macmillan, 1928), pp. 15–16.

34. *The Last Decade*, pp. 204–225.

35. See, for example, Mark L. Krupnick, "Lionel Trilling: Criticism and Illusion." *Modern Occasions*, 1971 (Winter), Vol. 1 (No. 2), 282–287. Krupnick, in a quite contradictory fashion, combines his accusation of "mandarin exclusiveness" and an "overripe aestheticism" with an image of Trilling's "straining after the quotidian." Written in the spirit of the 1960s, Krupnick's essay reflects the yearnings and the temper of that period, including the faith that personal problems will somehow be solved by identification with a radical movement of some sort. Trilling had been repeatedly clear about his position on such an issue, notably (but not exclusively) in his treatments of Dos Passos and Fitzgerald and in his introduction to Tess Schlessinger's *The Unpossessed*. Disagreement would be one thing; rather sullen name-calling, based on a central misunderstanding, seems quite another.

36. *Of This Time, Of That Place, and Other Stories*, pp. 72–116.

37. Robert Boyers, *Lionel Trilling: Negative Capability and the Wisdom of Avoidance* (Columbia, Mo.: University of Missouri Press, 1977), pp. 4–19.

38. *The Last Decade*, p. 228.

39. *The Last Decade*, p. 231.

40. See the discussion of Trilling on Keats and Joyce, especially the former, in chapter 5. In Trilling's essay on Keats in *The Opposing Self* (pp. 3–49), Negative Capability is the central subject of pp. 32–45.

41. T. S. Eliot, ed., *Pascal's Pensées* (New York: E. P.

Dutton, 1958). The *Pensées* were originally published
in 1669, seven years after Pascal's death. The *pensées*
quoted in this paragraph are No. 358 (p. 99), No. 418
(p. 111), and No. 427 (p. 114). The one in the following paragraph, cited by Trilling on pp. 29–30 of
Sincerity and Authenticity, comes from No. 434 (p.
121).

42. *Beyond Culture,* pp. 179–208.
43. Robert Boyers, *Lionel Trilling: Negative Capability
and the Wisdom of Avoidance* (Columbia, Mo.:
University of Missouri Press, 1977), *passim* and especially pp. 56–63.
44. Joseph Frank, *The Widening Gyre* (New Brunswick,
N.J.: Rutgers University Press, 1963), pp. 253–274.
45. *The Last Decade,* p. 140.
46. See Irving Babbitt, *Rousseau and Romanticism* (New
York: Meridian Books, 1955; first published Boston:
Houghton Mifflin, 1919); *Democracy and Leadership*
(Boston: Houghton Mifflin, 1924); and especially his
translation, with a long introductory essay, of *The
Dhammapada* (New York: New Directions, 1965;
first issued by the Oxford University Press in 1936).
There may be much to find fault with in Babbitt's
conception of a New Humanism, but Babbitt's stress
fell heavily and consistently on the volitional nature
of self-control and the will as crucial in the governing
of the passions. Similarly, in contrast to many current interpreters of Asian traditions, especially those
of Hindu and Buddhist origins, Babbitt noted and
advocated the centrality of spiritual vigor in Eastern
religion and thought. He was fond of identifying
"spiritual laziness" as the authentic original sin.
Frank's charges seem warped a little away from perceptiveness and accuracy by an irritation that may
possibly spring from ideological sources.
47. *The Last Decade,* pp. 148–159.
48. *The Liberal Imagination,* pp. 58–92.
49. William Chace, *Lionel Trilling: Criticism and Politics* (Stanford, Calif.: Stanford University Press,
1980), p. 187.
50. Chace, p. 188.

Bibliographic Essay

Although a deeply scholarly man, Lionel Trilling was in no sense a technical or formal scholar. For him, literature represented the most cogent and interesting language for capturing and reflecting upon human experience and the dynamics of culture. In consequence, the study of literature commanded his full seriousness; but the literary discipline enjoyed, in his eyes, far too great an importance to be restricted to discussions among academic peers. Both as critic and as teacher, Trilling drove for the widest audience he could reach, trying to ignite those concerns that literature embodies, that have a singular significance for our humanity, and that contribute to the more effective circulation of ideas in society. Preoccupied with the moral issues and the social dilemmas that he found so well illuminated in literary works, he assumed that thinking people would share his focus because of its intrinsic weightiness. Whether they shared his point of view or judgments was quite a different question that he seldom attended to.

Given his urge for the broadest possible audience, Trilling would be delighted with the Uniform Edition of his works, edited by Diana Trilling and published between 1978 and 1980 in twelve volumes by Harcourt Brace Jovanovich. The books, both in hard covers and paperback, are handsomely and sturdily manufactured, printed in readable type, and—most important—provide ready and pleasant access to all of his work except a few ephemeral pieces and some early articles and stories that add nothing to the riches now so happily available.

The Uniform Edition comprises the eight volumes that Trilling published during his lifetime: *Matthew Ar-*

nold, E. M. Forster, *The Middle of the Journey*, *The Liberal Imagination*, *The Opposing Self*, *A Gathering of Fugitives*, *Beyond Culture*, and *Sincerity and Authenticity*. In addition, it includes a collection of five short stories under the title of *Of This Time, Of That Place, and Other Stories*; *Prefaces to the Experience of Literature*, which include the commentaries that Trilling prepared for his big anthology, *The Experience of Literature*; and two collections of essays—*Speaking of Literature and Society*, which gathers together previously uncollected pieces published originally between 1924 and 1964, and *The Last Decade*, which contains the items that Trilling wrote during the last 10 years of his life, 1966 through 1975.

Only *Speaking of Literature and Society* appeared after the manuscript of *Lionel Trilling: Mind and Character* was completed. The last item in the Uniform Edition to see the light of print (in October, 1980), it would have saved a number of hours in libraries; but fortunately, everything necessary to the present book had been found in periodical form. The utility of *Speaking* rests not only on the increased accessibility of some of Trilling's most noteworthy essays, like those on Dos Passos and on "The Politics of T. S. Eliot"), but on a perceptive and revealing foreword by Mrs. Trilling and her biographical memoir, "Lionel Trilling: A Jew at Columbia," first published in 1977 in *Commentary* and the best publicly available source of information about Trilling's life.

For all practical purposes—and for the purposes that he most honored—the Uniform Edition defines Trilling's canon. But Trilling edited four books in addition to those that he wrote; he served as co-editor of the *Oxford Anthology of English Literature*, and two of the pieces that he later collected appeared originally as small books. For the record, the comprehensive list prior to the issuance of the Uniform Edition includes these items:

Matthew Arnold. New York: W. W. Norton, 1939. (Reprinted by the Columbia University Press, 1949, with a brief preface to the new edition.)

E. M. Forster. New York: New Directions Press, 1943.

The Middle of the Journey. New York: Viking Press, 1947. (Novel. Reissued in 1976 in paperback by Avon Books

with a new introduction. The introduction is collected
in *The Last Decade* as "Whittaker Chambers' Journey.")

The Portable Matthew Arnold. New York: Viking Press,
1949. (Edited with an introduction that adds nothing
to Trilling's insights into Arnold as set down in *Matthew Arnold*.)

The Liberal Imagination. New York: Viking Press, 1950.

The Selected Letters of John Keats. New York: Farrar,
Straus and Young, 1951. (Edited with an introduc-
tion included in *The Opposing Self* as "The Poet as
Hero: Keats in His Letters.")

The Opposing Self. New York: Viking Press, 1955.

Freud and the Crisis of Our Culture. Boston: Beacon Press,
1955. (Incorporated in *Beyond Culture* under the
title of "Freud: Within and Beyond Culture.")

A Gathering of Fugitives. Boston: Beacon Press, 1956.

Beyond Culture. New York: Viking Press, 1965.

The Experience of Literature. Garden City, N.Y.: Doubleday, 1967. (A selection of plays, stories, and poems to
each of which is attached a critical commentary. In
addition, Trilling included a large number of poems
"for further reading," without commentary. The commentaries have been collected as *Prefaces to the Experience of Literature*.)

The Life and Work of Sigmund Freud. New York: Basic
Books, 1970. (A one-volume abridgment, prepared
with Steven Marcus, of Ernest Jones's three-volume
biography.)

Literary Criticism: An Introductory Reader. New York:
Holt, Rinehart and Winston, 1970. (An anthology of
critical writing with an introduction reprinted in *The
Last Decade* as "What Is Criticism?".)

Sincerity and Authenticity. Cambridge, Mass.: Harvard
University Press, 1972.

Mind in the Modern World. New York: Viking Press,
1973. (The 1972 Thomas Jefferson Lecture in the
Humanities, given in Washington, D.C., under the
auspices of the National Endowment for the Humanities. Republished under the same title in *The Last
Decade*.)

The Oxford Anthology of English Literature. New York:

Oxford University Press, 1973. (Trilling served as one of several co-editors for this edition of a prestigious and widely used anthology. His specific contributions cannot be systematically isolated in the text from those of his fellow editors, a state of affairs both common and appropriate in enterprises of this kind.)

Trilling has himself been an object of critical attention, of course, since the appearance of *Matthew Arnold* in 1939. The first book-length study was Robert Boyers's *Lionel Trilling: Negative Capability and the Wisdom of Avoidance* (Columbia, Mo.: University of Missouri Press), issued in 1977. The most comprehensive to date is William Chace's *Lionel Trilling: Criticism and Politics* (Stanford, Calif.: Stanford University Press, 1980). *Art, Politics, and Will* (New York: Basic Books, 1977), edited by Quentin Anderson, Stephen Donadio, and Steven Marcus, began as a *Festschrift* for Trilling and became a memorial volume when he died in November, 1975. After the fashion of *Festschriften*, most of the essays that it contains develop, in only the most general way, themes with which Trilling was concerned. Anderson's piece on *The Middle of the Journey*, however, and Marcus's appreciative survey of Trilling's career, are directly relevant and of major importance.

Three Honest Men: Edmund Wilson, F. R. Leavis, Lionel Trilling, released only in Great Britain (Manchester: Carcanet New Press, 1980), comprises the transcripts of three radio programs put together by Philip French for the British Broadcasting Corporation. French conducted interviews about each of his subjects with a variety of well-informed persons and then assembled the comments that he evoked in a manner that gives the flavor of first-rate conversation. Contributors to the section on Trilling in this valuable little book are Daniel Aaron, Quentin Anderson, Jacques Barzun, Morris Dickstein, Stephen Donadio, John Hollander, Irving Howe, Alfred Kazin, Steven Marcus, and Norman Podhoretz. Nathan Scott's chapter on Trilling in *Three American Moralists: Mailer, Bellow, Trilling* (Notre Dame, Ind.: University of Notre Dame Press, 1973) has considerable provocative value by virtue of Scott's attack, at once rigorous and sympathetic, on Trilling's "humanism" from the standpoint of contemporary Christian theology.

Although Joseph Frank's judgments of Trilling may be wrongheaded and querulous, both his earned reputation and his clearly established sensibility require the citing of his "Lionel Trilling and the Conservative Imagination" in *The Widening Gyre* (New Brunswick, N.J.: Rutgers University Press, 1963) and his "Appendix (January, 1978)" to that piece in *Salmagundi*, 1978 (Spring), No. 41. Similarly, Robert Warshow's review of *The Middle of the Journey*, which may have turned Trilling away from the career that he coveted as a novelist, has high importance. It appears as a part of "The Legacy of the 30's" in Warshow's posthumous *The Immediate Experience* (Garden City, N.Y.: Doubleday, 1962).

Instructive and frequent references to Trilling appear *passim* in Daniel Aaron's *Writers on the Left* (New York: Harcourt, Brace and World, 1961), Leo Bersani's *A Future for Astyanax* (Boston: Little, Brown, 1976), Stanley Edgar Hyman's *The Armed Vision* (New York: Alfred Knopf, 1955), and Alfred Kazin's *New York Jew* (New York: Random House, 1978). Three essays from the periodical literature have a special utility for identifying the issues with which Trilling was intimately associated: R. P. Blackmur, "The Politics of Human Power," *Kenyon Review*, 1950 (Autumn), Vol. 12; Dennis Donoghue, "Trilling, Mind, and Society," *The Sewanee Review*, 1978 (Spring), Vol. 86; and Delmore Schwartz, "The Duchess' Red Shoes," *Partisan Review*, 1953 (January), Vol. 20. These three unfriendly treatments, like Joseph Frank's and Robert Warshow's, demonstrate something of the impact that Trilling had on the critical community at various stages of his life. For a much more cordial and comprehensive appraisal, see Robert Langbaum's "The Importance of *The Liberal Imagination*," *Salmagundi*, 1978 (Spring), No. 41, and the review by Richard Sennett of the first volumes of the Uniform Edition in *The New Yorker* for November 5, 1979.

Other references, as a representative sample of the extensive attention paid to Trilling, are provided in the Notes to the chapters of the present volume. It is quite possible that several book-length examinations of Trilling may soon appear. In *Three Honest Men*, Philip French remarks (p. 102) that "there are numerous books about him in various stages of completion—anything between seven and a dozen. Estimates of their number vary." Diana Trilling is assembling a collection of her husband's letters, and his papers have been deposited in the Rare Books and Manuscripts Division of the Columbia University Library in New York City.

Index

MODERN LITERATURE SERIES

In the same series (continued from page ii)